COMMON CORE BASICS

Building Essential Test Readiness Skills

READING

Mc Graw Hill Education

Bothell, WA • Chicago, IL • Columbus, OH • New York, NY

mheonline.com

Send all inquiries to:
McGraw-Hill Education
8787 Orion Place
Columbus, OH 43240

ISBN: 978-0-07-657520-6
MHID: 0-07-657520-9

Printed in the United States of America.

3 4 5 6 7 8 9 RHR 18 17 16 15 14 13

Contents

To the Student

Common Core Basics: Building Essential Test Readiness Skills, Reading will help you learn or strengthen the skills you need when you take any Common Core State Standards–aligned reading test. To answer some questions, you will need to focus on nonfiction documents such as instructions, memos, ads, editorials, magazines, and blogs. To answer other questions, you will need to concentrate on elements of fiction and of nonfiction prose such as biography.

Before beginning the lessons in this book, take the **Pretest**. This test will help you identify which skill areas you need to concentrate on most. Use the chart at the end of the Pretest to pinpoint the types of questions you have answered incorrectly and to determine which skills you need to work on. You may decide to concentrate on specific areas of study or to work through the entire book. It is highly recommended that you do work through the whole book to build a strong foundation in the core areas in which you will be tested.

Common Core Basics: Building Essential Test Readiness Skills, Reading is divided into five chapters:

- **Chapter 1: Functional Texts** introduces you to memos, forms, workplace documents, instructions, websites, graphic documents, and reference texts.

- **Chapter 2: Expository Texts** shows you the features of textbooks, newspaper and magazine articles, and technical texts.

- **Chapter 3: Persuasive Texts** teaches you about the language used in ads, editorials, blogs, and reviews—all designed to change your opinion about an issue.

- **Chapter 4: Literary Nonfiction** provides practice reading nonfiction prose, biographies, and autobiographies.

- **Chapter 5: Fiction** describes the elements of fiction—plot, setting, characters, point of view, literal and figurative language, theme, and text structure.

In addition, *Common Core Basics: Building Essential Test Readiness Skills, Reading* has a number of features designed to familiarize you with standardized tests and to prepare you for test taking.

- The **Chapter Opener** provides an overview of the chapter content and a goal-setting activity.

- **Lesson Objectives** state what you will be able to accomplish after completing the lesson.

- **Vocabulary** critical for understanding lesson content is listed at the start of every lesson. All boldfaced words in the text can be found in the Glossary.

- The **Key Concept** summarizes the content that is the focus of the lesson.

- In the lessons, the **Core Skill** and **Reading Skill** are emphasized with direct instruction and practice in the context of the lesson. The Core Skills align to the Common Core State Standards.

- In the lessons, the special features **21st Century Skills**, **Technology Connections**, **Workplace Connections**, and **Research It** will help you activate high-level thinking skills by using real-world application of these skills.

- **Think about Reading** questions check your understanding of the content throughout the lesson.

- **Write to Learn** activities provide you with a purpose for practicing your writing skills.

- End-of-lesson **Vocabulary Review** checks your understanding of important lesson vocabulary, while the **Skill Review** checks your understanding of the content and skills presented in the lesson.

- **Skill Practice** and **Writing Practice** exercises appear at the end of every lesson to help you apply your learning of content and skill fundamentals.

- The end-of-chapter **Review** and **Essay Writing Practice** test your understanding of the chapter content and provide an opportunity to strengthen your writing skills.

- **Check Your Understanding** charts allow you to check your knowledge of the skills you have practiced.

- The **Answer Key** explains the answers for the questions in the book.

- The **Glossary** and **Index** contain lists of key terms found throughout the book and make it easy to review important skills and concepts.

After you have worked through the book, take the **Posttest** to see how well you have learned the skills presented in this book.

Good luck with your studies! Keep in mind that knowing how to read and analyze various types of reading materials is a skill worth learning.

Reading

The Pretest is a guide to using this book. It will allow you to preview the skills and concepts you will be working on in the lessons. The Pretest is intended to be a check of your current level of knowledge and understanding. It will serve as a starting point as you work through these lessons and develop your reading skills.

The Pretest consists of 20 multiple-choice questions. These questions are based on informational texts and literary texts.

Directions: Read each question carefully. Then choose the <u>one best answer</u> to the question.

When you have completed the Pretest, check your work with the answers and explanations on page 9. Use the Evaluation Chart on page 10 to determine which areas you need to pay special attention to as you work your way through this book.

Reading

Directions: Questions 1–3 refer to the following passage.

The medium, or process, of our time— electric technology—is reshaping and restructuring patterns of social interdependence and every aspect of our

5 personal life. It is forcing us to reconsider and reevaluate practically every thought, every action, and every institution formerly taken for granted. Everything is changing— you, your family, your neighborhood, your

10 education, your job, your government, your relation to "the others." And they're changing dramatically.

Societies have always been shaped more by the nature of the media by which men

15 communicate than by the content of the communication. The alphabet, for instance, is a technology that is absorbed by the very young child in a completely unconscious manner, or by osmosis. . . . Words and the

20 meaning of words predispose [prepare] the child to think and act automatically in certain ways. The alphabet and print technology fostered and encouraged a fragmenting process, a process of specialism and of

25 detachment. Electric technology fosters and encourages unification and involvement. It is impossible to understand social and cultural changes without a knowledge of the workings of media.

30 The older training of observation has become quite irrelevant in this new time, because it is based on psychological responses and concepts conditioned by the former technology—mechanization.

—Excerpted from *The Medium Is the Message*, by Marshall McLuhan and Quentin Fiore

1. What is the main idea of this passage?
   A. Technology causes division in society.
   B. Technology changes our social relationships and personal lives.
   C. The alphabet is a technology that is absorbed by young children.
   D. Today's society is confused by electric technology.

2. Lines 16–19 say, "The alphabet . . . is absorbed by the very young child in a completely unconscious manner, or by **osmosis**." What is the meaning of the word **osmosis**?
   A. imagination
   B. hard work
   C. unconscious learning
   D. technology

3. According to the passage, which medium affects every aspect of our social and personal lives today?
   A. newspapers
   B. television
   C. books
   D. the alphabet

Reading

Directions. Questions 4–6 refer to the following passage.

"You're not scared, are you?" asked Max, when they were about to put on their helmets.

"Not enough to make a mess in my suit. Otherwise, yes."

5

Max chuckled. "I'd say that's about right for this job. But don't worry—I'll get you there in one piece, with my—what do you call it?"

"Broomstick. Because witches are supposed to ride them."

10

"Oh, yes. Have you ever used one?"

"I tried once, but mine got away from me. Everyone else thought it was very funny."

There are some professions which have evolved unique and characteristic tools—the longshoreman's hook, the potter's wheel, the bricklayer's trowel, the geologist's hammer. The men who had to spend much of their time on zero-gravity construction projects had developed the broomstick. It was very simple—a hollow tube just a meter long, with a footpad at one end and a retaining loop at the other. At the touch of a button, it could telescope out to five or six times its normal length, and the internal shock-absorbing system allowed a skilled operator to perform the most amazing maneuvers [movements]. The footpad could also become a claw or hook if necessary; there were many other refinements, but that was the basic design. It looked deceptively easy to use; it wasn't.

15

20

25

30

The airlock pumps finished recycling; the EXIT sign came on; the outer doors opened, and they drifted slowly into the void. *Discovery* was windmilling about two hundred meters away, following them in orbit around Io, which filled half the sky. Jupiter was invisible, on the other side of the satellite.

35

—Excerpted from *2010: Odyssey Two*, by Arthur C. Clarke

4. According the passage, which statement describes the relationship between Jupiter and Io?

A. It is smaller than Jupiter.
B. It is far from Jupiter.
C. It is the same size as Jupiter.
D. It is larger than Jupiter.

5. In lines 23–25, the author says, "it could **telescope** out to five or six times its normal length." What is the meaning of the word **telescope**?

A. focus
B. magnify
C. stretch
D. drift

6. Which of the author's techniques is the most effective in helping you identify the setting?

A. providing a description of a satellite and a planet
B. including dialogue in which characters discuss their feelings
C. contrasting the broomstick with a witch's broomstick
D. listing characteristic tools of several professions

Directions: Questions 7–9 refer to the following workplace document.

From: Martin Franzen <mfranzen@wp.com>

To: Carla Brown <cbrown@wp.com>

CC: Jeff Hall <jhall@wp.com>,
Meg Ruiz <mruiz@wp.com>,
5   Tanya Glass <tglass@wp.com>

Subject: Inclement Weather Policy

Department Heads:

Please inform your staff of the updated
policy regarding closings due to inclement
10 weather.

If there is a current or predicted severe
weather event, I will call each department
head by 6 a.m. You will call each of your staff
members. If you are not able to reach them,
15 you must attempt to leave a phone or
text message.

As a backup, I will send an e-mail to all staff
members, and I will post the office status on
our company website.

20 Employees registered to telecommute may
log in any hours they work from home.
Others should mark "Code 3" on their time
sheets for the day(s) of the closing.

On an unrelated note, all department heads
25 will meet in my office next Tuesday at 1 p.m.
to plan events for "Bring Your Child to Work
Day." I will supply refreshments.

Let me know if you have any questions.

Best regards,

30 Martin Franzen, President

7. Which statement best summarizes the
president's message?
   - **A.** All children are welcome at work.
   - **B.** E-mail is the most reliable means of
     communicating with staff.
   - **C.** Department heads are responsible for
     communicating to staff members.
   - **D.** Staff members don't know how to drive
     in inclement weather.

8. What is the purpose of this e-mail?
   - **A.** A department head wants to know
     what refreshments to bring to the
     meeting.
   - **B.** An employee wants to find out how to
     telecommute in bad weather.
   - **C.** An employee is asking to bring a child
     to work.
   - **D.** The president is alerting the
     department heads to a change in
     company policy.

9. Which of the following best describes this
workplace document?
   - **A.** official report of a workplace
     procedure
   - **B.** job performance review
   - **C.** causal memo between employees
   - **D.** meeting agenda

Reading

Directions: Questions 10–11 refer to the following instructions.

Congratulations on your purchase of your True Cut self-propelled field and brush lawnmower. Before using your mower for the first time, be sure to read the following procedures for the safe operation of your machine. As you read, refer to Figure 1 to familiarize yourself with the controls and features of your machine.

Start the Engine

5 Always check the oil and gas levels before you start to mow, and refill as necessary. To start the engine, first move the Shift Lever to the N, or neutral, position. Then move the Throttle Control to the Choke position. Next, turn on the key to start the engine. Be sure that the Blade Control Switch is down because the engine will not engage if the Blade Control Switch is up. After you move the Throttle Control to Run, move the Shift Lever into the gear you want to be in. Finally,
10 pull up the Blade Control Switch. Now the blade is engaged so it will cut the grass, and you are ready to mow.

Mow the Lawn

Your True Cut lawnmower has a four-speed transmission and a reverse gear. If you are mowing tall, wet grass or mowing on a slope, you should choose a low speed, which would be first or second gear. For wide-open areas, you can use a higher speed. If you need to back up, move the
15 shift lever to the R, or reverse, position.

Stop the Engine

When you are finished mowing, store your mower in a safe, sheltered area. To stop the engine, first disengage the blade by pushing the Blade Control Switch down. Then, move the Shift Lever to the N, or neutral, position. Put the Throttle Control in the Idle position. Finally, turn the key to the Off position so the battery will not discharge.

10. According to the information in the instructions, what would you do if you start to mow and the grass is not being cut?

   A. check the oil and gas levels
   B. move the Throttle Control to the Choke position
   C. put the Shift Lever into N, or neutral
   D. push down the Blade Control Switch

11. From what you have learned about this lawnmower, what advice would you give to someone using it for the first time?

   A. Never use the True Cut self-propelled lawnmower to mow a sloped field.
   B. Use fourth gear only if you are mowing soon after a heavy rain.
   C. If you are in a tight spot and need to make a sharp turn, use reverse.
   D. Put the machine into first gear before you turn the key to the On position.

Reading

Directions: Questions 12–14 refer to the following passage.

"He stares at me," she said. "He sighs and stares at me." I know what my wife looks like in the playground. She wears an old tweed coat, overshoes, and Army gloves, and a scarf is tied under her chin. The playground is a fenced and paved lot between a slum and the river. The picture of the well-dressed, pink-cheeked doctor losing his heart to Ethel in this environment
5   was hard to take seriously. She didn't mention him then for several days, and I guessed that he had stopped his visits. Ethel's birthday came at the end of the month, and I forgot about it, but when I came home that evening, there were a lot of roses in the living room. They were a birthday present from Trencher, she told me. I was cross at myself for having forgotten her birthday, and Trencher's roses made me angry. I asked her if she'd seen him recently.

10   "Oh, yes," she said, "he still comes to the playground nearly every afternoon. I haven't told you, have I? He's made his declaration. He loves me. He can't live without me. He'd walk through fire to hear the notes of my voice." She laughed. "That's what he said."

"When did he say this?"

"At the playground. And walking home. Yesterday."

15   "How long has he known?"

"That's the funny part about it," she said. "He knew before he met me at the Newsomes' that night. He saw me waiting for a crosstown bus about three weeks before that. He just saw me and he said that he knew then, the minute he saw me. Of course, he's crazy."

—Excerpted from "The Season of Divorce," by John Cheever

12. What is the main subject of this passage?
    - A. Ethel's behavior at the playground
    - B. a relationship between Ethel and Trencher
    - C. an argument between Ethel and her husband
    - D. Ethel's birthday

13. Which of the author's techniques is the most effective for developing Trencher's character?
    - A. comparing and contrasting Trencher and Ethel's husband
    - B. providing a physical description of Trencher
    - C. describing Trencher's feelings in Trencher's own words
    - D. including the characters' descriptions of Trencher's actions

14. Which statement best describes the narrator's feelings about Trencher's odd relationship with Ethel?
    - A. He takes no interest at first but becomes annoyed when Trencher sends roses.
    - B. His early annoyance gives way to a feeling of happiness for his wife.
    - C. He thinks it is funny that Ethel is imagining a relationship with Trencher.
    - D. He is upset that Ethel is making up lies about Trencher.

Reading

Directions: Questions 15–17 refer to the following editorial

Until now, Crystal Lake in Clearwater has been a private town lake open only to residents of the town. At last month's selectmen's meeting, a suggestion was made to open Crystal Lake to the public.

5

Crystal Lake is a glacial lake. It was formed when glacial ice was buried during the Ice Age. When the ice melted, the depression filled with the water that became Crystal Lake. Today Crystal Lake's water reflects its name. As a result, it is a popular place for swimming, sailing, canoeing, and kayaking. Such a peaceful, beautiful recreation area would attract visitors from all over.

10

15

Crystal Lake is free for all Clearwater residents. If the lake were open to the public, Clearwater could charge an admission fee similar to the fee at state parks. This fee would be charged to nonresidents only. Therefore, Clearwater residents could still use the lake free of charge. The money earned from nonresident visitors could help fund services and salaries in Clearwater. Thus, Crystal Lake could provide valuable income for the town.

20

25

Some people are worried about trash leading to pollution. If Crystal Lake established a carry-in, carry-out policy for trash, the town would not accumulate more waste. Another concern is additional traffic. Since the lake is located in the far northwest corner of town, additional traffic would not cause a problem in town.

30

Please come to the next selectmen's meeting and let your opinion be heard.

35

15. According to the arguments in this editorial, what can you conclude about the bias, or opinion, of the writer?

   A. Nonresidents should be charged a fee but allowed access to Crystal Lake.
   B. Only residents of Clearwater should be allowed access to Crystal Lake.
   C. Every visitor to Crystal Lake should pay an admittance fee to support the costs of operating the lake.
   D. Both residents and nonresidents should be allowed to sail free in the lake.

16. If the selectmen are discussing an issue involving the town forest, what do you think the writer of the editorial will likely do?

   A. move out of Clearwater
   B. spend the evening of the meeting at Crystal Lake
   C. attend the meeting and express an opinion
   D. discuss waste disposal issues for the town

17. On the basis of the opinions expressed in the editorial, which of these opinions is the writer likely to have?

   A. The selectmen should not listen to public opinion about the issue.
   B. Motorboats should be allowed at Crystal Lake.
   C. Nonresidents would overcrowd and thus cause water pollution.
   D. Charging admittance fees to nonresidents might lower town taxes.

Reading

Directions: Questions 18–20 refer to the following passage.

I was at first very uncomfortable in that strange country. Although I could handle the language well, I seemed to be making a lot of mistakes somehow. It was obvious that
5 people were beginning to think I was very cold, even though I felt very friendly toward them. Slowly it began to dawn on me that my sense of distance was different from theirs.

I saw a man I barely knew approaching
10 me on a road one day. He began to wave when he was still forty feet from me and was talking when he was yet twenty feet away. I did not respond at all until he was within ten feet of me: I waved. I began my hellos when
15 we were about five feet apart. I hadn't even realized that he had been waving at me from that great distance. I didn't know that he had been talking to me from twenty feet away. By the time I responded to seeing him, he had
20 already begun to think I had insulted him.

Another time, when I was being introduced to someone, I extended my hand to shake his. He held my hand so long that I began to feel uncomfortable and finally had
25 to pull away. The conversation didn't last long. The man thought me impolite. My own background had taught me that a handshake should last about two seconds; his culture prescribed a handshake of nearly a half-
30 minute with the last twenty seconds more like holding hands than a handshake.

Once I learned to begin waving from farther away and to hold a handshake for thirty seconds, people stopped regarding
35 me as cold. But I had to change the sense of distance I had grown up with. I had to understand that forty feet was close enough to wave and that holding hands with a stranger was nothing more than basic
40 courtesy.

18. What does this passage compare?
    A. two strangers on the street
    B. waving and shaking hands
    C. customs from two cultures
    D. time and distance

19. Why does the author become accustomed to waving from farther away and holding hands for a longer time?
    A. He does not want to offend anyone.
    B. He is tired of saying hello.
    C. It is required by law.
    D. He is learning a new language.

20. What was the author most comfortable with at first?
    A. ways to greet people
    B. the language
    C. changes in his diet
    D. the cold weather

Answer Key

1. **B.** The passage states that the medium of today is electric technology (lines 1–2) and that media shape society (lines 13–14).

2. **C.** The context clues tell you that *by osmosis* means "in an unconscious manner" (lines 18–19).

3. **B.** Television is an example of electric technology, which is the medium of our time (lines 1–2). Television has a big effect on our social and personal lives.

4. **D.** Because Io "filled half the sky" and Jupiter "was invisible" (lines 37–38), you can infer that Io is larger than Jupiter.

5. **C.** Since the broomstick is becoming longer, *stretch* is the best possible synonym for *telescope*.

6. **A.** Line 19 uses the term "zero-gravity" to describe a construction project. Line 36 describes *Discovery* as being "in orbit." Lines 37–38 say Io "half filled the sky" and Jupiter was "on the other side of the satellite."

7. **C.** In this workplace document, the president informs department heads they are responsible for notifying their staff members about the bad-weather policy.

8. **D.** This is a message from the president to the department heads telling them about the new policy regarding office closing in case of bad weather.

9. **A.** This is an official report of a workplace procedure. It outlines steps to be taken by the president, department heads, and employees.

10. **D.** The Blade Control Switch engages and disengages the blade. If the grass is not being cut, the Blade Control Switch is not engaged.

11. **C.** If you need to make a sharp turn, it may be easier to back up before making the turn. Use the reverse gear to back up.

12. **B.** Most of the description and all of the conversation deal with the relationship between Ethel and Trencher, the doctor who watches Ethel on the playground.

13. **D.** The narrator, Ethel's husband, describes how Trencher looks (line 4) and what Trencher does for Ethel's birthday. Ethel describes what Trencher does at the park ("He stares at me," line 1), what he says to her, and when he decided he loved her. That is how the reader learns about Trencher.

14. **A.** Until Trencher sent the roses, the narrator found this relationship "hard to take seriously" (line 5). But once he saw the flowers, he began asking questions.

15. **A.** All the arguments support allowing nonresidents to use the lake. It is clear that the writer wants the lake to be free for town residents but wants nonresidents to pay fees.

16. **C.** The writer seems to be interested in issues affecting the town and likes to express opinions about these issues. It is likely the writer would attend the selectmen's meeting

17. **D.** Since the writer gives arguments that support nonresidents using the lake if they pay a fee, the writer might be in favor of lowering taxes because of the new town revenue.

18. **C.** This passage emphasizes the differences between customs of the author's native land and the customs of the "strange country" (line 2).

19. **A.** The author mentions that before he changed his ways, people he met thought he was cold and impolite. The author's changed behavior corrected this situation.

20. **B.** In lines 2–3, the author mentions being comfortable speaking the language in this strange country.

Evaluation Chart

Check Your Understanding

On the following chart, circle the number of any question you answered incorrectly. Under each content area you will see the pages you can review to study the content covered in the question. Pay particular attention to reviewing those lessons in which you missed half or more of the questions.

Chapter	Item Number	Study Pages
Functional Texts	7, 8, 9, 10, 11	12–83
Expository Texts	1, 2, 3	86–113
Persuasive Texts	15, 16, 17	116–152
Literary Nonfiction	18, 19, 20	156–185
Fiction	4, 5, 6, 12, 13, 14	188–247

UNIT 1

Informational Texts

Functional Texts

You have the opportunity to apply for the job of your dreams. You are excited about presenting yourself and your abilities in the best possible way. Your first hurdle, however, is to fill out the company's job application form. It seems to go on forever! This is your best opportunity to highlight your skills and special talents, so you want to do your best.

Learning how to read and fill out functional documents can help you perform tasks in the workplace. It can also help you at home when you pay bills on the Internet, read instruction manuals, or apply to your school for financial aid.

Why study functional texts? In the job market today, companies seek employees who can understand company policies and rules, forms, and training information. The information in Chapter 1 provides tips and valuable information so you become familiar with the kinds of documents you will encounter in your workplace and your personal life.

In this chapter you will study these topics:

Lesson 1.1 Memos and Forms
Can you fill out an application to become a volunteer or to apply for a credit card? How do you request vacation time from your employer? You will encounter these kinds of documents on a daily basis. Learn how to use them effectively.

Lesson 1.2 How-To and Instructions
What if your computer printer breaks down just as you are finishing an important project? What can you do? By reading and following problem-solving instructions, you could get your printer going again and save your project.

Lesson 1.3 Websites
You can e-mail people in other countries with the click of a mouse. In a few seconds, you can find information on the Internet about almost any topic. Learn how websites help you navigate the information highway.

Lesson 1.4 Workplace Documents
Offices, factories, and other businesses use workplace documents such as forms and instructions. Knowing how to read and use them will help you be more effective at work.

Lesson 1.5 Graphic Documents
Graphic documents include signs, maps, and other visual images. Learn how to interpret the facts when reading visual formats.

Lesson 1.6 Reference Texts
Where would you look to find a synonym for a word? Where could you find detailed information about a research topic? Learn which reference text to use for a specific purpose.

Lesson 1.7 Comparing Texts in Different Media
You have a variety of media options you can use when searching for information—print, audio, video, and digital. Learning how to use the various formats will enhance your understanding of the topic.

Goal Setting

What do you hope to gain by reading this chapter? Think carefully about functional documents you have used at your job and at home. How can these lessons improve the way you use functional documents?

What kinds of functional documents do you use in your daily life? List as many as you can.

_____

_____

_____

_____

_____

Why do you think it is important to know how to read functional documents? How can this help you in everyday life?

_____

_____

_____

_____

Memos and Forms

KEY CONCEPT: Memos and forms are common documents employers use to share information with their employees.

Have you ever filled out an application for a new job or received a message from your employer? If so, you are familiar with memos and forms. These are two of the most common business documents you will encounter. When reading memos and forms, you need to interpret the information they provide so you can use them properly.

Informational Text

Informational text includes business documents. Two of the most common types of business documents are memos and forms.

One important way that companies communicate with their employees is by using memos. **Memos** are brief messages that can tell you about an upcoming meeting or about changes in employee policies. Today memos are usually sent by e-mail. A good memo will have the following information: the receiver's name, the sender's name, the date, and the subject.

This memo contains information about an employee's contract.

MEMO

To:	**Janice Gonzalez**
From:	**Ida Francese, Director of Human Resources**
Date:	**February 10, 2014**
Subject:	**Terms of Employment Agreement**

This certifies that Phoebe's Fitness Gym will employ Janice Gonzalez as an instructor. Ms. Gonzalez will work for three seasons this year—fall, winter, and spring. She will teach at least two basic courses each season. Duties will vary depending on the number of clients who request a personal trainer.

The employee may be dismissed by Phoebe's Fitness Gym for any of the following reasons:

- Repeated unexcused absences

- Repeated lateness

- Unprofessional behavior

Any complaints by clients about an employee will be discussed with the employee.

UNDERSTAND INFORMATION

You **encounter**, or come across, many kinds of information that affect your life on a daily basis. You look at bus or train schedules to figure out how to get somewhere on time. You read the instructions on a website to download your favorite music.

Information may be presented as visuals rather than as text. Charts, graphs, pictures, maps, and tables are examples. Visuals can help explain information in an easy-to-understand way. In a chart, for instance, numbers or facts are put in groups, called **categories**, based on what they have in common so you can compare the categories. These categories are usually organized into rows or columns.

Read the chart below. **Interpret**, or figure out, the information. What information does this chart provide? Who might use this information?

Occupation	Training and Requirements	Salary Range
Auto Service Technician	vocational school community college apprenticeship certification	$24,800–$43,600 per year
Licensed Practical Nurse	1 year vocational school; 1 year community college	$28,200–$53,500 per year
Postal Clerk	written exam; high school diploma or equivalency helpful	$43,800–$53,000 per year

The chart provides information about three occupations. It uses categories to compare the training required and the salary range for workers in each field. Such a chart would be useful to someone who is choosing a career path or thinking about a career change.

Reading Skill
Draw Conclusions

Memos that are sent to employees contain important information. The memo on page 14 was sent by the director of human resources to a person who was recently hired to work for the company. The memo explains the terms of employment that the employee and the company have agreed to.

As you read the memo, ask yourself: *What are the employee's responsibilities? What can she expect to receive if she fulfills her responsibilities? What can she expect if she does not fulfill her responsibilities?*

To buy something online or open a bank account, you need to be familiar with forms. Forms have blank lines to write or type on. They can also have a list of items for you to check off.

Forms are often used at work. For example, a timesheet records how many hours an employee worked in a week.

Follow these steps when completing forms to avoid making mistakes:

- Do not start to fill out the form until you have read all instructions.
- Notice headings that separate one section from another.
- Pay attention to **optional** sections, that is, sections you may not have to fill out.
- Look for numbers and letters that give steps in a sequence.
- Look up unfamiliar words in a dictionary.

WRITE TO LEARN

What if there were no forms? What if information had to be shared another way? Think about a form you have filled out. Would it be easier or more difficult to complete this task without a form?

Write a brief journal entry discussing the pros and cons of using that form.

Forms ask you to fill in information. They provide space for you to write or type in the information. Forms such as job applications are called **functional** documents because they have a specific function, or purpose—to provide required information in a certain format.

Read the business form below that lists possible violations to company policies. A **violation** is a failure to follow specific company policies.

Employee Disciplinary Action Form

Please complete this form and place it in the Human Resources in-box. Managers submitting forms may sign their own forms. Other employees must obtain a manager's signature before submitting this form. The information provided will remain confidential unless appropriate authorization is received.

Section A

Submitting Employee's Name: _____ Date: _____

requests disciplinary action against

Employee's Name: _____

Department: _____

Supervisor: _____ Hire Date : _____

Today's Date: _____ Date of Incident (if applicable): _____

Section B

Reasons for disciplinary action request (check all that apply):

_____ repeated lateness   _____ harassment of workers

_____ repeated absence   _____ disobeying authority

_____ violation of smoking policy   _____ personal use of company property

_____ violation of dress code

_____ other (please explain) _____

Section C

Please describe the incident(s) in detail below, including date, time, and context of incident, witnesses, and prior attempts at correcting behavior.

_____

_____

Section D (optional)

Additional Comments: _____

_____

Submitting Employee's Signature: _____

Manager's Signature: _____

THINK ABOUT READING

Directions: Answer the questions below.

1. What is the purpose of the Employee Disciplinary Action Form?

   A. to request a leave of absence
   B. to request a vacation
   C. to request a review of an employee's behavior
   D. to request that an employee be removed from the company

2. Under what circumstances would only one signature be needed at the bottom of the form?

   A. An employee submits the form.
   B. A manager submits the form.
   C. The violation of company policy is minor.
   D. The violation of company policy is major.

3. Which type of company policy violation is not specifically listed on this form?

   A. harassing a fellow worker
   B. wearing inappropriate clothing
   C. revealing confidential information to others
   D. using the office telephone to make personal calls

4. List three details that are required in Section C.

   _____

   _____

   _____

5. Name one section of the form that the employee submitting the form does not need to fill out.

   _____

   _____

WRITE TO LEARN

Read the *Disciplinary Action Form* on page 16. A *Disciplinary Action Form* is used to review an employee's behavior.

Imagine you are a manager who needs to submit a *Disciplinary Action Form* about an employee who is continually late for work. In a notebook, make a list of the required information you will need to provide to complete this form.

TECHNOLOGY CONNECTION

Online Forms

Today almost anything can be done online. You can register your car, pay taxes, apply for insurance, and manage credit card bills. To do these things, though, it is necessary to complete forms.

Online forms often look like paper forms. Instead of writing information on blank lines, however, online forms usually require you to type information into blank boxes. All other rules for using forms apply to both paper and online versions.

Vocabulary Review

Directions: Use these words to complete the following sentences.

categories   violation   functional   encounter   optional

1. Organizing information into _____ is a way to compare information.

2. You _____ many kinds of information on a daily basis.

3. A form providing specific information is a(n) _____ document.

4. Filling out Section C on this application form is _____.

5. Tanya was fired because of a major _____ of company policy.

Skill Review

Directions: Read the following excerpt from an employee handbook. Then answer the questions.

Memo to Zoo Employees

The Metropolitan Zoo prides itself on meeting the needs of its employees and their families. If a serious medical condition, such as a scheduled surgery or the birth of a child, prevents you from working for more than 10 consecutive workdays, you may take a medical leave of absence from your job. This leave of absence may be extended for up to one year. It is available to full-time employees after six months of employment.

Employees who take a medical leave of absence may be asked to do the following:

- Obtain a medical evaluation from a physician selected by the zoo.

- Complete the forms required by the human resources department.

- Join a rehabilitation program, if necessary (see section 5A on Substance Abuse).

- Obtain a physician's release note before returning to work.

If a sudden and serious medical condition develops (for example, appendicitis) that requires an extended absence, you (or a family member) must notify your supervisor as soon as possible and maintain contact with him or her throughout your absence. If your absence will exceed 10 consecutive days (a medical leave of absence), then your supervisor may need to arrange for temporary coverage of your job duties. Therefore, advance notice (when possible) of such absences is greatly appreciated.

When you return to work after your medical leave of absence, you will return to your former position, if it is available, or to a similar position. If other positions are available at the Metropolitan Zoo at that time, you may apply for them.

Skill Review (continued)

1. How long must an employee work at the Metropolitan Zoo to qualify for the extended medical leave policy?

    A. one year
    B. one month
    C. six months
    D. six weeks

2. Which of the following is not something a zoo employee might be asked to do during an extended medical leave?

    A. attend physical therapy sessions
    B. fill out paperwork
    C. get a doctor's permission to return to work
    D. attend substance abuse support group sessions

3. Why is an employee handbook a good place to include a Medical Leave document?

    _____

    _____

    _____

    _____

4. You work at the Metropolitan Zoo and have been asked to create a form that an employee can submit to a manager when applying for a medical leave. What information would you include on this form?

    _____

    _____

    _____

    _____

    _____

    _____

    _____

    _____

    _____

    _____

    _____

Skill Practice

Directions: Choose the one best answer to each question. Questions 1 through 4 refer to the following business memo.

MEMO

To: Employees of Peyton Discount Stores
From: Samantha Peyton, Owner of Peyton Discount Stores
Date: January 30, 2014
Subject: Shoplifting Reminders

In the wake of the shoplifting attempt in the hardware department of our Louisville store last month, I would like to take this opportunity to remind you of the proper procedures for handling a suspected shoplifter in one of our stores.

5   Please be advised that in a situation where a suspected shoplifter is still present in the store, all efforts should be made to delay his or her departure from the store to allow time for the proper authorities to arrive at the scene. However, at no time should human safety be at risk. The shoplifter should not be confronted, accused, or physically prevented from leaving the store.

10   If a shoplifter leaves the store, employees should remain inside the store and follow the instructions of the store manager. These instructions may include noting the make, model, and license plate number of any vehicle the suspect uses to leave the store and attempting to assess the physical appearance of the suspect, including height, weight, hair color, and any distinguishing physical features. In an effort to make our store "unfriendly" to shoplifters, remain visible to customers at all times. This can deter

15   potential shoplifters, who usually prefer to remain unnoticed by store employees.

Your cooperation with these safety procedures is greatly appreciated.

Skill Practice (continued)

1. What is the best description of this document?

   A. a leave-of-absence request form
   B. a company policy memo
   C. an employment application
   D. a letter of complaint

2. If a suspected shoplifter has left the store, which action are store employees advised to take?

   A. leave the store and wait for police outside
   B. confront the shoplifter
   C. follow the suspect to his or her vehicle
   D. follow their manager's instructions

3. What is Samantha Peyton's job?

   A. She is a security guard.
   B. She is a cashier.
   C. She is the head of the human resources department.
   D. She is the store owner.

4. Store employees are urged to "make our store 'unfriendly' to shoplifters" (lines 13–14). What does this mean?

   A. Use practices that discourage shoplifting.
   B. Make customers feel unwelcome.
   C. Follow customers throughout the store.
   D. Place shoppers' safety at risk.

5. What is the main purpose of business memos?

   A. to entertain
   B. to confuse
   C. to inform
   D. to criticize

Writing Practice

Directions: Imagine you are the president of a small company and you have good news to share with your employees. For example, you might want to share the news that profits were up last year, so everyone will get a raise. Write a memo to your employees sharing your good news and explaining what happened. Use the memo from this lesson as a model.

How-To and Instructions

Lesson Objectives

You will be able to

• Recognize the correct sequence of steps

• Follow directions and instructions

• Understand how directions and instructions are organized

Skills

• **Core Skill:** Understand Diagrams

• **Reading Skill:** Sequence Events

Vocabulary

diagram
instructions
résumé
sequence

KEY CONCEPT: How-to texts and instructions explain how to make something or how to do something.

Imagine that you just bought a new computer program. Before you can use the program, you have to install it on your computer. To figure out how to install the program, what would you do? You would probably start by reading the instructions on the back of the box. Every time you read an owner's manual, follow a recipe, or read directions, you are reading instructional texts.

How-To and Instructions

Instructions explain how to do something. When reading instructions and how-to texts, it is helpful to remember these steps:

1. Read all of the steps before you do anything.

2. Then return to the beginning and reread each step one at a time. Make sure you understand what each step is asking you to do. Complete one task before beginning the next step.

3. As you read, keep in mind the task you are trying to do. That will help you understand the steps.

4. Always follow the steps in **sequence**, or in order. Look for signal words such as *first*, *next*, or *finally* or numbers that show you the order of the steps.

Read the following instructions for changing a flat tire. Look for signal words to help you follow the sequence.

How to Change a Flat Tire

Imagine you are in the car on the way to a friend's house. All of a sudden, the car seems difficult to steer. It's bumping and seems unbalanced. When you pull off to the side of the road, you realize the car has a flat tire. Don't panic—a flat tire is easy to fix.

Choose a Safe Spot

First, pull the car off the road so that it is out of traffic. Make sure you are on a straight part of the road so other cars will see you. You need to be on a level spot because it is unsafe to jack up a car on a slope, or slight incline. Then turn on the hazard lights to signal to other drivers that you are repairing your car. Hazard lights blink to show other drivers that the car is not operating. The switch for these lights is usually near the steering wheel.

FOLLOW A SEQUENCE OF STEPS

How-to texts and instructions describe the steps for completing an activity. Before following a sequence of steps, start by reading all of the instructions. You will often find that you need to understand everything in the sequence before you begin.

Depending on the activity, you may need to gather supplies or information before you begin. In many workplace tasks, you may not be able to stop to look something up or find materials once you have begun a task. You may have to start over from the beginning, or you may inconvenience others who are waiting.

There may also be times when steps are written out of order. If you read all instructions at the beginning, you will be able to identify this problem. Then you can figure out the correct order of steps.

Read these instructions for making a three-way telephone call. What is the matter with the instructions?

Placing a Three-Way Call

Call the first participant.

Dial the second participant.

Place the first caller on hold by pressing the conference button.

Press the conference button again.

Readers will not be able to follow these directions. They cannot call the second participant before putting the first participant on hold.

Now revise the directions above so that the steps are in the correct sequence.

Did you use the words *first*, *next*, *then*, and *finally*? Using number and word clues can help a reader understand directions and follow them successfully.

When you are following a sequence of steps, try to put each step in your own words to make sure you understand it. You may find it helpful to keep track of the steps by making a numbered list of the steps. Read your list to make sure you did not leave out any steps.

Read the instructions on this page for changing a tire. In a notebook, write a numbered list of the sequence of steps in your own words.

WRITE TO LEARN

Think about a task you do every day that requires several steps. It could be something simple, such as making and packing your lunch, or something more complicated.

In your notebook, write a how-to text that explains the steps in sequence. Have a classmate read your how-to text and see if it is easy to follow.

Get Your Tools

Once the car is in a safe spot, you are ready to change the tire. Get the spare tire, the jack, and a lug wrench. If you aren't sure where these things are in your car, look at the owner's manual. This guide will tell you where to find the tools you need.

Change Your Tire

First, if the car has hubcaps, you need to remove them. Then, use the lug wrench to loosen the lug nuts, but not all the way. You want them to hold the tire as you raise the car. Now you are ready to jack up the car. Look at the owner's manual to see where to position the jack. Put the jack in the correct spot under the car and jack up the car until the tire is about 6 inches off the ground. Now remove the lug nuts and pull the wheel off the car. Replace the flat tire with the spare tire, and tighten the lug nuts just enough to hold the tire on as you lower the car. Lower the car with the jack until the car is resting on all four tires. Finally, use the lug wrench again to tighten the lug nuts all the way.

This picture shows where to place the jack when changing a tire.

Clean Up

First, put the flat tire where the spare tire was. Then put away the tools and double-check to make sure you are not leaving anything behind.

THINK ABOUT READING

Directions: Answer the questions that follow.

1. Which pair of steps is in the correct sequence?

   A. Remove the lug nuts. Then take off the hub cap.
   B. Loosen the lug nuts. Then jack up the car.
   C. Tighten the lug nuts all the way. Then lower the car.
   D. Turn on your hazard lights. Then pull the car off the road.

2. Which step in changing a flat tire can the photograph help you understand?

   _____

Directions: Read this passage. Pay careful attention to the sequence of steps in the instructions.

Clearing a Paper Jam in a Copy Machine

If you have ever used a copy machine, chances are you've experienced a paper jam. Office copy machines use a lot of paper, and sometimes paper gets caught inside the machine. If a paper jam occurs while you are using a copy machine, it is a good idea to clear, or fix, the paper jam so the next person using the machine won't be inconvenienced.

Clearing a paper jam is usually quite easy. However, there are some steps you should follow to do it correctly. It is important to follow these steps so you don't damage the copy machine.

First, you should try to find the location of the paper jam. Carefully open the cover of the copy machine and the paper tray to see exactly where the paper is jammed. Once you have located the jam, turn off the copy machine.

Once the power is off, try to pull the paper out of the machine. Pull gently! If you pull too hard, the paper may rip or you may damage the inside of the copy machine. It is important to pull the paper the opposite direction that it was fed into the copier.

Next, check to make sure the entire sheet of paper was removed. Make sure there are no paper fragments or torn pieces still stuck in the machine. Carefully check to make sure none of the copier parts are loose or broken.

Then replace the cover and the paper tray and turn the machine back on. Press the button to cancel the paper jam message. The display on the machine should tell you which button to push.

Finally, it is a good idea to test to be sure the jam is fixed by copying one sheet. If you have no problem making that copy, the jam is cleared. If you get another error message, you may have to repeat the steps above.

Happy copying!

Core Skill
Understand Diagrams

Diagrams are pictures that show what something is, what the parts of something are, or how something is organized.

To understand a diagram, read the title and the labels. The title will tell you what the diagram is about. The labels will identify the parts of the diagram. There are usually lines or arrows from a label to the part it describes.

This is a sequence diagram. It shows the order of steps.

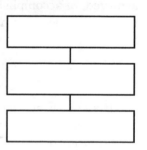

In a notebook, create a sequence diagram that shows the steps for clearing a paper jam.

THINKING ABOUT **READING**

Directions: Answer the questions in the space provided.

1. What should you do first to clear a paper jam?

   _____

2. In what situation would you have to repeat these instructions?

   _____

   _____

Directions: Read this selection and answer the questions that follow.

How to Write a Résumé

Whether you are applying for your first job or trying to get a better job, a good résumé can help you stand out from the crowd. A **résumé** is a list of all your qualifications, or skills, for doing a job. Your résumé is your first chance to make a good impression on an employer, so take the time to do it right.

First, type your name, address, phone number, and e-mail address. Make sure you type this information correctly. An employer needs accurate information about how to get in touch with you.

Next, write your objective statement. This is a sentence or two that tells what kind of job you want. Be sure to match this statement to the job you are applying for. For example, if you are applying to be a waitress, you might write: *I want a service career in the restaurant industry.* Write your objective statement carefully. It's one of the first things an employer will see.

Now you are ready to list your work and education history. Start with your most recent job. State your position title and the dates you had this job. Then tell what you achieved, or accomplished, in this position. If you are applying for your first job, list volunteer experience or school activities. Describe what you did when you participated in these activities.

Next, list your education. Name the schools you have attended and give their location. List any degrees or certificates you have received.

If you have special skills, list them next. You can include computer programs you know how to use. You can also list any special training you have, such as CPR or lifeguard certification, and any volunteer activities you participate in.

Finally, include references. References are people that your future employer can call or contact to learn more about you. References can be people you have worked for, teachers, or people who have known you for a long time. Choose people who can explain why you would be a good employee.

Before you send your résumé, review it carefully. Check that it is neat, organized, and free from mistakes. Remember that your employer will use your résumé to decide whether he or she will interview you for a job. Your résumé represents you. Make sure it shows why you are the best person for the job.

Joseph Kline
12 Main Street • Anytown, NY 12201
555-1234 • joseph_kline@email.com

OBJECTIVE
An administrative assistant position requiring strong organization and planning skills to provide exceptional support to a vice president in the financial industry.

WORK EXPERIENCE
Buy Stuff Here, Colonial Mall, Anytown, NY
Sales Associate, December 2011 – Present

• Maintain and restock inventory
• Provide customer service
• Operate computerized cash register system

EDUCATION
Anytown High School, Anytown, NY
September 2009 – May 2012

SPECIAL SKILLS
• Proficient with Microsoft Word, Excel, and PowerPoint

REFERENCES
• Carla Mendez, Store Manager, Buy Stuff Here: 555-2121
• Dr. Louis Jones, English teacher, Anytown High School: 555-8989

Skill Review (continued)

1. What is the first thing you should do when you write a résumé? Why is this important?

   _____

2. Why should you write an objective?

   _____

   _____

3. What should you list on a résumé after you have described your education?

   _____

   _____

4. Look at the diagram at the end of the selection. What does this diagram show you?

   _____

5. According to the passage and the diagram, what comes after your objective?

   _____

Vocabulary Review

Directions: Use these words to complete the following sentences.

diagram   instructions   résumé   sequence

1. The _____ showed Amir how to put a bookshelf together.

2. A well-written _____ is an important tool in finding a new job.

3. The numbers showed the _____ of the steps to connect the DVD player.

4. It is important to read all of the _____ before beginning.

Skill Practice

Directions: Choose the one best answer to each question. Questions 1 through 4 refer to the following passage.

Using the Self-Timer on a Digital Camera

How many times have you taken pictures of your friends and family and wished you could be in the picture too? Once you learn how to use the self-timer button on your digital camera, you can always be a part of a group picture.

First, organize the people you want in the picture into a group. Leave a space for
5   yourself. Then, turn on the self-timer button on your camera. It will probably look like a clock timer.

Set your camera on a flat, even surface. Now, push the shutter button halfway to focus the camera. Check your screen to make sure the picture is the way you want it. Then, push the button the rest of the way and move into your spot. As you push the
10   button, make sure you don't move the camera from its position.

You will have about 10 seconds to get into your spot.

1. According to the passage, what is the first step for using the self-timer on a digital camera?

   A. Move into the spot you have left for yourself.
   B. Set your camera on a flat, even surface.
   C. Turn on the self-timer button on your camera.
   D. Organize the people who will be in the picture.

3. What might happen if you push the shutter button all the way instead of halfway?

   A. Your picture will not be in focus.
   B. Your timer won't be set.
   C. There will not be space for you in the picture.
   D. Your camera will not be on a flat, even surface.

2. What might happen if you forget to do both parts of the first step?

   A. You will forget to get into the picture.
   B. Your picture will not be in focus.
   C. There will not be room for you in the picture.
   D. The self-timer button will not work.

4. What should you do after you push the shutter button halfway?

   A. Push the button all the way down.
   B. Get into your spot for the picture.
   C. Check to make sure the picture is the way you want it.
   D. Make sure your camera is on a flat, even surface.

Writing Practice

Directions: Think about something you read recently. It could be a story or novel, a newspaper article, or an e-mail from a coworker. As you read this text, you had to analyze and make sense of what it said. This process involves several steps. Think about what you need to do to analyze and understand a text. Then write a how-to text or set of instructions for how to do this successfully. When you are finished, share your instructions with friend or classmate. Can he or she follow the steps?

Websites

KEY CONCEPT: A website is a collection of web pages that give information about a topic.

Suppose you are planning a vacation. You will probably want to know what attractions to see, where to eat, and where to stay. You can find all the information you need on the Internet. Websites give information about topics, and they may also link you to other sites about your topic. Websites make it fast and easy to gather information.

Websites

Websites are different from other sources of information. That is because anyone can put anything on the **Internet**, a worldwide system of computer networks. Therefore, it is very important to check the **reliability** (accuracy) of any website you use for information. Ask the following questions:

- Does the website have an author? Is the author an expert, or someone whose job it is to know about the topic?

- Is the information accurate? Are dates and facts correct?

- Is the website up-to-date? When was it last updated?

- What is the purpose of the website?

One way to judge the reliability of a website, is to look at its address, or **URL**. Museums, science centers, and other organizations usually have website addresses that end in *.org*. The URLs for schools and universities usually end in *.edu*. Web addresses for government offices end in *.gov*. The URLs for businesses end in *.com*.

When you are doing research, sites with addresses ending in *.edu* or *.gov* will probably be the most reliable sources of information. Be aware that sites with addresses ending in *.com* are in the business of trying to persuade you to buy something. The information on these sites may not be reliable.

SCAN TO FIND INFORMATION

When you perform a search in an online search engine, don't read every item that appears in the list of results. Instead, move your eyes down the screen to find words or phrases that relate to your topic. This is called **scanning**. When you scan a text, you don't read every word. You look quickly to find specific information.

Scanning is useful when you are looking at a **reference source**, such as an encyclopedia or a website, that contains factual information. By scanning the page, you can quickly determine whether the text has the information you are looking for. If it does, you can go back and read more closely.

When you scan, look for

- **key words**, words that are central to the main idea
- definitions
- numbers and dates
- headings and links
- specific examples, including graphs, charts, and diagrams

Scan the following paragraph. Underline terms that quickly give you important information about a Global Positioning System.

> Cars are "smarter" than ever before. One new device that many cars have is called a **Global Positioning System**, or **GPS**. GPS was developed in 1973. It uses satellites to track the location of a vehicle. Drivers can enter the address they want to go to, and the GPS maps the trip. The best route appears on a screen.

You might have underlined *GPS*, *1973*, *satellites*, and *route*. Now you can read the paragraph more carefully to learn what GPS is.

TECHNOLOGY CONNECTION

Internet News

Look at the front page of your local newspaper or a national newspaper. Now visit the website for that same newspaper.

Compare and contrast the two versions. Are the headlines and photographs the same? Is there information available in one version but not the other?

Make a list of the similarities and differences between the two versions. Then write one conclusion you can draw about the differences between news websites and printed newspapers.

THINKING ABOUT READING

Directions: Answer these questions.

1. What is the purpose of a website with an address ending in *.com*?

   _____

2. Where can you find the most reliable sources of web information?

   _____

   _____

When you are scanning a website, text features can help you locate important ideas quickly. Look for **boldfaced** or *italic* text.

Study the website on this page. Notice that the headings and key words are boldfaced. Boldfaced type makes these words stand out so they are easily seen.

Some websites show key ideas on tabs that appear across the top of the page or in the **margin** (narrow column on the side of a page). These tabs are also called menu bars.

In a notebook, list three tabs on this website and describe what you would find when you click on each of these tabs.

Scanning for Information

When you are looking at a website, you usually want to find a specific piece of information. Before you begin searching the Internet and reading websites, be sure you are clear about what you are seeking. Scan the website below. Think about what questions you could answer by looking at this page.

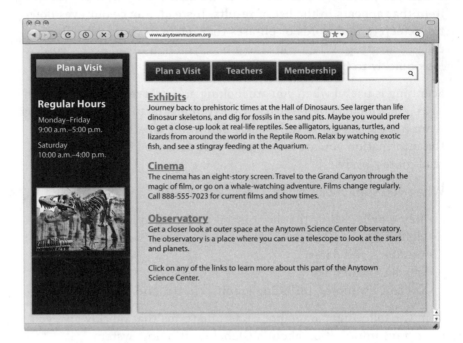

THINK ABOUT **READING**

Directions: Look at the website on this page. Then answer the questions.

1. What should you do if you want to learn more about the Anytown Science Center Observatory?

   _____

2. What features help you scan the information on the website?

   _____

   _____

WRITE TO LEARN

Write a paragraph telling about a website you are designing for your favorite restaurant. Make a list of the information that must be included. Describe how you might organize the information and visuals on the page to encourage people to visit your website. Tell about special features you would include.

Reliability of Information

The most important questions to ask yourself while scanning and reading websites are *Who is providing the information to me?* and *Why?* As you read the website below, keep these questions in mind.

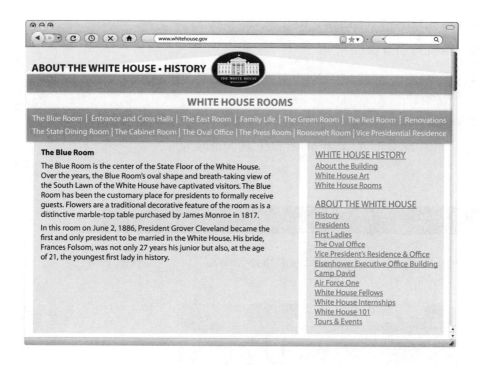

When doing research, you should always look at more than one source. Then you can **synthesize** (combine) ideas and use them to create your own new idea.

Before beginning your research, write several questions that you want answered. As you read, take notes related to your questions. Then synthesize the information to answer your questions.

You might look at the website on this page if you were trying to answer the question *What does the White House look like inside?*

Often websites will include links to related sites. This site will link you to White House Art or First Ladies.

Write one question you would like answered about the White House. Then go online to find two more sources of information related to this topic. List these website addresses in your notebook.

THINKING ABOUT READING

Directions: Write a short response to each question.

1. Scan this web page for information about the White House. What is the main thing you will learn from visiting this page?

_____

2. What happens in the Blue Room? Look at the links in the margin. Which link would you click on to learn more about the rooms in the White House?

_____

_____

3. Is this website reliable? How do you know?

_____

Vocabulary Review

Directions: Match the words to their definitions.

1. Internet

2. key word

3. margin

4. reliability

5. reference source

A. a word that is important to the main idea

B. the side of a page

C. a large computer network that links smaller computer networks

D. accuracy and honesty

E. a book or website that gives factual information

Skill Review

Directions: Scan these two websites. Then answer the questions that follow.

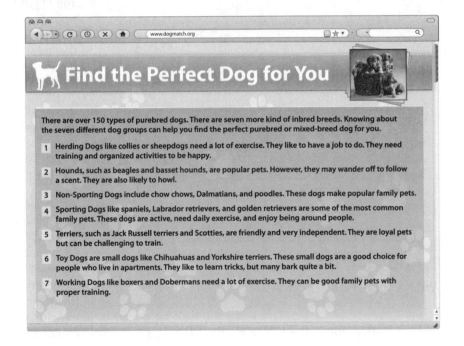

www.dogmatch.org

Find the Perfect Dog for You

There are over 150 types of purebred dogs. There are seven more kind of inbred breeds. Knowing about the seven different dog groups can help you find the perfect purebred or mixed-breed dog for you.

1 Herding Dogs like collies or sheepdogs need a lot of exercise. They like to have a job to do. They need training and organized activities to be happy.

2 Hounds, such as beagles and basset hounds, are popular pets. However, they may wander off to follow a scent. They are also likely to howl.

3 Non-Sporting Dogs include chow chows, Dalmatians, and poodles. These dogs make popular family pets.

4 Sporting Dogs like spaniels, Labrador retrievers, and golden retrievers are some of the most common family pets. These dogs are active, need daily exercise, and enjoy being around people.

5 Terriers, such as Jack Russell terriers and Scotties, are friendly and very independent. They are loyal pets but can be challenging to train.

6 Toy Dogs are small dogs like Chihuahuas and Yorkshire terriers. These small dogs are a good choice for people who live in apartments. They like to learn tricks, but many bark quite a bit.

7 Working Dogs like boxers and Dobermans need a lot of exercise. They can be good family pets with proper training.

Skill Review (continued)

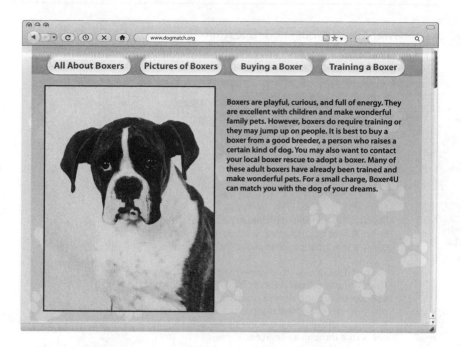

1. In website 1, how many groups of purebred dogs are there? How did the author help you find this information quickly?

_____

_____

2. Scan website 1 and list four or five key words.

_____

_____

3. Which site would be better to use to help you decide what kind of dog is best for you? Explain.

_____

_____

4. What can you conclude about boxers from these websites?

   A. Boxers are working dogs that need training.
   B. Boxers are the perfect dog for everyone.
   C. Boxer4U is the best way to find a dog.
   D. Boxers are sporting dogs that can be bought from breeders.

Skill Practice

Directions: Choose the <u>one best answer</u> to each question. <u>Questions 1 through 4</u> refer to the following websites.

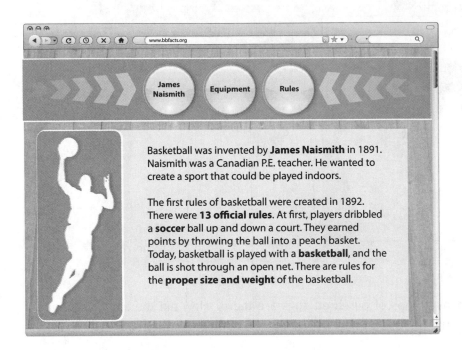

Basketball was invented by **James Naismith** in 1891. Naismith was a Canadian P.E. teacher. He wanted to create a sport that could be played indoors.

The first rules of basketball were created in 1892. There were **13 official rules**. At first, players dribbled a **soccer** ball up and down a court. They earned points by throwing the ball into a peach basket. Today, basketball is played with a **basketball**, and the ball is shot through an open net. There are rules for the **proper size and weight** of the basketball.

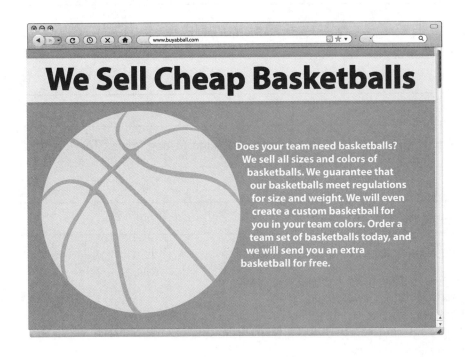

We Sell Cheap Basketballs

Does your team need basketballs? We sell all sizes and colors of basketballs. We guarantee that our basketballs meet regulations for size and weight. We will even create a custom basketball for you in your team colors. Order a team set of basketballs today, and we will send you an extra basketball for free.

Skill Practice (continued)

1. Imagine you are creating a new website about James Naismith. What information would be most important to include?

   A. the rules of basketball
   B. the proper size of a basketball
   C. the date Naismith invented basketball
   D. what Naismith thought about other sports

2. Which is the best website to use for a report about basketball?

   A. Website 1, because it gives facts and details about the history of basketball
   B. Website 1, because it also mentions other sports, like soccer
   C. Website 2, because it describes basketballs
   D. Website 2, because it mentions the size and weight of basketballs

3. What product does website 2 advertise?

   A. Basketball hoops
   B. Colored basketballs
   C. Team uniforms
   D. Basketballs signed by professionals

4. What is the purpose of website 1?

   A. to persuade you to buy a basketball
   B. to explain the rules of basketball
   C. to describe kinds of indoor sports
   D. to give information about basketball

Writing Practice

Directions: Think of a school or company you know only a little bit about. Visit the website of that school or company. Scan the home page and quickly read several of the other pages on the site. How helpful is the website? Can you find information easily? Is it attractive? Write a letter to the school or company, describing your thoughts—either positive or negative—about its website.

Workplace Documents

KEY CONCEPT: Workplace documents are written papers (print or digital) used in offices, factories, and other places where people work. They include instructions or forms.

At your job, you may have read and written many e-mails. Have you ever read job applications or instructions for how to do something? In the workplace, these types of documents are very common. It is important to understand the purpose of documents such as employee handbooks and agendas.

Lesson Objectives

You will be able to

- Recognize the purpose of common workplace documents

- Explain and apply information from common workplace documents

Skills

- **Core Skill:** Summarize Information

- **Reading Skill:** Determine Author's Purpose

Vocabulary

agenda
alternative
design
documents
employee handbook
identify
structure
summarize

Workplace Documents

People encounter workplace documents almost daily, whether they are employed in a government office, a store, a factory, or a school. **Documents** such as e-mails, **employee handbooks** (which explain company rules), **agendas** (which tell what will be discussed at meetings), and safety guidelines provide information needed on the job. The **design**, or appearance, of the documents should help the reader understand the information that is presented.

Some workplace documents are listed here. They fall into two groups: documents you might encounter on a daily basis and documents providing specific information about your job or your workplace.

Everyday Communication	Specific Workplace Documents
E-mail	Job announcement
Memo	Job description
Business letter	Job performance review form
Meeting agenda	Self-assessment form
Request form	Employee handbook
	Safety guidelines

It is important to **identify**, or recognize, the purpose of a workplace document and the audience it was written for.

> Why was the document written? (What is its purpose?)

> Who is supposed to read it? (Who is the audience?)

Once you know a document's purpose and audience, it is helpful to identify the **structure** of the document. In other words, how is information organized? Recognizing the structure of the document makes it easier to find the information you need. Bullet points, numbered steps, section heads, and charts or tables are commonly used to organize information in workplace documents.

DETERMINE AUTHOR'S PURPOSE

An author's purpose for writing a text **varies**, or changes, depending on what is being communicated. Authors generally write to entertain, to inform or teach, or to persuade or convince their readers.

It is important to figure out the purpose of any workplace document you read. Ask yourself: Who wrote the document? What information does it contain? What does the author want me to do after reading the document?

Directions: As you read each document, identify the author's purpose for writing the document.

To: Marketing team

From: Fernando Torres

Subject: Model IP300 product launch meeting

Marketing team,

Good morning! I just want to remind everyone about today's meeting. Let's gather at 2:00 in the conference room on the third floor. Please bring some fresh ideas for the upcoming launch of our new Model IP300!

Fernando Torres
Director, New Product Development

Marketing Meeting Agenda

Here is the agenda for today's 2:00 meeting.

1. Team Update: Shelly (10 min)

2. Results of Online Survey: Jermaine (10 min)

3. Introduction of IP300 New Product Launch: Fernando (20 min)

4. Brainstorming Session: all team members (30 min)

5. Discussion of Next Steps: Fernando (10 min)

Fernando Torres
Director, New Product Development

In a notebook, answer the following questions about each document. Who is the author? What is the author's purpose for writing? Who is the audience? What does the author want the audience to do after reading the document? **Compare** and **contrast** the documents. How are they similar? How are they different?

TECHNOLOGY CONNECTION

Online Workplace Documents

Workplace documents are increasingly available online or in digital form. In some cases, paper documents are being replaced by digital **alternatives**, or substitutes. Because e-mail is faster and more convenient than typing and mailing business letters, e-mail has replaced most typewritten letters.

Employers can e-mail their workers interactive documents, such as questionnaires. Employees read, fill out, and return these forms without ever handling a piece of paper.

In your notebook, compare and contrast reading text on paper with reading text on a computer screen. How are the experiences different? How are they similar? Explain why the workplace is more likely to use online documents than paper documents.

When you **summarize** information from a text, you briefly state the text's main points. Summaries do not include personal opinions or information that was not part of the text. Writing a summary will help you understand and remember the text.

As you read, look for the main idea in each paragraph or section. Watch for places where the author has repeated certain ideas. When you have finished reading, you will be able to write a summary statement that answers this question: What does the author want you to understand and remember?

The process for summarizing information in workplace documents is the same as summarizing other nonfiction texts. As you read the job description on this page, think about the information in each section. What does the author want you to understand about this job? What are the most important parts of the job? Make a chart like the one below to record your summary.

Important Idea	Important Idea
Summary	

Directions: As you read this workplace document, think about its purpose and intended audience. Then answer the question below.

Job Description: Administrative Assistant

Job Purpose: Provides office services by implementing administrative systems and monitoring, or keeping an eye on, administrative projects

Job Duties:

- Manages department schedule by maintaining, or keeping up-to-date, calendars for department supervisors

- Arranges meetings, teleconferences (telephone meetings), and travel

- Prepares department reports, e-mails, invoices, and other documents, using word processing or other computer software

- Opens and distributes, or hands out, incoming correspondence

- Handles incoming phone calls and receives departmental visitors

- Files department's documents

- Maintains office supplies, placing orders for supplies when necessary

Skills/Qualifications: Written and verbal communication skills; organization, scheduling, computer, and office management skills; professionalism

---

THINK ABOUT **READING**

Directions: Review the job description above. What is the purpose of this document? Who is the audience? Answer these questions in the space provided.

_____

_____

_____

_____

_____

Directions: As you read this document, think about its purpose and consider how the document is used in the workplace.

CONFERENCE ROOM RESERVATION REQUEST

**This form must be submitted
at least 3 business days before the event date.**

General Information

Department

Event Date(s)

Contact person

Start Time

E-mail

End Time

Phone

Estimated Attendance

Fax

Equipment Required

Title of Event

Event Type
• Please check the word(s) that best describe your event.

☐ Meeting   ☐ Lecture   ☐ Film/Movie

☐ Seminar   ☐ Webinar (online   ☐ Breakfast
                       presentation)

☐ Reception   ☐ Lunch

                                        ☐ Dinner

Submit

Reading Skill
Determine Author's Purpose

The form on this page is a common type of workplace document. Think about the author's purpose for creating this form. The form requests information from its reader. Other forms that require you to fill in information include W-4 forms for payroll tax deductions and application forms for health insurance.

Many of these forms are available online. Often they are designed to be completed and returned through the Internet or by e-mail.

Compare and contrast online forms with the same forms printed on paper. Is one version more convenient than the other?

In a notebook, write about a time you filled in a form on paper. Do you think you could have provided the same information by using an online form? Why or why not? How is completing a paper form similar to and different from completing an online form?

THINKING ABOUT READING

Directions: What is the purpose of the Conference Room Reservation Request document? How will using this document make work easier for company employees? Answer these questions in the space provided.

_____

_____

_____

_____

Read the message on this page. Imagine that the person sending this e-mail is your supervisor. Write a response in which you answer each of her questions.

Set up your response so it looks like an e-mail message. Since you are the author of this document, think about your purpose for writing. Keep your audience (your supervisor) in mind and use appropriate language.

Directions: As you read this document, identify the author, audience, and purpose in the workplace. Doing this will help you answer the questions that follow.

From: Carolyn Smith <csmith@workplace.com>
To: Brian Yamamoto <byamamoto@workplace.com>
Cc:
Subject: Board of Directors Meeting

2:42 p.m.

Brian,

Happy Monday! I hope you had a nice weekend.

We need to start thinking about next week's meeting with the Board of Directors. I'd like to schedule time today or tomorrow to sit down and talk about your presentation. We can brainstorm to come up with some ideas. Maybe we'll think of something amazing!

Do you think we'll need a computer for the meeting? Do you want to project anything on screen? Will you show a video? If so, we'll have to request the equipment so it's set up on time.

On an unrelated note, did you remember to complete your time sheet for last week? I need to approve it by the end of the day.

Thanks!

Carolyn

Carolyn Smith
Director, Resources
ABC Corporation
123 Main St., New York, NY

THINK ABOUT READING

Directions: Answer these questions about the e-mail from Carolyn Smith to Brian Yamamoto.

1. What is the purpose of this e-mail?

   A. A supervisor wants to ask about an employee's weekend.
   B. A supervisor is checking with an employee about an upcoming meeting.
   C. An employee is checking with a supervisor about an upcoming meeting.
   D. An employee is asking a supervisor a question about his time sheet.

2. What is the purpose of the questions that Carolyn asks in the third paragraph?

   A. to remind Brian to fill out his time sheet
   B. to find a time to set up a meeting
   C. to convince Brian to include visual media
   D. to help Brian plan ahead and prepare for the meeting

3. Which of the following best describes this workplace document?

   A. everyday oral communication
   B. official report of a workplace event
   C. everyday written communication
   D. technical document

4. Which details in the document identify the author? What is the author's relationship to the audience?

   _____

   _____

   _____

Vocabulary Review

Directions: Match each vocabulary word with its definition.

1. _____ agenda
2. _____ alternative
3. _____ design
4. _____ document
5. _____ employee handbook
6. _____ identify
7. _____ structure

A. text that explains a company's rules and workers' benefits
B. to recognize something
C. list of subjects for discussion
D. the look or appearance of an item
E. a text or piece of writing
F. the form and organization of a text
G. a replacement of one thing for another

Directions: Read the documents below. Then answer the questions that follow.

Memorandum to all ABC Company Facilities

ABC Company Safety and Health Policy

The purpose of this policy is to develop the highest possible standard of safety in all operations of ABC Company. Our management gives top priority to the prevention of occupational injury or illness.

It is our intention here at ABC Company to initiate and maintain comprehensive accident-prevention and safety-training programs. Employees are responsible for their health and safety and for the health and safety of their coworkers. By accepting mutual responsibility to operate safely, each of us contributes to the well-being of all employees.

Sincerely,

Shaundra Wright
CEO
ABC Company

ABC Company Safety Program Outline

Safety Orientation: All new employees will be given a safety orientation, or introduction, so they will be familiar with our safety rules and accident-prevention program.

All employees must follow these basic safety rules:

- Never do anything that is unsafe. If a task is unsafe, report it to your supervisor. We will find a safer way to do that job.

- Do not remove or disable any safety device.

- Never operate equipment until you have been trained and authorized to use that equipment.

- Use your personal protective equipment when required.

- Obey all safety warning signs.

- Working under the influence of alcohol or illegal drugs or using them at work is prohibited.

- Neither firearms nor explosives are allowed on company property.

- Running and fighting are prohibited.

- Clean up spills immediately. Replace all tools and supplies after use.

- If you are injured or become ill on the job, report this to your supervisor immediately.

- All supervisors must have first-aid training.

Skill Review (continued)

1. What is the purpose of the first document? Who is the intended audience?

_____

_____

_____

2. Compare and contrast the two workplace documents. How are they similar? How are they different?

_____

_____

_____

_____

_____

3. Summarize each of the two documents. State the main points simply and clearly.

_____

_____

_____

_____

_____

4. How does the structure of each document help the audience understand the information presented?

_____

_____

_____

_____

Directions: Read the following document. Then choose the <u>one best answer</u> to each question.

Department of Public Safety Recruitment Announcement

Recruitment for	State Training Center
Classification	Personnel Clerk (contractual; no benefits)
Salary	$13.50 per hour
Closing Date	Open until filled
Position Duties	This position will provide support to the Human Resources Department. The employee will perform a variety of clerical tasks to assist the department in efficiently providing human resources services for all employees.
Education	Graduation from an accredited high school or possession of a high school equivalency certificate
Experience	One year of general clerical or administrative support
Special Qualifications	Must have computer experience, including use of Microsoft Office, and must possess the following skills:

- Knowledge of business English, including accurate spelling, grammar, and punctuation

- Knowledge of standard office procedures and use of equipment

- Ability to understand and **interpret**, or explain, personnel policies and rules

- Ability to prepare and maintain personnel records

- Ability to follow departmental procedures

- Ability to maintain confidentiality for all personnel-related activities

- Ability to communicate and maintain effective working relationships with employees, management, public officials, and the general public

---

Skill Practice (continued)

1. Which of the following words are evidence that this job requires a certain level of schooling?

   A. "The employee will perform a variety of clerical tasks"

   B. "Graduation from an accredited high school"

   C. "One year of general clerical or administrative support"

   D. "Ability to maintain confidentiality"

2. What is the purpose of this document?

   A. to describe workplace duties to an employee

   B. to announce new responsibilities to employees

   C. to search for a new employee

   D. to inform employees about changing roles and expectations

3. According to the document, which of the following skills is required for this job?

   A. advanced computer expertise

   B. public speaking

   C. a second language

   D. organizational skills

4. Who is the intended audience of this document?

   A. current employees of the Department of Public Safety

   B. current supervisors for the Department of Public Safety

   C. a future employee of the Department of Public Safety

   D. a future supervisor for the Department of Public Safety

Writing Practice

Directions: Choose a workplace document from the lesson or another workplace document you are familiar with. Write a summary of the document. Then write a paragraph in which you state the author's purpose for writing the document and explain what the audience is supposed to do after reading the document.

Graphic Documents

KEY CONCEPT: Graphic documents use a variety of visual formats to present factual information.

Signs, maps, and pictures surround us. We are all familiar with road signs that tell us how fast to drive or where to turn. Have you ever seen a map that shows campgrounds, roads, and cities? How often do you see posters telling the date and place of an upcoming concert? These documents that use pictures, symbols, and charts are all graphic documents.

Graphic Documents

Graphic documents present information in a visual format, using pictures instead of words. Visual formats include photos, drawings, signs, graphs, charts, diagrams, and maps. Some graphic documents use only pictures, while others combine pictures and text. The text is often just a few important words, perhaps only a title. The reader must **infer**, or figure out, the meaning of the document by studying the pictures and the text.

Some graphic documents that are common in the workplace are **bar graphs**, **line graphs**, **pie charts**, **layout maps**, **organization charts**, and **safety signs**. Bar graphs and line graphs use bars or lines of different lengths to represent information such as sales or population. Pie charts are circular diagrams with "slices" representing parts of a whole. Layout maps are floor plans such as a map showing where the departments in a store are located. Organization charts show the roles or functions of company employees. Safety signs are visual representations of potentially dangerous environments.

The illustrations in some graphic documents are **concrete**, or realistic. A photo of a person, an animal, or an object is a concrete image. However, many graphic documents use a **symbol**, a simple sign or image, to represent an item or an idea. For example, an "H" on a map may be a symbol used to indicate where hotels are located.

To determine the meaning of a graphic document, it is helpful to ask the following questions.

• What images does the graphic show? What do they mean?

• Does the graphic include text? If so, what does the text say? Why is this text important? What does it mean?

• Where is the graphic document located—in a newspaper article, on a bulletin board, or in a textbook? Why is this location important?

ANALYZE VISUAL INFORMATION

Most documents present information through the use of words. In both fiction and nonfiction texts, an author uses language to communicate ideas. The audience reads the author's words to understand those ideas.

By contrast, graphic documents use few—if any—words to present information. Instead, they use images to show information visually. Just as you need to use reading skills to understand written texts, you must use certain skills to "read" and understand graphic documents.

The graphic documents that are the easiest to understand are those with concrete images, since their meaning is straightforward. Graphic documents that use symbols can be more challenging to understand.

Examine the following graphic documents. Try to determine the meaning and purpose of each. What do the bar and line graphs represent? How might theater managers use the information in the pie chart to help them decide which films to screen? In a notebook, write one sentence about where you might find each of these documents.

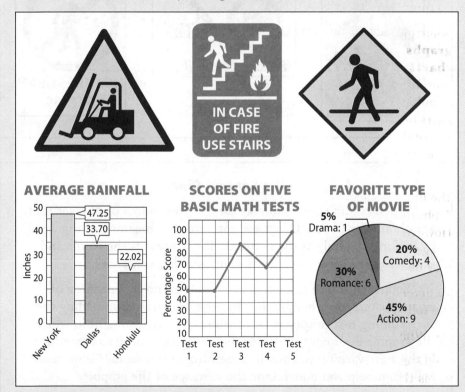

The first sign might be in a lumber yard, where small vehicles move supplies. The second sign could be in any building that has elevators. The third sign is seen on streets where many people walk. The bar graph could be used in a weather report. The line graph might be posted in a school. The circle graph could be in a magazine story about new movies.

TECHNOLOGY CONNECTION

Icons and Emoticons

Elements of graphic documents are found on the Internet, and they are used often in modern technology. The users of computers and mobile devices must learn to recognize the meaning of the various graphic images that are displayed on screens and in messages.

Mobile devices that have small screens employ **icons**, symbols that suggest what will happen if you click on the image.

People who send e-mails, instant messages, and text messages may use **emoticons**, or symbols made by combining keystrokes or using a device's picture characters. They express emotions such as humor and sarcasm.

In a notebook, draw three commonly used emoticons. Then write a sentence explaining why each might be used.

Workplace safety signs use simple images to get their message across. How do the images make these graphics easy to understand? What if these signs used no words? Could viewers easily infer their meaning?

For each sign displayed on this page, write a sentence explaining why both words and images are used to convey the message.

Directions: As you examine the workplace safety signs below, think about their purpose and the information they provide. In a notebook, write the message each sign conveys.

Use Context Clues

When reading text, you may come across words or phrases that are unfamiliar to you. Often you can infer the meaning of the word by looking carefully at the **context**. The context is the words and phrases in the sentence or in the surrounding sentences.

You can also use context clues to determine the meaning of signs, posters, or other graphic documents. Instead of reading the surrounding text, **analyze**, or consider, the environment in which the graphic document is located. Is the sign pointing to something? Is the sign warning you about something in the room? These clues will often help you understand the message of the graphic.

Look again at the workplace safety signs on this page. For each sign, write a sentence explaining why the sign might be necessary in a work area.

THINK ABOUT READING

Directions: Use the graphic documents on the previous page to answer these questions.

1. What is similar about graphics 1 and 2?

_____

_____

_____

2. Which of these graphic documents must be placed in a particular location in order to be understood?

   A. graphic 2
   B. graphic 3
   C. graphic 5
   D. graphic 6

3. What is similar about graphics 3 and 6?

_____

_____

_____

4. Evaluate the effectiveness of safety signs such as these. Why do these signs use graphics and very little text?

_____

_____

5. Design a graphic sign that could be used to present a specific message. Your sign may contain a few words of text.

Core Skill
Analyze Visual Information

Graphic documents present information that can be read quickly and easily. A workplace evacuation map, for example, clearly shows where to go in case of an emergency. A written evacuation plan would contain more detail, but it would be much less convenient—especially during a real emergency. In an emergency, people need simple, clear instructions about what to do and where to go.

In a notebook, write a sentence describing a graphic document that you have seen on the road, in a store, in a classroom, or on the job. Be sure to include the document's purpose. Then write a sentence explaining what makes the document easy to understand or how it could be improved.

Select two graphic documents that you have recently seen. Think about the purpose of each of these documents. Write one paragraph about each of the graphic documents you have chosen.

First, describe the image and the text, if any, on the graphic document. Then, describe the environment, or context, where you saw the graphic document. Analyze why the graphic document is or is not well suited for its purpose.

Directions: Graphic documents, like other texts, have a purpose. They might be created to inform, to entertain, to explain, or to persuade. As you examine the graphic documents below, think about their purpose and the information they represent. In a notebook, write one sentence stating the primary purpose of each of these graphic documents.

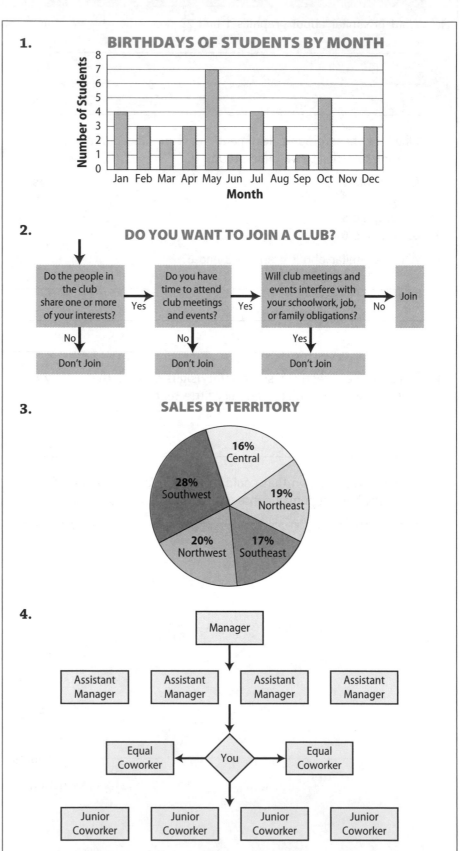

1. **BIRTHDAYS OF STUDENTS BY MONTH**

2. **DO YOU WANT TO JOIN A CLUB?**

3. **SALES BY TERRITORY**

4.

THINK ABOUT READING

Directions: Use the graphic documents on the previous page to answer these questions.

1. Which of these graphic documents represents the organization, or structure, of a group?

   A. graphic 1
   B. graphic 2
   C. graphic 3
   D. graphic 4

2. What is the purpose of graphic 2?

   A. to show cause and effect
   B. to compare and contrast people who do and don't like clubs
   C. to show how a decision is made
   D. to support an idea

3. Compare and contrast graphics 1 and 3. How are they similar? How are they different?

   _____

   _____

   _____

4. Determine the effectiveness of these graphic documents. Why have the authors chosen to use graphic documents rather than text?

   _____

   _____

Vocabulary Review

Directions: Match these words with their definitions.

1. _____ symbol

2. _____ bar graphs

3. _____ concrete

4. _____ context

5. _____ graphic

6. _____ infer

7. _____ pie charts

A. relating to pictures and images

B. simple sign representing an object or idea

C. graphics showing parts (slices) of a whole (circle)

D. to figure out from evidence and reasoning

E. realistic or true-to-life

F. graphics using rectangles to compare amounts

G. the environment or surrounding information

Directions: Analyze the graphic documents below. Then answer the questions that follow.

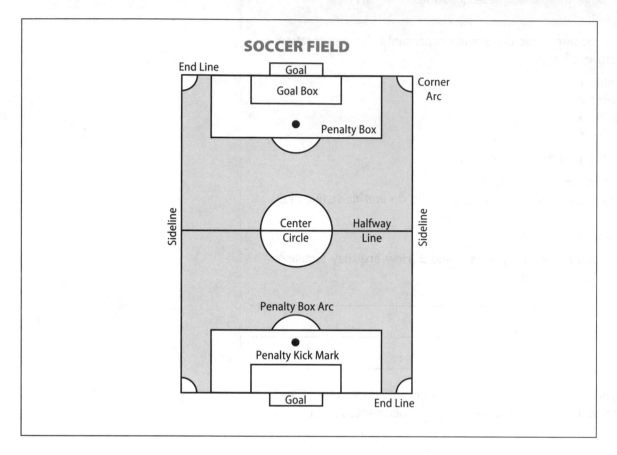

SOCCER FIELD

End Line

Goal

Goal Box

Corner Arc

Penalty Box

Sideline

Center Circle

Halfway Line

Sideline

Penalty Box Arc

Penalty Kick Mark

Goal

End Line

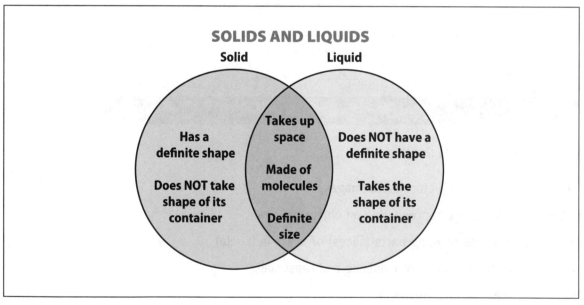

SOLIDS AND LIQUIDS

Solid   **Liquid**

Has a definite shape

Does NOT take shape of its container

Takes up space

Made of molecules

Definite size

Does NOT have a definite shape

Takes the shape of its container

Skill Review (continued)

1. Compare and contrast the two graphic documents. How are they similar? How are they different?

_____

_____

_____

_____

_____

2. Summarize the two documents. What information does each present?

_____

_____

_____

_____

_____

3. How does the format of each graphic document help the audience understand the information?

_____

_____

_____

_____

_____

4. Analyze the second graphic document. Then create a similar diagram that compares and contrasts cell phones and landline telephones.

Directions: Analyze the graphic document below. Then answer the questions that follow.

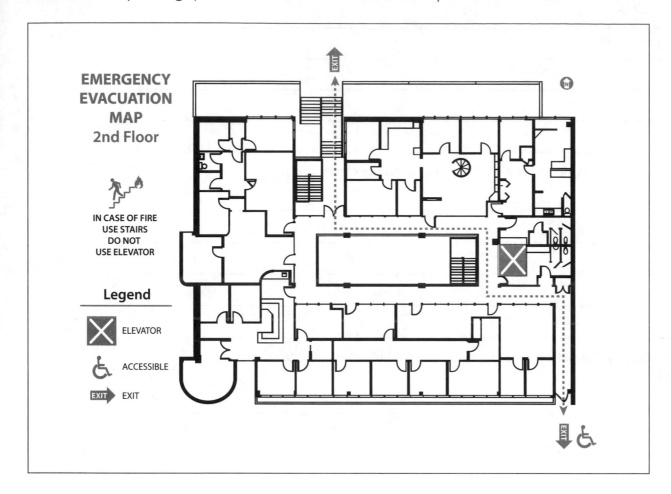

EMERGENCY
EVACUATION
MAP
2nd Floor

IN CASE OF FIRE
USE STAIRS
DO NOT
USE ELEVATOR

Legend

⊠ ELEVATOR

♿ ACCESSIBLE

▶ EXIT

Skill Practice (continued)

1. Which of the following best describes this graphic document?

   A. graphic with text
   D. graphic without text
   C. bar graph
   D. pie graph

2. What is the primary purpose of this document?

   A. to provide a useful workplace map
   B. to indicate the location of fire extinguishers
   C. to help people leave the building during an emergency
   D. to identify people's offices

3. Explain why this visual document would be much less effective if it were a written document.

   _____

   _____

   _____

   _____

4. Draw a simple emergency evacuation map for your home, classroom, or workplace.

Writing Practice

Directions: Choose one of the graphic documents from this lesson. Think about the purpose and meaning of the document. Then write a paragraph that could be used in place of the graphic document. Keep in mind the purpose of your document and the audience. Which version is the more efficient way to communicate this information? Explain your answer.

Reference Texts

Lesson Objectives

You will be able to

- Consult reference materials, such as dictionaries and thesauruses

- Gather information from different media

- Determine author's purpose

Skills

- **Core Skill:** Analyze Text Structure

- **Reading Skill:** Evaluate Content in Different Formats

Vocabulary

digital
entry
evaluate
online
preview
reference text
specialized
synonym
volumes

KEY CONCEPT: A reference is a source of factual information. Reference texts include dictionaries, encyclopedias, thesauruses, atlases, directories, and handbooks. These references may be print or digital.

Are you unsure about the meaning of a word you have read? Do you need to research a topic for a report? Would you like to find an expert to help you set up your new sound system? Knowing how to use reference texts can help you with school assignments, workplace responsibilities, and everyday tasks.

Reference Texts

When you need information about a topic, you can look in a **reference text**. A reference text is a source of factual information. Many types of reference texts are found in libraries, in schools, in workplaces, and at the offices and websites of various businesses and government departments. They are available in print form and in digital form.

Purpose of Reference Texts

Reference texts may be written by just one author or by groups of people. Whether a reference text is created by one person or by a team, the purpose of the text is to provide the reader with factual information. These authors usually do not include their opinions about a topic; they are not trying to persuade the reader. Instead, the authors' purpose is to present facts in a straightforward way. Reference texts serve as an educational resource.

Common types of reference texts and their purposes are shown in this chart.

Reference Text	Purpose
Dictionary or Glossary	Provides information on word meanings, spelling, pronunciation, plurals, and more
Thesaurus	Provides **synonyms**, or words with the same or similar meanings
Encyclopedia	Provides informational articles on a variety of topics
Atlas	Provides maps of the world, continents, countries, and states. Some atlases focus on one subject, such as historical maps.
Handbook or Manual	Provides information on rules, procedures, step-by-step instructions, or product details
Directory	Provides information, such as phone numbers and websites, about groups of people, organizations, or businesses

Analyze Text Structure

All reference texts provide factual information. However, to deliver this information effectively, different reference texts may **structure**, or organize, information in different ways. To understand text structure, examine the following example of the text structure commonly used in dictionaries.

Dictionary

A **dictionary** contains a great deal of information about each **entry**, or word listed. The information is structured in the same way for each entry. Follow these steps to use a dictionary.

1. **Preview** the parts of the dictionary. To preview text, browse through it to see how information is organized.

2. Use the dictionary's **text features**, such as the table of contents and the **guide words**, to find what you are looking for.

3. Guide words, found at the top of each page, show the first and last entries on the page. For example, you will find the word *strategy* on the page that has these guide words:

strand • stratus

4. Decide what information you need. Then **analyze**, or examine, the entry structure to find the data you want.

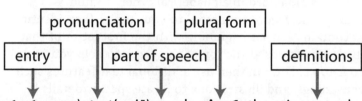

strat·e·gy \strat'-ə-jē\ *n.*, pl. **-gies 1:** the science and art of using political, economic, and military forces to gain support for adopted policies in peace or war. **2:** a careful plan of action.

- Do you want to know how to **pronounce**, or say, the word? Look at the respelling that uses special symbols. The **pronunciation key** explains the sound that each symbol represents.

- Do you want to know how to use the word in a sentence? Look for the **part of speech**. Parts of speech are abbreviated, using *n.* for noun, *v.* for verb, and *adj.* for adjective, for example.

- Do you want to know the word's definition? The entry often provides several definitions.

Directions: Use the pronunciation key to sound out these words:
an·a·lyze \a'-nə-līz\, **syn·o·nym** \si'-nə-nim\, **struc·ture** \strək'-chər\.

\ ə \ as **a** in abut	\ a \ as **a** in ash	\ i \ as **i** in chin
\ ə \ as **u** in abut	\ s \ as **c** in ace	\ ē \ as **ea** in easy
\ ə r \ as **ur/er** in further	\ ch \ as **ch** in chin	\ ī \ as **i** in ice

Glossary

A **glossary** is a text feature of nonfiction books. It identifies important vocabulary words and phrases found in the text. Like a dictionary, a glossary is arranged alphabetically, but it does not include as much information as a dictionary. Usually it gives the meanings of words and phrases only as they are used in the book.

Thesaurus

A thesaurus is a reference text that lists words with their **synonyms**, or words that have the same or similar meanings. You can use a thesaurus when you need to find just the right word to express an idea. You can also use a thesaurus when you want to avoid repeating a word over and over.

Directions: Choose a word from the following thesaurus entry to replace the word *eat* in this sentence:

I am so hungry I could eat this entire dinner in one gulp.

> **eat:** consume, ingest, put away, swallow, devour, take in, dispose of

Encyclopedia

An encyclopedia is a set of **volumes**, or books, that contain factual articles. Some encyclopedias cover a wide variety of subject areas, such as history, biography, geography, sports, and science. Other encyclopedias are **specialized**—that is, they focus on just one subject area.

A print encyclopedia is organized in alphabetical order. To find information, think of a key word connected to your topic. Then identify the volume that contains articles beginning with the first letter of that key word. Use the guide words at the top of the pages to help you find the article on your topic. You can then use additional text features such as headings, subheadings, and illustrations to locate specific details in the article.

The last volume of an encyclopedia is the index. It lists topics in alphabetical order. You can use the index to quickly find the volume that contains the main article about your topic. The index also lists additional articles related to your topic.

Atlas

An atlas is a book that contains maps. There are many kinds of maps. The types of maps you are likely to use most often are political maps and physical maps. **Political maps** show the boundaries between countries and states. They also show other details such as cities, rivers, and roads. **Physical maps** show landforms, oceans, and other natural features of an area. Atlases may include other types of maps, such as maps that focus on oceans, climate, or historical events.

Directions: Examine the political map shown here and name the states that **border**, or touch the edge of, Iowa.

MIDWESTERN AND GREAT PLAINS STATES

THINK ABOUT READING

Directions: If you are thinking of moving to another city for a job, how would you use an encyclopedia to get information about that city? What additional information would you find in an atlas? Write your answers on the lines below.

_____

_____

_____

_____

_____

WRITE TO LEARN

The Impossible is a movie that tells the story of the December 2004 Southeast Asian tsunami from the point of view of one family that survived the disaster.

Use an encyclopedia to gather details about that tsunami and the areas in Southeast Asia that were affected by it. **Evaluate**, or make a judgment about, whether your reference is up-to-date.

Use a print or online atlas to find physical maps of the area surrounding the Indian Ocean where the tsunami did the most damage. Find a physical map that shows the area's elevation above sea level. What do these physical maps show you about the lands that were hardest hit by the tsunami?

Write a three-paragraph factual article that could be used in a newspaper on the anniversary of the tsunami.

Handbook or Manual

A handbook or a manual is a reference text that provides detailed information or instructions about specific subjects. You may have used or seen some of the following examples of handbooks and manuals:

Employee handbooks explain a company's rules of conduct, workplace procedures, and safety policies.

Grammar handbooks list rules of language usage.

Technical manuals provide details and step-by-step instructions on how to repair items such as vehicles or major appliances.

User manuals give information about how to use electronic devices such as computers, smartphones, and e-book readers.

Handbooks and manuals are written by experts. They are updated frequently to include new information. You can find handbooks and manuals online or in the reference section of your library.

Directions: Read the following questions. In a notebook, name the kind of handbook or manual that would likely contain the information needed to answer each question.

- What features does my smartphone have?

- How can I install software on my computer by myself?

- What is a noun?

- What are the duties and responsibilities of a US mail carrier?

Directory

A directory is a book or online resource that lists names, addresses, and other information about people, businesses, or organizations. A telephone book is an example of a directory. You can find a directory for almost any type of organization or location.

Directions: Read the list of types of directories below. Then discuss with a partner how these directories are used in business and in everyday life.

- Professional directories provide lists of lawyers, dentists, business executives, builders, and other specialized workers.

- School directories give information about location, type, size, and courses available.

- Some directories focus on places; for example, there are directories of airports, parks, hospitals, and restaurants.

- Other directories focus on organizations; for example, government offices, businesses, and volunteer organizations.

THINK ABOUT READING

Directions: Answer the following questions.

1. Which of the following is the best resource to use for finding a list of doctors' names and phone numbers?

   A. a manual
   B. a handbook
   C. a directory
   D. a map

2. Which of the following best describes the kind of information you would find in a technical manual?

   A. names, addresses, and phone numbers
   B. company rules and policies
   C. restaurant locations and ratings
   D. product details and step-by-step instructions

3. Why is it important to use the most up-to-date handbooks and manuals?

   _____

   _____

   _____

Vocabulary Review

Directions: Match these words with their definitions.

1. digital
2. entry
3. online
4. reference
5. specialized
6. synonym
7. volumes

A. focused on one particular subject

B. a term listed in a reference source

C. available on the Internet

D. a source of information

E. books

F. a word that is similar in meaning to another word

G. relating to computer technology

Directions: Look at the example of a dictionary entry below. Then answer the questions that follow. <u>Questions 1 through 5</u> refer to the example.

> **crazy • creek**
>
> **cra·zy** /krā′-zē/ *adj.* 1. affected with madness; insane.
> 2. impractical. 3. being out of the ordinary. 4. infatuated.
> **cream** /krēm/ *n.* 1. the yellowish fatty part of milk.
> 2. a pale yellow. 3. the choicest part.
> **cred·i·ble** /krĕd′-ə-bəl/ *adj.* 1. capable of being believed.
> 2. worthy of confidence.

1. Look at the guide words on the dictionary page above. Which of the following words will you find on that page?

   creaky, creepy, crate, crease, crescent, creature, crash, credence

   _____

2. Which meaning of the word *cream* matches the meaning of *cream* in the following sentence?

   The walls are painted a rich cream, which gives the room a warm, open feeling.

   _____

3. Which words in the dictionary example are adjectives?

   _____

4. Does the *a* in *crazy* rhyme with the *a* in *cape* or the *a* in *cat*?

   _____

5. How many definitions, or meanings, does *credible* have?

   _____

6. How is a glossary similar to and different from a dictionary?

   _____

   _____

   _____

7. How is the reason you use a thesaurus different from the reason you use a dictionary?

   _____

   _____

   _____

Skill Review (continued)

Directions: Choose the <u>one best answer</u> to each question.

8. Creating a list of topics and key words is helpful when looking for information in which reference text?

    A. a thesaurus
    B. an atlas
    C. an encyclopedia
    D. a dictionary

9. What is the best way to find specific information in a long encyclopedia article?

    A. Read the entire article and take notes.
    B. Read only the first and last paragraphs of the article.
    C. Look at the illustrations and photographs and read the captions.
    D. Look for headings related to your topic and read those sections.

10. How could you determine which states border a particular state?

    A. Consult a political map in an atlas.
    B. Use key words to find the information in an encyclopedia.
    C. Look for a useful chart in a transportation manual.
    D. Look up the specific state in a dictionary.

11. Which resource should you use if you want to know who is in charge of your local health department?

    A. a communications handbook
    B. a manual of public health
    C. a directory of local government officials
    D. a glossary in a health textbook

12. In what way do businesses benefit from being listed in directories?

    A. They can be fined if they are not listed in a directory.
    B. Directories increase business by providing publicity.
    C. Directory publishers pay for their listings.
    D. People know that only the best businesses are listed in directories.

Skill Practice

Directions: Fill in the blanks with words or short answers to complete the sentences for questions 1 through 8. Write a short response for questions 9 and 10.

1. If you encounter an unknown term in a text, you should check to see if the text has a(n) _____ that tells the meaning of the word.

2. If you want to add excitement to a report you are writing, you can use a(n) _____ to find an interesting _____ to substitute for an uninteresting or overused word.

3. A print encyclopedia is a set of _____ that contains information that is organized in _____ order.

4. You can use the guide words at the top of dictionary pages and encyclopedia pages to _____.

5. If you want to know whether a city you plan to visit is near a beach, you can find out by consulting a(n) _____.

6. One reason you might want to use a political map is to see _____.

Skill Practice (continued)

7. In order to make repairs, an auto mechanic may need to refer to _____.

8. The most important information for a business to list in a directory is _____.

9. What types of information would you expect to find in a company's workplace procedures and safety handbook?

   _____

   _____

   _____

10. Evaluate the differences between digital dictionaries and print dictionaries. In what ways are they the same? In what ways are they different?

    _____

    _____

    _____

Writing Practice

Directions: Choose a city or region that you would like to visit. Use reference texts to gather information about the region. Use the information you have gathered to write three paragraphs that include important or interesting facts about the place you have chosen.

Comparing Texts in Different Media

KEY CONCEPT: Comparing how the same text is presented in different media can provide a deeper understanding of a text.

You often read texts that are meant to help you understand how to do a task or how to make a choice. These are called functional texts. An application form can tell you how to apply for a job, and a menu can tell you what choices are available for lunch. Sometimes seeing or hearing the same information in a different form can be helpful. Have you ever read a set of instructions and wished you could see them demonstrated? When text is presented in different media, you may find new layers of meaning.

Texts in Different Media

People use different **media**, or systems of communication, to access entertainment, news, and other information. Books, newspapers, magazines, television, radio, billboards, advertisements, and the Internet are types of media. Each medium has its own advantages and disadvantages.

Reading a written text is a direct way to connect with an author's message. When you read, you are free to use your imagination to **visualize**, or picture, what an author describes. An author uses words to help readers "see" and "hear" the message.

However, exploring a different version of that same functional text can greatly **enhance** (improve or add to) your understanding of the text. Reading a wedding invitation is a different experience than hearing the same invitation directly from the bride. The bride might give you exactly the same information about the time and place of the wedding, but her body language and the emotion in her voice might affect the way that you respond to the invitation.

Each person's understanding of a text depends, in part, on the knowledge and values that person brings to the text. An advertising writer may **interpret**, or understand, the text of an advertisement in a different way than you would interpret it. That is why it is important to **analyze**, or carefully examine, the ways that a text is affected by the medium in which it is presented.

EVALUATE CONTENT IN DIFFERENT MEDIA

When you compare different versions of a text, look for ways the versions are alike and different. How you respond to audio and video versions is affected by the choices that performers and directors make. An **audio**, or sound, version may build mood through sound effects or music. Performers affect the mood through their **tone**. By speaking in a stern tone or a friendly tone, performers help the audience understand the text. The rhythm of an actor's speech adds another effect. Directors influence video versions through setting, lighting, and camera work.

Read this weather warning that might appear on a website.

Online version

Your Weather Web, webmaster Rosita Ruiz

Travel Advisory

- Drivers in Virginia and North Carolina should take care. Black ice has covered many roads due to yesterday's snow.

- Farther north, Philadelphia, New York, and Buffalo have blizzard conditions. Drivers are advised to stay off the roads.

Tomorrow's Weather

- A cold front will move down from Canada through the Great Lakes and the Ohio Valley. The frigid air will be pushed along by winds of 30 to 40 miles per hour, causing falling tree limbs and possible power outages in some areas.

Now read aloud the following audio version, as a radio announcer would read it. Use expression and emphasize the words in **italics**, or slanted type. Notice how the audio version differs from the print version.

Audio version

Good morning! I'm Rosita Ruiz with your weekend weather report. This morning, drivers in Virginia and North Carolina will have to *watch out* for *black ice* from yesterday's snow. Farther up the coast, folks in Philadelphia, New York, and Buffalo are *still battling that monster blizzard.* So stay *indoors* and *keep warm! Tomorrow* a *huge cold front* will *blast* down from Canada, all the way through the *Great Lakes* and the *Ohio Valley.* Winds of *30 to 40 miles per hour* will *push that frigid air along,* which may cause falling tree limbs and possible *power outages* in some areas.

The audio version adds language not found in the original text. What is the effect of these changes? How does emphasizing certain words affect their impact? Which version makes it easier for you to visualize the serious weather situation? Which version is more informal?

Reading Skill
Evaluate Content in Different Media

When you examine different media versions of an informational text, review the content to determine if there are any differences between the two versions.

If the information included in an audio, video, or digital version of a text differs from the information in the print version, determine whether the difference affects the message. Does the **adapted**, or changed, version still represent the author's viewpoint or values?

Think about why the changes were made. Was the original text too long or too short? Was the tone too formal or too informal? Does the addition of photos, art, videos, maps, or charts change the way you understand the text?

In a notebook, list the main ideas of the online and audio versions of this weather report. Make note of any ideas that have been changed or omitted.

To draw conclusions about a text, first analyze the parts of the text. In the written announcement about on-the-job training, the headings lead you to bullet points that add details about who might be interested in on-the-job training, why on-the-job training is helpful, and what workplaces commonly offer on-the-job training.

In the video version, the **presentation**, or demonstration, is enhanced by the onscreen captions that repeat the narrator's speech.

Studying both the video and print versions of the on-the-job training information helps you understand various aspects of this type of instruction.

After analyzing the text, discuss the following questions with a classmate:

What conclusion can you draw about the usefulness of on-the-job training?

From the video, what can you infer about on-the-job training from the examples of people learning on the job?

Do you have a positive or negative impression of the value of on-the-job training? Explain your view.

Directions: Read this announcement about an employment option. Pay attention to the headings and the way the text is organized. When you have finished reading the announcement, write one sentence stating the author's purpose.

Looking for a Job? Consider On-the-Job Training!

What is on-the-job training?

On-the-job training is instruction provided to employees while they are working. This training teaches skills that will help employees do their jobs safely and efficiently.

Are you a candidate for on-the-job training?

You may be a candidate if you are
- a young person entering the workforce
- a worker laid off due to downsizing
- a military serviceperson returning from active duty
- a person hoping to change careers without lengthy preparation

What advantages can on-the-job training offer you?

On-the-job training offers you
- the chance to begin earning an income while learning new skills
- the opportunity to learn job skills through instruction, demonstration, and hands-on practice
- the acquisition of skills that can transfer from one job to another and help you build a professional career

What industries offer on-the-job training?

On-the-job training is often offered in
- the communications, automotive, steel, and construction industries, for example
- many government agencies

To explore employment offering on-the-job training, go online and visit your state's employment development website. These websites contain information about employers and on-the-job training.

Directions: Watch an online video about on-the-job training at this link. Under the heading *Work Option Videos*, click on the title *Requiring On-the-Job Training.*

http://www.careeronestop.org/Videos/WorkOptionVideos/
work-option-videos.aspx

THINKING ABOUT **READING**

Directions: Use the space provided to explain why you think the information about on-the-job training is more effective in the written text or in the video version?

_____

_____

Clear written instructions can guide you through everyday tasks, such as making popcorn or changing a tire. Written instructions can also teach you more complicated skills, such as cardiopulmonary resuscitation, or CPR.

Directions: Read the CPR instructions below. Look carefully at the headings and the illustrations. Then close your book and write a brief description of the C-A-B steps.

Guidelines for Basic CPR

The three steps of CPR

Compressions: Push hard and fast on the center of the victim's chest.

Airway: Tilt the victim's head back and lift the chin to open the **airway**, or breathing passage.

Breathing: Give rescue breaths to the victim by exhaling your breath into the victim's mouth.

To perform CPR on an adult

Check and Call: Check the victim for responsiveness. If the victim is not conscious, is not breathing, or is gasping for breath, call 911 for emergency medical help. Then begin CPR.

Compress
- Put your hands one on top of the other in the center of the chest. Push 30 times, pressing down at least 2 inches.
- Push at the rate of 100 pushes per minute.

Breathe
- To open the victim's airway, tilt the head back and lift the chin.
- Pinch the victim's nostrils closed so air will not escape.
- Put your mouth over the victim's mouth and give 2 breaths.

Continue
- Continue sets of 30 pushes followed by 2 breaths.
- When emergency medical personnel arrive, they will take over the victim's care.

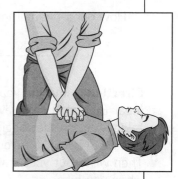

Imagine you live in Chicago, Illinois, and frequently travel by car around the state. You may use a printed map when you are traveling. However, you may get more up-to-date information if you use an online map.

An interactive Illinois highway map can be found at this website:

http://www.gettingaround illinois.com/gai.htm

Click the *Road Closed* and *Construction Zone* icons in the box on the right side of the map to show road construction on major highways.

Then click the + icon on the left side of the map to change the size of the map. Enlarge the map until you see the names of streets so you can find the exact location of road construction sites.

In a notebook, explain how accessing this map before starting out on a trip would help you plan your route.

A **multimedia** presentation uses two or more types of media. These may include audio, video, still images, text, and **animation** (movement). The illustrations and text on the web page listed below show basic CPR steps. The animation created by the arrows helps you visualize the movements used when doing CPR.

Directions: Go to the website and review the text and illustrations. Then, in a notebook, answer the questions that follow.

http://depts.washington.edu/learncpr/quickcpr.html

What additional instructions are provided when you click the words "unresponsiveness" and "push"?

How does the multimedia format enhance the CPR training steps?

Directions: Imagine you are living in the Minneapolis, Minnesota, area (near Big Lake) and travel around by bike and commuter train. You are taking a class that begins at 8:00 a.m. Your school is a 10-minute walk (3-minute bike ride) from Fridley Station. Study the train schedule below. Then write out your travel schedule for days when you walk and days when you bike.

Route Number	Big Lake Station	Elk River Station	Ramsey Station	Anoka Station	Riverdale Station	Fridley Station	Target Field Station
1	2	3	4	5	6	7
AM							
888	5:01	5:11	5:16	5:22	5:26	5:34	5:50
888	5:51	6:01	6:06	6:12	6:16	6:24	6:40
888	6:21	6:31	6:36	6:42	6:46	6:54	7:10
888	6:51	7:01	7:06	7:12	7:16	7:24	7:40
888	7:21	7:31	7:36	7:42	7:46	7:54	8:10

Directions: Now that you have read the printed version of this train schedule, go online and explore the differences between the print text and the information available online.

http://metrotransit.org/schedules/webschedules .aspx?route=888

Click *Weekday* to access the desired schedule. This schedule is the same as the print text. Now click *View/Print Detailed Route Map*. Read the information on pages 1 and 2 of the map. Then, in a notebook, make a list of the information provided online that does not appear in the printed schedule.

THINK ABOUT READING

Directions: Use information from the online detailed route map to answer these questions.

1. What options do you have for what to do with your bike when you are traveling from home (Big Lake) to school (Fridley)?

   _____

   _____

2. You want to attend the Memorial Day parade, which starts near the Target Field Station at 9:00 a.m. Which train should you catch in order to be on time?

   _____

   _____

3. Your roommate, who drives a car, has signed up for the same class you are taking. He is trying to decide whether to drive to school or take the train. What advantage would he have by driving to Big Lake Station and then taking the train?

   _____

   _____

   _____

4. The map shows the names of the train stations. What additional information does the map show about the stations?

   _____

   _____

   _____

Vocabulary Review

Directions: Match these words with their definitions.

1. _____ animation   **A.** a demonstration

2. _____ italics   **B.** movement

3. _____ enhance   **C.** systems of communication

4. _____ interpret   **D.** to add to or improve

5. _____ media   **E.** slanted type

6. _____ multimedia   **F.** to understand a text

7. _____ presentation   **G.** using several forms of communication

Directions: Read the text of the recipe. Then go to the website listed below to watch a video of a chef preparing the recipe. To find the *Spaghetti and Tomato Sauce Video*, write "spaghetti and tomato sauce" in the box that says "Enter search terms..."

http://www.stjoeslivingston.org/body_howell.cfm?id=4611&action=list&t =Health-eCooking&d=recipe&w=trinity&tid=1&cid=143

Tasty Tomato Sauce Pasta

Makes 4 servings

Ingredients

2 tsp. (teaspoons) olive oil

$\frac{1}{2}$ cup chopped onion

1 garlic clove, finely chopped

$\frac{1}{2}$ tsp. salt

$\frac{1}{4}$ tsp. black pepper

2 (16 oz.) cans crushed tomatoes

1 Tbsp. (tablespoon) chopped parsley

12 oz. spaghetti

2 Tbsp. grated Parmesan or Romano cheese

Preparation

Fill a large pot $\frac{2}{3}$ full with water. Heat the water over high heat until it boils. Keep water hot while you make the sauce.

Pour olive oil into a large frying pan and heat over medium heat until the oil is hot. Add the onion, garlic, salt, and pepper. Cook for 4 to 5 minutes.

Add the tomatoes to the pan and let the sauce come to a boil. Reduce heat to low and stir the mixture occasionally until the sauce becomes thick. This will take about 15 minutes. Add the parsley and cook on low for 5 more minutes, stirring occasionally.

Add spaghetti noodles to the pot of boiling water and cook until tender, about 9 minutes. Drain the water from the spaghetti. Place one serving of spaghetti on each plate and spoon sauce over the top. Sprinkle cheese over each plate and serve.

Directions: Answer these questions.

1. What effect does the video version of the recipe have on your interest in preparing the recipe?

_____

_____

_____

2. In what ways does the video version give you more information than the written text? In what ways does the written text provide more information than the video version?

_____

_____

_____

3. If you were preparing the recipe, what suggestions from the video version would you use? What ways might you change the recipe to make it your own?

_____

_____

_____

4. What people "see" and "hear" when reading a text may be different from what they see and hear when viewing a video version of that text. Why is that so?

_____

_____

_____

5. When a television cooking show demonstrates how to make recipes, the television director will often cut, or stop the action, at the point that a partially prepared dish is being placed into the oven or into the refrigerator. The director will then come back to the action when the dish comes out of the oven or refrigerator. Why do you think this may be so?

_____

_____

_____

6. How might a print version of an instructional text be more helpful than a multimedia version? How might a multimedia format make instructional text easier to understand?

_____

_____

_____

_____

Directions: Read the following document. Then answer the questions that follow.
<u>Questions 1 and 2</u> relate to the poster.

ROCKLINE COUNTY FAIR
Anytown, Oklahoma
August 17–30

Fun for the Whole Family!

Come and enjoy
Main Street Parade
Live Bands
Giant Carnival Midway
4-H Food Auction
Livestock Judging Contest
All-Breed Dog Show
Open Youth Rodeo
High Plains Barbershop Chorus
Amateur Flat Track Racing
Nightly Fireworks Display

Visit www.rocklinefair.com for
• Ticket Outlets and Advance Ticket Information
• Complete Details of all Fair Activities

1. If the organizers of the Rockline County Fair put a video of the fair on their website, what advantages might the video have over this print flyer?

_____

_____

_____

Skill Practice

2. Which events mentioned in the print flyer do you think should be featured in a video to interest more people in attending the fair?

_____

_____

_____

3. Evaluate the differences between using a print train schedule and an online train schedule. In what ways are the texts the same? In what ways are they different?

_____

_____

_____

4. What types of information would you expect to find on a printed road map? What information would you expect to find in an online interactive map?

_____

_____

_____

Writing Practice

Directions: Choose a print text from the lesson or another functional document you are familiar with, such as a product information sheet, an application form, an advertisement, or a schedule. Write a paragraph in which you state the author's purpose for writing the document and describe the audience that would read the document. Then write a one-paragraph summary of the document. Finally, write a paragraph explaining why the text might be more effective in a different medium, such as an audio, video, or multimedia presentation.

Directions: Choose the one best answer to each question. Questions 1 through 4 refer to the following passage.

The Importance of a Receipt

At one time or another, you will probably buy something that is not what you really want. You will then need to return the item to the store. Returning an item is easy if you have a receipt. You can simply return the item to customer service and receive a store credit or get your money back. However, if you do not have a receipt, here is what to do.

1. First, if the item has parts, make sure you have all the pieces.
2. Then, neatly fold or repack the item in its original packaging.
3. At the store, go immediately to the customer service desk before you do any other shopping. If you walk through the store with the item, a sales clerk cannot be sure that you brought the item into the store.
4. Explain that you want to return the item but you do not have a receipt. If you used a credit card, show the employee the card you used. The store may have a record of your purchase.
5. Tell the employee whether you would like to exchange the item for something else or would like store credit. A store credit would allow you to buy something from the store at a later time for the amount of the credit.
6. Do not expect to get your money back. Most stores will not give you money without a receipt.
7. At home, create a receipt box to save receipts from future purchases. Then you will have the receipt the next time you need to make a return.

---

1. How is returning an item with a receipt different from returning an item without a receipt?

    A. It is easier to return an item with a receipt.
    B. It is easier to return an item without a receipt.
    C. You will get store credit only if you have a receipt.
    D. You do not need to go to customer service if you have a receipt.

2. Why should you go straight to customer service when you walk in the store?

    A. It will give you more time to shop.
    B. You will get your refund faster.
    C. Store employees will know you already bought the item.
    D. You will not have to wait in line.

3. Which people would find the advice in this passage most useful?

    A. customer service employees
    B. customers who have a receipt for an item they want to return
    C. customers who do not have a receipt for an item they want to return
    D. customers who is happy with what they bought

4. What might happen if you skip step 1?

    A. You might get store credit instead of a refund.
    B. You might get a refund instead of store credit.
    C. You may forget to fold or repack the item properly.
    D. You may forget a piece and not be able to return the item.

Review

Directions: Questions 5 through 8 refer to the following passage

---

GZ Mattress Company Mission Statement

Our Goal: To be the top manufacturer of mattresses in the world. To meet this goal, we must constantly seek innovations and new designs to ensure that our products are superior to all others.

Our Pledge: We will provide cost-effective, high-quality mattresses internationally in order to improve the quality of our customers' sleep. This pledge exemplifies our reason for being in business in the mattress industry and represents the way we will go about realizing our goal.

Our Professionalism: Our standards for professionalism are reflected in the way we do business. They include a commitment to courtesy, pride, superiority, innovation, determination, honor, and philanthropy. We expect all our employees to adhere to these standards when working with one another and with people outside of our company.

---

5. What type of mattresses does this company plan to sell?

   A. the cheapest mattresses possible
   B. well-made, reasonably priced mattresses
   C. mattresses in several colors
   D. mattresses that can also be used as couches

6. What is the GZ Mattress Company's main goal?

   A. to be the top US manufacturer of mattresses
   B. to produce and sell the least expensive mattresses in the world
   C. to produce the most comfortable mattresses in the United States
   D. to sell mattresses that are superior to every other mattress

7. To reach its goal, what must GZ Mattress Company do?

   A. produce its mattresses outside the United States
   B. produce mattresses that are inferior to other mattresses
   C. use innovation and new design
   D. use cheap labor and shortcuts to produce better mattresses

8. What does this employer expect from its employees?

   A. They should adhere to the company's standards of professionalism with all people.
   B. They do not need to follow the company's standards when dealing with people outside the company.
   C. They should follow the company's standards only when dealing with people inside the company.
   D. They should follow the company's standards only when dealing with supervisors.

Directions: <u>Questions 9 through 12</u> refer to the following website.

9. Is this website the best place to get just the facts about the game between the Sonics and the Tornadoes?

   A. No, because it tells what a Tornadoes fan thought of the game.
   B. Yes, because it is a website for a local newspaper.
   C. No, because it tells what a Sonics fan thought of the game.
   D. Yes, because it gives the score of the game.

11. How does the website help you find important information?

   A. It uses pictures.
   B. It uses italic type.
   C. It uses boldfaced type.
   D. It uses numbers.

10. Which link should you click on to read news updates?

   A. www.citysonicsnews.com
   B. Hector Rivera
   C. Lee Chen
   D. Tony Hutchinson

12. Where should you click if you wanted to see a list of the City Sonics games?

   A. News
   B. Schedule
   C. Tickets
   D. Meet the Players

Review

Check Your Understanding

On the following chart, circle the number of any question you answered incorrectly. Under each content area you will see the pages you can review to learn the content covered in the question. Pay particular attention to reviewing those lessons in which you missed half or more of the questions.

Chapter 1 Review

Lesson	Item Number	Review Pages
How-to and Instructions	1, 2, 3, 4	22–29
Websites	9, 10, 11, 12	30–37
Workplace Documents	5, 6, 7, 8	38–47

ESSAY WRITING PRACTICE

Memos and Forms, How-To and Instructions, Workplace Documents, and Reference Texts

Directions: Write an essay in response to one of the prompts below. Review Lessons 1.1, 1.2, 1.4, or 1.6 for help with planning, writing strategies, and text structure.

MEMO

Memos are a quick and easy way for people to communicate in the workplace. These documents can include questions about work assignments, changes in company policies, announcements about company events, and so on.

Create a memo about an upcoming company Family Day Picnic. Outline the details of this event. Keep in mind that this memo will go to everyone in the company. It should include all of the information employees need to know about when and where the event will take place.

HOW-TO AND INSTRUCTIONS

Some workplace tasks may be complex or involve many steps. Instructions and how-to manuals are useful guides that list each step in a process. Reading these guides and following them carefully will help you successfully complete your assignments.

Your supervisor has asked you to create a set of instructions for a new employee. Write a list of instructions with at least five steps about a process of your choice. For example, you could write out the steps for your department's process for ordering supplies, or your process for customer care. For each step, include enough detail that someone new to the job would know how to complete the task safely and correctly.

WORKPLACE DOCUMENT

Within a workplace environment, employees use many types of documents to convey information. Part of your daily routine might involve writing and responding to e-mails and memos, following performance and safety guidelines, or completing forms.

Write a two-paragraph report to your supervisor in which you summarize a meeting you attended. List the main points discussed at the meeting and tell what was decided about each of the points. Use proper punctuation and appropriate language to maintain a professional tone.

REFERENCE TEXTS

A key part of doing research is choosing proper reference materials. You can use a variety of reference texts, such as dictionaries, encyclopedias, thesauruses, atlases, directories, handbooks, and manuals. Many of these texts are available online as well as in print.

Choose a topic that interests you and determine which types of reference texts you would use to find information on that topic. List at least three texts you would use for your research. For each text, tell what kind of information you would find. Then explain the advantages of using this type of reference text.

ESSAY WRITING PRACTICE

_____

_____

_____

_____

_____

_____

_____

_____

_____

_____

_____

_____

_____

_____

_____

_____

_____

Expository Texts

Suppose you want to find the score from last night's baseball game between your favorite team and a rival? Where would you look? Suppose you needed to complete an assignment on the latest discovery in stem-cell research? What would be the best source to read? Suppose you needed to study for a US history test? What source would you use? In all these instances, you are looking for factual information. Expository writing is factual writing that communicates knowledge. The expository writer's job is to explain information clearly.

Expository texts include magazine articles you read for fun, textbooks you read for information, and technical texts you need for job training. Magazine and newspaper articles and textbooks are the most common kinds of expository texts. Technical texts provide specialized information for a particular group of people. Using the tips given in this chapter for the various types of expository texts will help you become a more effective reader of the sources of information you come across each day.

In this chapter you will study these topics:

2.1 Textbooks and Other Educational Materials
Books that are used for the study of a particular subject—history, math, science, literature, languages—are textbooks. They can help you gain a thorough understanding of a particular subject area. Learn how headings, subheadings, captions, and graphics are useful when you are analyzing information.

2.2 Magazine and Newspaper Articles
Do you read a daily or weekly newspaper so you stay informed about current events? Newspaper and magazine articles provide up-to-date information. They are designed to catch and hold your interest. These articles vary widely—from human-interest stories and sports analysis to political reports and entertainment reviews.

2.3 Technical Texts
Have you ever read instructions that helped you use your computer, TV, or mobile phone? Technical texts provide the information you need to perform a specific procedure or to learn how a process works. Learning how to read technical texts will make using these texts more effective.

Goal Setting

Why is it important to know how to read expository texts?

_____

_____

_____

To help you set goals for learning as you study this chapter, use this checklist as you read the material in each lesson.

☐ What does the title tell me about the general topic?

☐ Is the opening paragraph interesting?

☐ Are explanations accurate, complete, and clear?

☐ Do the visuals provide useful additional information?

☐ Is the information presented in a logical order?

☐ Does each paragraph have a main idea? Do all the details support the main idea?

☐ Does the passage have an introduction, a body, and a conclusion?

Textbooks and Other Educational Materials

Lesson Objectives

You will be able to

- Identify the stated main idea
- Gain information from textbooks and other educational material

Skills

- **Core Skill:** Analyze Visual Information
- **Reading Skill:** Summarize Text

Vocabulary

classify
details
main idea
stated
survey
topic sentence

KEY CONCEPT: Textbooks and other educational materials are instructional texts used in mathematics, science, social studies, and other fields of study.

In almost every class you have ever taken, you have probably had a textbook. At first glance, a textbook can seem a little intimidating. After all, it's usually bigger, thicker, and heavier than books you read for fun. Once you know some strategies for reading textbooks, you will have the confidence to start learning about a new topic.

Educational Materials

Textbooks, encyclopedias, reference books, technical manuals, and educational websites present information about a variety of topics. These are usually considered reliable sources. This means that someone has checked that every fact is true. The information is presented without bias, and the reader can easily determine who is responsible for the content. However, it is important to check the publishing dates of these materials, since the date of publication can affect the accuracy of some facts.

Most printed books are divided into chapters. Because the purpose of these materials is to give information, they often include special features to help readers locate information. Many educational websites have the same features.

- Titles and headings give show the topic of a section.
- Important words and vocabulary words are often written in **boldfaced** type.
- Graphs, tables, charts, illustrations, and photographs present information in a visual way.

Here is a basic strategy for reading educational materials. It is called *SQ3R*.

Survey Before you read, **survey** (scan) titles, headings, and boldfaced words.

Question As you read, ask yourself questions about what you are reading. For example, you might ask yourself, "What is the main idea?" By turning titles and subtitles into questions, these headings can help you find the main idea. For instance, this section is titled "Educational Materials." Turn that heading into a question by asking yourself, "What are examples of educational materials?"

Read Read to find important ideas and facts. Focus on finding answers to the questions you wrote.

Recite Write or say aloud the answers to your questions as you find them.

Review Go back and look again at main ideas, important supporting details, and key concepts.

FIND MAIN IDEA AND DETAILS

Books, chapters, and paragraphs all have a **main idea**. The main idea is what the book, chapter, or paragraph is mostly about.

Many times, main ideas are directly **stated**. The reader can find the main idea directly in the text. Stated main ideas often appear as the **topic sentence** in a paragraph. The topic sentence can appear anywhere in the paragraph, but it is usually the first or last sentence of the paragraph. Stated main ideas are supported by **details**, which give more information about the main idea.

Read the following passage from a textbook. Find the stated main idea.

> A number of developments took place that made the 1400s the right time for the global age to begin. The first development, or influence, was the Crusades. Large numbers of Europeans went to the Holy Land to fight the Muslims. Their travels showed them the marvels of other places. When they returned home, they told stories of what they had seen. The ships that returned from the Holy Land carried luxury goods like spices and silks. These goods were sold in European markets. Marco Polo's journal also told Europeans about life outside Europe.
>
> —Excerpted from *Contemporary's World History*

The main idea of this paragraph is stated in sentence 1: "A number of developments took place that made the 1400s the right time for the global age to begin." Sentences 2 through 5 give more information about what happened in the 1400s.

21st Century Skill
Global Awareness

With the Internet, it is possible to access materials from all around the world. It is easy to read, watch, and listen to educational materials such as textbooks, newspaper and magazine articles, radio and television programs, and nonfiction books from almost every country.

A global perspective can provide different points of view and a unique focus on both familiar and unfamiliar topics.

Use a search engine to find an Internet newspaper article about a country you are interested in. In a notebook, record the name of the article, the name of the newspaper, and the date of the article. Then write the main idea of the article.

THINK ABOUT **READING**

Directions: Number the steps for reading educational materials in the order in which you would do them.

_____ Ask yourself questions.
_____ Write answers to your questions.
_____ Scan titles, headings, and boldfaced words.
_____ Read for facts and ideas.
_____ Look again at main ideas, details, and concepts.

When you summarize a text, you retell the main ideas in your own words. A good summary includes the main idea and the most important details.

The main idea is often stated in a topic sentence. Headings and titles give a clue to the main idea. The sentences that follow a stated main idea provide supporting details. Use your judgment to determine the most important details to include in a summary.

After reading the selection on this page, summarize the selection. In a notebook, write the main idea. Then restate the important supporting details in your own words.

Directions: Use the SQ3R strategy as you read the following excerpt from an online resource about China. As you read, identify the main idea and supporting details of the passage.

Filial piety governed life in the extended family.

The Importance of Family in China

The family was the basic unit of Chinese society and the most important unit. Each family member had a duty and a responsibility to every other family member. This duty was known as **filial piety**. It governed the relationships among family members. Sons and daughters were to obey their parents. Parents were to obey their parents.

All family members were to obey the oldest male of the family. He was the head of the **extended family**. An extended family contains all the related members of a family—grandparents, parents, children, aunts, uncles, and cousins. The oldest male member of an extended Chinese family might have been a great-great-grandfather.

THINK ABOUT **READING**

Directions: Answer the following questions.

1. Survey the text. Which two terms will be important for you to understand?

   _____

   _____

2. Write one question based on the heading.

   _____

3. Put a check next to the sentence that states the main idea of the first paragraph.

   _____ This duty was known as filial piety.

   _____ Parents were to obey their parents.

   _____ The family was the basic unit of Chinese society and the most important unit.

Directions: Read this excerpt from a textbook on Egyptian society and summarize the information presented in the chart.

Egyptian Society and Daily Life

At the top of Egyptian society was the pharaoh and other members of the royal family. Next came the upper class of priests and nobles. The priests took care of the temples and celebrated religious ceremonies. The nobles oversaw the government. The ruling, or upper, class was small in number.

The middle class was slightly larger. It was made up of merchants, craftworkers, scribes, and tax collectors. The **scribes** used **hieroglyphics** to keep records. This was the writing system that the ancient Egyptians developed.

The largest class of people were peasant farmers. Land belonged to the pharaoh who gave some of it to the nobles and priests. The farmers worked the fields for the upper class. They also maintained the irrigation systems. Both men and women worked in the fields. The women were also responsible for taking care of the home and the children. During nonfarming seasons, farmers worked on the pharaoh's building projects. Slaves were the lowest social class, below the peasants.

Hieroglyphics was an early form of Egyptian writing.

Achievements of the Ancient Egyptians

Some concepts (general ideas), such as writing, did not develop in one region and spread to other world regions. Often a concept developed independently in different parts of the ancient world.

Inventions	Concepts
• papyrus, a paper-like material • mummification • medical advances, such as surgery and the use of splints for broken bones • copper, bronze, and gold work	• hieroglyphic writing • geometry concepts for measurement • calendar of 12 months, each containing 30 days with 5 days at the end

THINKING ABOUT READING

Directions: Answer the questions in the space provided.

1. What is the topic of this passage?

   _____

2. What are two important words from this section of the text? How do you know?

   _____

Core Skill
Analyze Visual Information

Tables and charts present information in a visual way. They put ideas and data side-by-side so you can **classify**, or arrange, important ideas or numbers and compare and contrast them. To understand a table or a chart, follow these steps:

• First, read the title. This will tell you what the table or chart is about.

• Then, read from left to right across the first row to learn what people, places, or events are being described.

• Finally, read down the first column to see what information is given about the people, places, or events.

Look at the table on this page about the achievements of ancient Egyptians. In a notebook, write the names of the two categories of things that are being described.

WRITE TO LEARN

Scan, or survey, the text on Egyptian society on this page. Look for special features of textbooks that help readers locate information.

In a notebook, list those text features and explain how they helped you understand the information in the text.

Vocabulary Review

Directions: Match these words with their definitions.

1. _____ details
2. _____ main idea
3. _____ stated
4. _____ survey
5. _____ topic sentence

A. something that is said directly
B. a statement that gives the main idea
C. more specific information about a topic
D. the most important idea
E. scan

Skill Review

Directions: Read the passage below from an online encyclopedia. Answer the questions.

Religion of the Byzantine Empire

Just as there were political tensions between the capitals of Rome and Constantinople, disagreements over religion also occurred. Two groups formed within the Christian Church, and they argued over beliefs and practices. Some of these, such as whether a priest should have a beard, do not seem important to us now.

There was also a disagreement about the power of Rome over the Eastern churches. The pope claimed to rule over all Christian churches. Not surprisingly, the head of the Church at Constantinople, who is called a patriarch, disagreed. In 1054, the pope and the patriarch broke their relationship. This was known as the Great Schism. The Eastern church became known as the Eastern Orthodox Church. The Western church became the Roman Catholic Church. The split continues to this day.

---

1. After reading the title of this section, what topic would you expect to read about?

_____

_____

2. Look at the first paragraph. Underline the sentence that states the main idea.

3. What is the main idea of the second paragraph?

   A. The Eastern church became known as the Eastern Orthodox Church.
   B. The pope claimed to rule over all Christian churches.
   C. The Western church became the Roman Catholic Church.
   D. There was also a disagreement about the power of Rome over the Eastern churches.

Directions: Look at the following table from a cultural guidebook to India. Then answer the questions that follow.

FIVE MAJOR CATEGORIES OF ARYAN SOCIETY

Caste*	Members	Work
Brahman	• priests • highest caste and smallest in number	• oversaw religious ceremonies
Kshatriya	• warriors	• defended kingdom
Vaishya	• commoners, or ordinary people	• mostly farmers and merchants
Sudra	• largest group of people • non-Aryans	• earned a living by doing farm work and other manual labor
Untouchable	• outside the caste system • about 5 percent of the people	• did jobs no one else would do, such as garbage collecting • lived separate from others

*caste: a social group

4. What three things does the table show about Aryan society?

_____

_____

_____

5. According to the table, what are the castes in Aryan society?

_____

_____

6. Which caste was ranked the highest?

_____

Skill Practice

Directions: Choose the one best answer to each question. Questions 1 through 4 refer to the following textbook excerpt and the chart.

Hammurabi, Ruler of Babylon

In 1792 BC, Hammurabi decided to create an empire. He was the ruler of Babylon, a city-state in Sumer. He and his army set out to unite Mesopotamia under his rule. He succeeded in taking over much of central and southern Mesopotamia. Many other kings attempted to control parts of Mesopotamia before and after Hammurabi. He is remembered, however, because of his code of laws.

Hammurabi was the first ruler to **codify**, or bring together, a set of laws. He did not write the laws. He gathered them from many parts of his empire. The 282 laws were then carved on stone pillars and placed throughout the Empire. By reading the laws, Hammurabi's subjects knew what was lawful and what was not.

The laws set up a strict system of justice. Those who broke the law were punished. Often the punishment was severe. Punishments were worse for public officials and wealthy men than for peasants. The laws also regulated marriage and the family. Every marriage was governed by a marriage contract. Fathers had absolute rule over the family. Women had fewer rights than men.

—Excerpted from *Contemporary's World History*

ACHIEVEMENTS OF MESOPOTAMIA

Many different people lived in Mesopotamia over the centuries. They made important discoveries. They also developed many important ideas.	
DISCOVERIES	**CONCEPTS**
• the arch • the dome • the wheel • bronze and copper for tools, weapons, and jewelry • iron for tools and weapons	• cuneiform writing • alphabet • division of the circle into 360 degrees • geometry concepts for measurement • calendar • code of laws

Skill Practice (continued)

1. Which of the following is most likely to be an important word or a vocabulary word?

    A. gathered
    B. strict
    C. punished
    D. codify

2. Which of the following would be the best heading for paragraph 3?

    A. Breaking the Law
    B. A Strict System of Justice
    C. Marriage and Family
    D. The Rights of Women

3. Which of the following best states the main idea of paragraph 1?

    A. Babylon is a city-state in Sumer.
    B. Every empire needs a code of laws.
    C. Hammurabi decided to create an empire.
    D. Many other kings attempted to control parts of Mesopotamia.

4. What is the purpose of the table?

    A. to list the achievements of Mesopotamia
    B. to show how tools were made
    C. to explain the beginning of writing and the alphabet
    D. to show why the Mesopotamians invented things

Writing Practice

Directions: Think about a subject that interests you. Write an essay describing how you could learn more about this subject. Include the types of resources you would use and where you could find them. Explain what you would like to learn about this subject and tell why you find it interesting. Make sure to use transitions to link your ideas together.

Magazine and Newspaper Articles

KEY CONCEPT: Magazine and newspaper articles provide current information about events and other topics.

Lesson Objectives

You will be able to

- Explain text features and graphics and their purpose
- Read magazine and newspaper articles to gain information

Skills

- **Core Skill:** Evaluate Content in Different Formats
- **Reading Skill:** Analyze Text Structure

Vocabulary

byline
caption
graph
heading
legend
visual

Imagine you are planning to buy a new car. There are so many cars to choose from. One way to find current information about your choices is to read an article in an automobile magazine. Magazine articles are good places to find information about various topics. Newspaper articles give information about current events. If you want to know what is happening in the world around you, a newspaper is a good source.

Magazine and Newspaper Articles

When you read a magazine or newspaper article, you are reading to learn something. You may also be reading because the topic interests you, but your main purpose is to gain information. Magazine and newspaper articles usually include the following features:

- A title, which tells what the article is about
- A **byline**, which tells who wrote the article
- Headings, which give the main idea of each section of an article
- Photographs, illustrations, and captions, which help you picture ideas in the text
- Magazine and newspaper articles may be divided into two or more columns. Read the entire left column first. Then move to the next column to the right.

When you read a magazine or newspaper article, you may be reading about new or unfamiliar ideas. Here are some ways you can make sense of the information.

- Read the title or headline. This will tell you quickly what the article is about.
- Read the headings. They relate to the main ideas covered in the article.
- Look for the main idea in each section. Often the main ideas are stated in the first or last sentence of a section.
- Use photographs, illustrations, and other visuals to help you picture the information.

TEXT FEATURES: HEADINGS AND CAPTIONS

Magazine and newspaper articles about a topic include special text features such as headings and captions. A **heading** is a brief phrase, usually in boldface type, that states an important idea. Headings can often help you set a purpose for reading. To do this, turn the headings into questions.

Heading: Ways to Conserve Water
Question: What are some ways to conserve water?

Captions are the words underneath a **visual**, such as a photograph or an illustration. These words explain the visual and help you understand the relationship between the visual and the text.

Look at the following excerpt from a magazine article. First, turn the heading into a question in order to set a purpose for reading. Then, identify new information that is provided in the caption.

Flying Trains

Did you think airplanes were the only way to fly? Think again. Today's high speed trains really do fly. Reaching speeds of more than 300 miles per hour, the trains do not touch the tracks. Strong magnets let the trains float above the rails.

In 1990, the TGV Atlantique reached a speed of 321.8 mph.

One question that can be formed from the heading is "What are flying trains?" New information contained in the caption is "In 1990, the TGV Atlantique reached a speed of 321.8 mph."

©Frederic Pitchal/Sygma/Corbis

Directions: Read the article below that reports new findings about the death of the emperor Napoleon. Then answer the questions that follow.

Powerful Leader Napoleon May Have Been Poisoned

Was It Murder?

The French emperor Napoleon died in 1821, in the prime of his life. One of the most powerful European leaders of all time, he ended his days in exile, a tragic figure. History tells us that the cause of his death was stomach cancer. However, recent evidence suggests that he was murdered.

New Findings

In the book *The Murder of Napoleon*, Sten Forshufvud, a Swedish author, makes a strong case that Napoleon was poisoned by his longtime rival and fellow officer, Count Charles Tristan de Montholon.

Napoleon was a famous French emperor.

The evidence points to arsenic poisoning. The autopsy revealed an enlarged liver, a telltale sign of an arsenic overdose. While in exile on the island of St. Helena, Napoleon showed symptoms of chronic arsenic poisoning. Family members reported that he complained of sleepiness, insomnia, swollen feet, and excessive weight gain.

Shocking Evidence

Dr. Forshufvud chemically analyzed strands of Napoleon's hair, which showed abnormally high traces of arsenic.

The most startling evidence of murder actually came to light in 1840. Napoleon's body was moved to Paris. When the coffin was opened, observers were shocked to see a well-preserved body instead of bones and dust. One of the most unusual effects of arsenic is that it greatly slows the decay of living tissue.

WRITE TO LEARN

Summarize the article about Napoleon. When you summarize, you retell the main points in your own words. Use the headings to be sure you have included the most important ideas.

THINK ABOUT **READING**

Directions: Answer the questions in a notebook.

1. What is this article mostly about? How do you know?

2. What was the most surprising evidence to support Dr. Forshufvud's case? Where in the article did you find this information?

3. Who is in the painting? How do you know?

Library of Congress Prints and Photographs Division [LC-USZC2-2870]

Directions: Read this newspaper article and study the table. Notice the text features. Write a sentence about why each feature is useful.

Table Source: U.S. Department of Education, National Center for Education Statistics,(2011). Digest of Education Statistics, 2011, Table 200.

THE BAKERSVILLE DAILY CHRONICLE
Wednesday, June 22, 2014

More Adults Going Back to School
by Rodney Donaldson

For the first time in history, there are more students enrolled in colleges as part-time students than are enrolled full-time. Most of these part-time students are working people between the ages of 25 and 45; many have families.

Older Is Sometimes Better

Universities and colleges are glad to see these new, older students because they bring to their campuses a kind of maturity that younger students do not always possess. Because of their work and family responsibilities, older students often make better, more disciplined students than the younger ones.

Going Back to School

Adults are in school for various reasons. Some who already hold degrees are taking classes to broaden their knowledge in a certain area. Other adults with degrees return to school to prepare for career changes or to get another degree. Colleges are especially interested in such students.

Experience Counts

Some colleges offer life-experience credits to students. They give suitable credit for work they did either as an employee or as a volunteer. Other colleges change the requirements for students studying in a liberal arts program. An older adult's experience is broader than that of a younger freshman; thus, it takes less time to set up a program for study.

The graph below reflects the increase in the number of adults who are returning to college for their degrees.

Total fall enrollment in degree-granting institutions, by age: Selected years, 1990 through 2016 [in thousands]							
Year	**1990**	**1995**	**2000**	**2005**	**2007**	**2010**	**2015[1]**
Total	13,819	14,262	15,312	17,487	18,248	21,016	22,612
14 to 17 years old	177	148	145	187	200	211	211
18 and 19 years old	2,950	2,894	2,531	3,444	3,690	4,119	4,282
20 and 21 years old	2,761	2,705	3,045	3,563	3,570	4,052	4,278
22 to 24 years old	2,411	2,411	2,617	3,114	3,280	3,674	4,083
25 to 29 years old	1,982	2,120	1,960	2,469	2,651	3,196	3,510
30 to 34 years old	1,322	1,236	1,265	1,438	1,519	1,823	2,083
35 years and older	2,484	2,747	2,749	3,272	3,339	3,941	4,165

[1] Projected numbers

THINK ABOUT READING

Directions: Answer the questions that follow.

1. Scan the headings. In which section would you find information about life-experience credits?

_____

2. According to the table, which group of adults is likely to have the greatest number enrolled in college by 2016? _____

Vocabulary Review

Directions: Match these words with their definitions.

1. _____ byline   **A.** an explanation of a photograph or other visual

2. _____ caption   **B.** information in the form of a picture or diagram

3. _____ graph   **C.** a visual that compares numbers

4. _____ heading   **D.** a phrase above a section of text that refers to the main idea

5. _____ legend   **E.** a line that tells who wrote an article

6. _____ visual   **F.** a key that explains what symbols represent

Skill Review

Directions: Read the article and study the graph that is included in the article. Then answer the questions that follow.

SHOULD RESTAURANTS HAVE TO PROVIDE NUTRITION INFORMATION?

With the problems of overweight teens and adults on the rise, many states are now thinking about requiring restaurants to post the calorie counts of the food they serve. This law would require fast-food restaurants to post the number of calories in an item next to its price on the menu. Lawmakers hope that displaying the calorie counts would encourage people to make more nutritious, or healthy, food choices.

The Importance of Menu Labeling

According to recent studies, people are suffering from the disease diabetes in record numbers. The rise of this disease is because of the food choices people are making. People are eating out more and more. Unfortunately, when people eat out, they frequently make poor choices. They eat more calories, fat, and salt than they would at home. Menu labeling may help people make smarter choices and help reduce the rise in diabetes.

Your Right to Know

People who support menu labeling say it is a consumer's right to know what they are putting in their bodies. Without labels, there is no way to know how many calories you are consuming or how much fat or salt are in your restaurant meal choices. The clothing you wear has labels. If you buy food at a grocery store, it has a nutrition label. People who dine out should have the same access to information.

Making Better Choices

New York is one state that requires restaurants to post nutrition information. Eighty-six percent of New Yorkers were in favor of menu labeling. Eighty-six percent were also surprised by calorie counts in the foods they ordered. Ninety-seven percent said they were higher than expected. Posting this information helps people make more responsible choices. A study at a popular fast-food chain showed that people ordered an average of 52 fewer calories when nutrition information was posted. Who knows? You, too, might think twice about what you order when you can see exactly what an extra-large order of fries does to your diet.

Skill Review (continued)

Directions: Study this graph, which shows people's reactions to an online poll about labeling menus. Then answer the questions that follow.

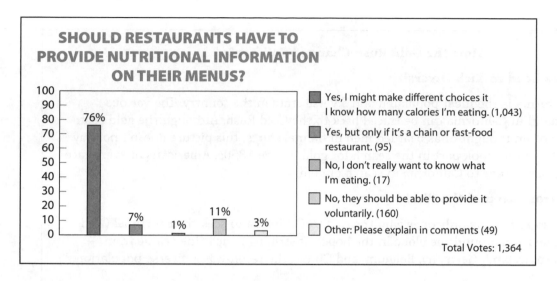

1. In which section would you look for information about how menu labeling affects people's food choices? How do you know?

   _____

   _____

2. What are three topics you would expect to read about in this article?

   _____

   _____

3. What does the online poll show?

   _____

   _____

4. What conclusion can you draw from the bar graph?

   A. Most people make better choices when nutritional information is available.
   B. Most people prefer that menus do not list nutritional information.
   C. Most people think restaurants should have the right to decide whether to post nutritional information.
   D. Most people have no opinion about whether restaurants post nutritional information.

Skill Practice

Directions: Choose the one best answer to each question. Questions 1 through 5 refer to the following article.

How the Gold Rush Changed California

Golden Dreams Lead to Rich Diversity

1   Today California is the most populated and diverse state in the country. The various cultures found in California can be traced back to the Gold Rush. Although the gold rush miners are often thought of as bearded men in flannel shirts, this picture doesn't portray all the cultures that took part in the search for gold. In the 1850s, Americans of every race and background went to California in search of gold.

Gold Seekers from Around the World

2   Americans were not the only ones who traveled to California to seek their fortune. Gold seekers came from around the globe in the hopes of striking it rich. They came from Mexico, Peru, Ireland, Germany, Belgium, and China. The result was a diverse population.

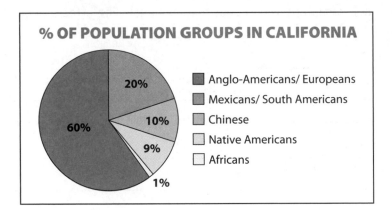

3   Although many people traveled to California with golden dreams, most left disappointed. Life in the mines was difficult, and many miners did not find gold. Life was especially difficult for miners from other parts of the world. Foreign miners had to pay taxes that American miners did not. Many of them were harassed, or bothered, by American miners. Still, many of them stayed in the California towns and cities that developed because of the gold rush.

Skill Practice (continued)

1. In paragraph 2, the writer says that gold seekers "came from Mexico, Peru, Ireland, Germany, Belgium, and China. The result was a diverse population."

   Which definition of diverse is intended in the sentence above?

   A. having similar language and experience
   B. having various levels of education
   C. coming from different economic classes
   D. of many ethnic and cultural backgrounds

2. Which would be the best heading for paragraph 3?

   A. Shattered Dreams
   B. Traveling to California
   C. Striking It Rich
   D. California Today

3. How did the gold rush affect California's population?

   A. It got smaller because people left after not finding gold.
   B. It became more diverse because people came there from around the world.
   C. It became less diverse because people were taxed.
   D. It did not change.

4. What is the author's purpose in this article?

   A. to persuade people to search for gold
   B. to tell humorous stories about the gold rush
   C. to give information about the gold rush
   D. to explain how to find gold

5. Which group or groups made up the second largest percentage of the population in California in 1852?

   A. Chinese
   B. Native Americans
   C. Mexicans/South Americans
   D. Anglo-Americans/Europeans

Writing Practice

Directions: Write a review of a newspaper or magazine article you have read recently or one of the articles in this lesson. Include a short summary of the information in the article. Then clearly state your opinion, positive or negative, of the article. Include examples to support your opinion. End with a conclusion that restates your opinion.

Technical Texts

KEY CONCEPT: A technical text is a document that provides particular group of people information about a specialized subject.

Have you ever used instructions to install software on your computer or to change an ink cartridge on a printer? If so, you are already familiar with some types of technical texts. Instruction manuals, workplace flowcharts, and product warranties are all technical texts. These texts are useful tools for understanding specific, often work-oriented, topics.

Determine Author's Purpose in Technical Texts

A **technical** text provides detailed information on a specialized subject. The purpose of the text is to provide professional instructions to a targeted group. One example of a technical text would be a process flowchart. Such charts show a **process**, or series of actions, that is repeated in a business or technical setting. For example, a process flowchart for an online retailer's call center might begin with an incoming phone call. Later items in the chart would be a series of yes/no questions such as "Is the merchandise in stock?" and "Does the customer want overnight delivery?"

Use Text Structure to Determine Author's Purpose

Like textbooks and other educational materials, the primary purpose of a technical text is to inform and explain. However, technical texts explain how to perform specific procedures or how certain processes work. The text may contain instructions and definitions of technical terms. There may be text features such as numbered steps, bulleted lists, illustrations, and **diagrams**, or technical drawings. Text features make information easier to understand, and they reinforce the instruction in the document.

There are several types of technical texts. Each type has a structure, or format, that fits the purpose of that text. A process flowchart uses text and symbols to describe a process. Instruction manuals often include numbered steps and graphics. **Regulations**, or rules, may break text into sections that use numbers and letters to show the order of ideas. Consumer information tells **consumers**, or buyers, about the products they buy and use. For example, the label on a bottle of a pain reliever might tell consumers the dosage and possible side effects of the drug.

INTERPRET WORDS AND PHRASES IN TECHNICAL TEXTS

Both the structure and the language of a technical text reflect the purpose of the text. For this reason, some of the words and phrases in the text will be technical and specific to the topic. These words may be unfamiliar to many readers. To keep the message of the text clear, the words and phrases surrounding the technical vocabulary must be as simple and direct as possible.

Examine the following information from an instruction manual for installing a washing machine. Step number 7, shown below, explains how to connect the washing machine hoses to the water supply. As you read the text, consider these questions: Which words are specific to this instruction manual? Where does the writer deliberately use simple, clear wording so the text will be easy to understand? What symbols and illustrations help clarify the process?

In a notebook, list two examples of each of these characteristics: specific vocabulary, simple wording, and graphics.

7. CONNECT INLET HOSES TO WATER FAUCETS

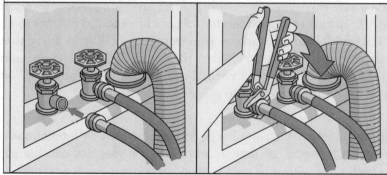

Use new inlet hoses to connect washing machine to water faucets.

Attach first hose to hot water faucet. Screw on coupling until it is seated on washer. Tighten coupling with pliers. Repeat to attach second hose to cold water faucet.

IMPORTANT: Do not use tape or sealants on valve. Damage can result.

Specific vocabulary in this technical document includes "inlet hoses" and "coupling." The wording seems simple because the sentences are so short. The arrow in the drawing shows exactly what the directions refer to.

Technical texts usually include key terms that are specific to the topic. In the instruction manual for installing a washing machine, you must understand the meaning of *inlet* and *coupling* to accomplish your task.

When you come across a technical word, try using context clues and graphics to determine the word's meaning. If you're still stumped, you can often find the meaning of a word by doing an online search.

Locate the consumer information for a product you currently own. If you do not have the owner's manual, you can usually find this information at the manufacturer's website.

Skim the text to find words or terms you do not know. Next, read the surrounding text to see if you can figure out what these words mean. Write the unfamiliar words and your definitions for them in your notebook. Finally, do an online search to check the definitions you created.

To understand what you are reading, you must often read between the lines—that is, you must think about what the writer wants you to understand. When you use information stated by the writer and your own experience to form a new idea, you are drawing a conclusion.

Study the driving regulation below. Look for facts and details that let you draw a conclusion about the need for the regulation. In a notebook, state the conclusion you can draw about why this rule was formed. Then list several facts that you used as evidence in order to draw your conclusion. Finally, write a sentence that tells how your own knowledge and experience helped you to draw your conclusion.

Distracted Driving Safety Act of 2004

Beginning July 1, 2004, it is illegal for motorists to use a mobile phone or other electronic device while driving in the District of Columbia, unless the telephone or device is equipped with a hands-free accessory. The Distracted Driving Safety Act of 2004 is designed to improve traffic safety in DC.

Draw Conclusions

When you read, you often draw conclusions about the people, events, and ideas in the text. A **conclusion** is an opinion or decision that you form after thinking about what you have read. To draw a conclusion, you must use evidence from the text, selecting the facts and details that will help you to make up your mind. You can add your own experience and knowledge to this evidence in order to draw a conclusion.

A Rule by the National Park Service **on** 01/23/2012

ACTION   Final Rule

SUMMARY   This rule designates off-road vehicle (ORV) routes and authorizes limited ORV use within Cape Hatteras National Seashore in a manner that will protect and preserve natural and cultural resources, provide a variety of safe visitor experiences, and minimize conflicts among various users.

You read in the ruling from the National Park Service that the use of off-road vehicles (ORVs) has been limited to protect a natural resource and provide a safe experience for visitors. After analyzing that information, you may conclude that park service officials have found visitors to the Cape Hatteras National Seashore who were using ORVs in a way that was not safe. You may also conclude that the use of ORVs was threatening the beach's sand dunes and other natural resources. Finally, you may conclude that the new rule is an effort to solve these problems.

Directions: Look at the Drug Facts document below. In a notebook, write a conclusion that you can draw from it. Use the graphics and the evidence in the text along with your own knowledge and experience to draw your conclusion.

DRUG FACTS

Active ingredient (in each tablet)   *Purpose*
Chlorpheniramine maleate 2 mg .... Antihistamine

Uses Temporarily relieves these symptoms caused by hay fever and other upper respiratory allergies:
■ itchy throat or eyes   ■ sneezing   ■ runny nose   ■ watery eyes

---

Directions: Study the two documents on this page. In a notebook, state the author's purpose for writing each text. Then list several technical words that you must know the meaning of in order to understand the document.

Compare Words and Phrases in Technical Texts and Other Informational Texts

Technical vocabulary surrounded by simple text is a common feature of technical documents and other informational texts. In addition, the formatting styles used in technical texts (bullet points, subheadings, and boldfaced type) are often used in these texts. You can apply the skills you use when reading technical texts to reading other informational texts.

Directions: Look at the sample texts below. Some similarities between the technical text and the informational text are noted. In a notebook, write one difference between the instruction manual and the recipe.

WRITE TO LEARN

Write instructions for a process you do often at home, at work, or at school. Follow the examples shown on this page.

After completing your instructions, do a mental walk-through of the task to be sure you have included all the necessary steps and have put the steps in order.

Instruction manual for recharging a camera battery	Similarities	Recipe for Low-Fat Cornbread
1. Open the hatch. 2. Slide the battery pack into the battery charger. 3. Insert the charger's plug into a power outlet.	• numbered points • terms specific to task • use of commands	1. Preheat oven to 350 degrees. Lightly grease an 8 × 8-inch baking pan. 2. In a bowl, mix 1 cup flour, 1 cup cornmeal, ¼ cup sugar, 1 tsp. baking soda, and ½ tsp. salt. 3. Combine 2 egg whites, 1 cup low-fat buttermilk, and ¼ cup applesauce. Add wet and dry mixtures together and stir just until moist.

THINK ABOUT READING

Directions: Answer these questions.

1. Which of the following word lists would you expect to find in a regulation about importing fresh citrus fruit from Uruguay into the US?

   A. monitor, inspect, require, allow

   B. connect, measure, attach, repeat

   C. use, doctor, ingredients, dose

   D. ask, decide, check, complete

2. How does an instruction manual organize its information?

   A. Symbols and words show repeating events.

   B. An outline style shows relationships between parts of the text.

   C. Numbered sections show the order and importance of information.

   D. Poetic language helps explain specific terms.

Directions: Match these words with their definitions.

1. _____ consumers   **A.** drawing

2. _____ diagram   **B.** laws or rules

3. _____ process   **C.** series of steps

4. _____ regulations   **D.** buyers

Skill Review

Directions: Study this passage from an instruction manual. Then answer the questions.

6. Lay the Boards

Once you have cleared the floor of debris, you can begin to lay your floor. Use your chalk line as a guide to place your first long board on the ground. Drill pilot holes in each end of the board and nail it down. This will provide a strong base for matching up the remaining boards.

Choose boards that are random lengths to add variety to your floor. Each board will be grooved, allowing for easy sliding and snapping in place.

1. Where would you most likely find this information?

_____

2. Why does the step include an illustration?

_____

3. What are three technical words or phrases are used to describe the process?

_____

Skill Practice

Directions: Answer the following questions.

1. What is the purpose of a technical document?

    A. to persuade readers that a certain viewpoint is true
    B. to entertain with an engaging story
    C. to give facts and information about a person's life
    D. to provide information on a specialized subject

2. How is a technical text usually structured?

    A. It always has numbered steps.
    B. The format varies depending on the purpose of the text.
    C. A technical document does not need illustrations.
    D. It is organized so readers do not need to drawing conclusions.

3. Which is one of the best ways to determine word meaning in a technical text?

    A. Review the surrounding sentences for context clues.
    B. Skip the word and read over the remaining text.
    C. Remove the word from the sentence and continue reading.
    D. Substitute words until the sentence makes sense.

4. Why is it important that consumer information be presented clearly?

    _____

    _____

Writing Practice

Directions: Choose a project that requires you to use a technical document. Find a technical document that guides you through the steps of your project. In an essay, discuss the format of this technical document and explain how that format helps you to understand the information. Consider the language, graphics, and organization of the document.

Directions: Choose the <u>one best answer</u> to each question. <u>Questions 1 through 4</u> refer to the following textbook passage.

Black Hawk, famous chief of the Sauk Indians, refused to leave Illinois after white men arrived in the late 1700s. When the Sauk and Fox tribes gave their lands to the US government in 1804, Black Hawk would not accept the contract. He believed that the white men got the chiefs drunk with firewater to trick them. The chiefs agreed to sign the contract, but Black Hawk was convinced that they had not really wanted to give up their land.

The high point of Sauk resistance came in the Black Hawk War. In 1832, Black Hawk's tribe remained in Illinois and Wisconsin. The other Indians had moved west to reservations. The Black Hawk War did not last long, and the casualties on both sides were light. Black Hawk and his tribe were strong fighters, but they were defeated. Black Hawk and his sons were sent with their tribe to a reservation near Fort Des Moines.

The story of Black Hawk continues because of his love for the land. "Keep it as we did," he said to his captors.

Date	Important Event
Late 1700s	White men arrived in Illinois
1804	Sauk and Fox tribes gave up their land
1832	

1. Why did Black Hawk refuse to leave his land?

   A. Hunting was better in Illinois than in Wisconsin.
   B. The US government did not have a signed contract.
   C. He felt the chiefs had been tricked into giving away their land.
   D. He had won the land from the Fox in the Black Hawk War.

2. How did Black Hawk show his love of the land?

   A. He fought for his land.
   B. He gave up his land.
   C. He was defeated in battle.
   D. He drank firewater before signing the contract.

3. Which statement should appear in the table under "Important Event" for 1832?

   A. The story of Black Hawk lives on.
   B. The Black Hawk war took place.
   C. Black Hawk would not accept the contract.
   D. The chiefs drank firewater and gave up their land.

4. What might have happened if Black Hawk had won the war?

   A. He would have been set free by the US government.
   B. He could have moved to a different reservation.
   C. His story would have lived on.
   D. He could have kept his land.

Review

Directions: Questions 5 through 8 refer to the following magazine article

Advertising plays a vital role in the nation's economy. Americans spend more than $149 billion a year on this enterprise. No other country in the world invests in advertising as the United States does.

Advertising is found in media ranging from newspapers to billboards. About 85 percent (or 85 cents out of every dollar) of newspaper advertising is paid for by local businesses and individuals. Radio receives about 70 percent of its advertising income from the local community. National advertisers, such as automobile manufacturers and large drug companies, prefer to advertise in magazines and on television.

The following graph shows how much money is spent on different kinds of advertising.

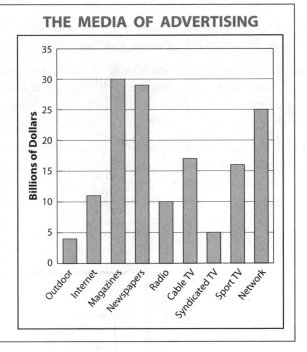

THE MEDIA OF ADVERTISING

5. If you want to sell your refrigerator, where would be the best place for you to advertise the sale?

   A. radio
   B. a magazine
   C. a newspaper
   D. television

6. General Gadget Corporation wants to tell the country about the latest in its new line of gadgets. According to the article, which would be the most effective form of advertising for the company to use?

   A. television
   B. newspapers
   C. outdoor signs
   D. direct mail

7. According to the graph, which type of media is the least amount of money spent on?

   A. Outdoor
   B. Syndicated TV
   C. Radio
   D. Internet

8. Which would be the best heading for the first paragraph?

   A. $149 Billion a Year
   B. A Vital Part of the Economy
   C. Top Three Types of Media
   D. How Other Countries Advertise

Directions: <u>Questions 9 through 12</u> refer to the following newspaper article.

Since the year 2004, studies done on polar bears have shown an increase in polar bear drownings. Since polar bears are good swimmers, why is this happening?

Polar bears hunt on giant blocks of ice. As temperatures have increased, the blocks of ice have begun to melt. Polar bears are drowning because they have fewer and fewer blocks of ice to hunt and live on. Also, animals that polar bears hunt, such as seals, are moving farther out to sea. With fewer blocks of ice to hunt on, the journey for food has grown long and difficult.

Earth's temperature naturally rises and falls over time. However, in recent years, it has been rising steadily. This is called global warming. One reason for this rise in temperature is an increase in carbon dioxide in the air. Carbon dioxide is a gas that is released from burning coal and oil. The graph below shows how the amount of carbon dioxide has increased.

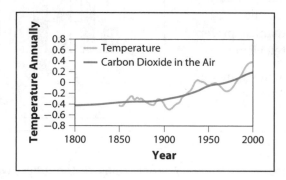

One Arctic researcher said, "It is a phenomenon that frightens the native people that live around the Arctic. Many fear their children will never know the polar bear." You may be wondering why you should care about polar bears. Polar bears are one of the first animals to be directly affected by global warming. Since all life on Earth is connected, you can assume that one day humans, too, will feel the effects of rising temperatures.

9. Why are polar bears drowning?

   A. There is less ocean for them to swim in.
   B. Warmer temperatures have made it harder for them to swim.
   C. The ice blocks they live on are melting.
   D. There is less food for them to eat.

10. Why does the author quote an Arctic researcher in the article?

   A. to make the article longer
   B. to use the words of an expert to support his argument
   C. to provide a different point of view
   D. to prove that the research was necessary

11. According to the article, what is one change people could make to help decrease the amount of carbon dioxide in the air?

   A. stay away from melting ice blocks
   B. help polar bears find food closer to home
   C. use less coal and oil
   D. increase the amount of carbon dioxide they breathe

12. According to the graph, what has happened to the amount of carbon dioxide in the air?

   A. It has decreased.
   B. It has stayed the same.
   C. It has increased.
   D. It increased and then decreased.

Review

Check Your Understanding

On the following chart, circle the number of any question you answered incorrectly. Under each content area you will see the pages you can review to learn the content covered in the question. Pay particular attention to reviewing those lessons in which you missed half or more of the questions.

Chapter 2 Review

Lesson	Item Number	Review Pages
Textbooks and Other Educational Materials	1, 2, 3, 4	86–93
Magazine and Newspaper Articles	5, 6, 7, 8, 9, 10, 11, 12	94–101

ESSAY WRITING PRACTICE

Expository Texts

Directions: Write a passage of informative or explanatory text in response to one of the prompts below. Review Lessons 2.1 and 2.2 for help with the structure and purpose of these kinds of writing.

TEXTBOOKS AND OTHER EDUCATIONAL MATERIALS

People who want in-depth information about a subject often use specialty libraries and collections. Digital libraries also make this kind of information easily available, if you know where to look.

At the library where you volunteer, you are on the committee that is creating a guide called "How to Research American History Online." You are writing a section on the Library of Congress's American History collection. Go online and visit the Library of Congress website (www.loc.gov). On the home page, in the "Topics" section, click the "American History" link. Study the information you find on that page. Open various articles so you understand how the site works.

Then write two paragraphs telling readers how to use the American History link on the Library of Congress site. Describe the path you took to reach the American History collection, give a brief description of how the American History collection is organized, and make two recommendations of topics that readers can explore on that site.

MAGAZINE OR NEWSPAPER ARTICLE

Magazine and newspaper articles provide current information about local, national, and world events. Their topics range from politics and world affairs to science and the world of entertainment.

The work of the National Aeronautics and Space Administration (NASA) is widely reported in magazines and newspaper articles. NASA's website provides coverage of its current, past, and future missions related to space research and technology. Visit the website (www.nasa.gov) and select one of NASA's current or future missions. After reading about the mission, write a two-paragraph article that describes the mission for a weekly news magazine. Tell why the mission important and what its contribution to science will be. Be sure to give your article a headline that clearly states what the article is about.

ESSAY WRITING PRACTICE

_____
_____
_____
_____
_____
_____
_____
_____
_____
_____
_____
_____
_____
_____
_____
_____
_____
_____
_____
_____
_____
_____
_____
_____
_____
_____
_____
_____
_____
_____
_____

Persuasive Texts

What problems do you and your friends face? What problems do you see in your school or your community? Do you worry about pollution or endangered animals? Maybe you are concerned about the homeless and wonder how you can be helpful. Do you feel there is too much violence in movies and on TV? Have you ever had an idea that could improve the world, if only someone would listen? A good way to get your message across effectively is to use persuasive language and persuasive texts.

In this chapter you will learn how authors use persuasive language in blogs, ads, editorials, and reviews. To evaluate persuasive texts, you need to recognize the difference between fact and opinion. The lessons in this chapter provide you with skills so you can evaluate arguments and sort facts from opinions.

In this chapter you will study these topics:

Lesson 3.1 Ads
Are you ever confused about the recommendations in ads? One ad tells you to buy a product because it is better than others. Another ad tells you not to listen to a competitor's claim—to buy its product instead. How do you figure out what is the best product for you? Learn about recognizing facts and opinions in this lesson.

Lesson 3.2 Editorials
Editorials express opinions about current issues. They may be long articles that appear on the editorial page of a newspaper. They can also be letters from the public supporting or disagreeing with a position. A news story about an election would report the positions that the candidates represent. However, an editorial about the election might urge readers to vote for one candidate instead of another.

Lesson 3.3 Blogs
People today have many more ways of communicating with one another than they did just ten years ago. Are you familiar with Facebook and Twitter? How do you network? Learn what is a blog and what a blog is used for. Learn how to read and use the information in a blog.

Lesson 3.4 Reviews and Commentaries
You are probably familiar with movie and television reviews. Newspapers and magazines regularly feature reviews of movies, books, television shows, and radio programs. A review can help you decide whether you would enjoy a particular book, program, or film.

Goal Setting

What do you already know about persuasive texts?

_____

_____

_____

What do you hope to learn about persuasive texts that you don't know?
List three things you would like to know.

1. _____

2. _____

3. _____

How will learning this information help you to become a better reader?

_____

_____

_____

To help you set goals for learning, use the following checklist as you read
the persuasive texts in this chapter.

☐ Does the author state the problem clearly?

☐ Does the author support his or her opinions with facts?

☐ Does the author state the solution or conclusion clearly?

☐ Does the author use strong, clear language to help readers follow
the argument?

Ads

KEY CONCEPT: Ads are persuasive messages that try to convince people to buy or use something or to think or act in a certain way.

As you travel around town, you are probably surrounded by ads. Billboards, big roadside signs, and small posters on buses and trains urge you to buy a hamburger, visit a theme park, or see a movie. Magazines and newspapers are also filled with ads for everything from clothing to cars. Whether they are big or small, funny or serious, all ads have one thing in common—they want to convince you of something.

Ads

Advertisements, more commonly called ads, are persuasive messages that try to convince you to buy a product, use a service, think a certain way, or do something. You can watch ads on television, hear them on the radio, and see them in magazines and newspapers. Thinking about an ad's purpose can help you understand how advertisers sell products and help you decide whether the product is something you really need. To analyze an ad, ask yourself these questions:

• What does the ad want me to think, buy, or do?

• Who created this ad?

• Who is the audience for this ad? Who does the advertiser want to persuade?

Look for the persuasive words and phrases used in the ad. The ad may contain words such as *best*, *must*, and *everyone* to convince you that you will be missing out if you do not buy a product or do something. Pay attention to **logos**, which are symbols used by a company. Watch for **slogans**, or sayings. Look carefully the images in the ad.

Ads often use bold words, colorful pictures, and photos of celebrities to capture your attention. Sometimes they include **testimonials**, statements people make about the high quality of a product. When the testimonials are made by celebrities, they can be especially appealing.

Considering all these elements can help you evaluate the ad. Then you can decide whether you want the product or need the service.

Read the following ad. Think about what is being sold and how the author presents the information.

For Sale: Used Grill—Great Condition!

This is a slightly used gas grill in great condition. It's a few years old, but it's only been used twice. You won't find a better deal than this! It has a three-burner main grill with a smaller side burner. All the burners are in working condition. This is your chance to get a great grill at a great price! Get it now, and you could be eating the most delicious grilled hamburgers and hot dogs this summer! Propane tank not included. **Price: $100.00**

Call Desi at (555) 555-5555.

DISTINGUISH FACT FROM OPINION

When authors write, they may use a mix of facts and opinions. A **fact** is a statement that can be proven. An **opinion** is a statement that shows someone's feelings, judgments, or beliefs. An opinion cannot be proven.

Authors often use signal words and phrases to show that they are expressing an opinion. These words can help readers distinguish opinions from facts. Words and phrases that signal opinions include *I think*, *I believe*, *I feel*, *best*, *worst*, *always*, *should*, and *never*. Descriptive words such as *beautiful*, *important*, *terrible*, and *surprising* can also signal opinions.

Read the following statements. Underline the facts, and circle the opinions.

1. This shirt is made of 100 percent cotton.
2. Cotton is the best material for T-shirts.
3. Everyone should own a nice white T-shirt.
4. This shirt is also available in black.

You should have underlined sentences 1 and 4. These statements are facts. They can be proven. You can look at the label of the shirt to prove sentence 1 and check a catalog to prove sentence 4. You should have circled sentences 2 and 3. These sentences are opinions, and they cannot be proven. *Best* in sentence 2 and *should* in sentence 3 signal that these statements are opinions.

REAL WORLD
CONNECTION

Analyze Visual Elements

People who write ads use visual elements designed to grab the public's attention. Ads often contain bright colors, eye-catching designs, and memorable photos.

The first job of an ad—regardless of where it appears—is to get your attention. The designs and colors must make you want to learn more. The visual elements should relate to the ad.

Find two ads in magazines or newspapers. With a partner, make list of the visual elements that make you notice this ad and want to read it.

All ads are a combination of fact and opinion. It is important to distinguish facts from opinions. When you find an opinion, look for the facts and reasons that support the opinion. As a reader, you must decide whether the opinion makes sense.

As you read the paragraph below, look for signal words that help you distinguish between facts and opinions.

(1) Yesterday I went to Miser's Grocery and Drug Store. (2) It seems to me that Miser's is the cheapest supermarket in town. (3) Cluck's chicken soup is 10 cents less there than at Buy Right Grocery. (4) Fancy Farms whole wheat bread is two cents a loaf cheaper than at Buy Right Grocery. (5) Miser's offers the best value.

THINK ABOUT READING

Directions: Answer the following questions.

1. Which sentences in the paragraph are facts?

   _____

2. Which sentences in the paragraph are opinions?

   _____

3. Which words helped you to distinguish between fact and opinion?

   _____

   _____

Directions: Read the ad below. Look for key words or phrases that signal opinions or facts.

HOME ENTERTAINMENT SUPER STORE

Home of the highest quality home entertainment equipment at the best prices

The Home Entertainment Super Store Memorial Day Weekend sale is on now. We are offering brand-new MP3 players, speakers, and, and tuners at up to 50% off our regular prices. Our salespeople are the best around. They will help you find the perfect equipment for your audio needs.

On Memorial Day ONLY, we will be offering our DVD players and high-definition flat screen televisions at 30% off.

All at 30% off!

Televisions

HD Flat screen TVs
Plasma Televisions
3D Televisions

Home Theater/Audio

Sound Bars
Wireless Streaming Speakers
Surround Sound

Video DVD Players

Blu-ray players

Isn't it time to upgrade your home entertainment systems TODAY?!

Home Entertainment Super Store 390 Colonial Drive (010) 555-3333

THINK ABOUT READING

Directions: Read the following statements from the Home Entertainment Super Store ad. Label each statement as *F* for fact or *O* for opinion.

1. _____ We are offering brand-name MP3 players, speakers, and tuners at up to 50% off our regular prices.

2. _____ Our expert salespeople are the best around.

3. _____ Home of the highest quality home entertainment equipment at the best prices.

4. _____ On Memorial Day ONLY, we will be offering our DVD players and high-definition flat screen televisions at 30% off.

You have probably heard the saying "Don't believe everything you read." That is especially true when the author's purpose is to convince you of something.

In an ad, the writer presents an **argument**, or reason, why you should do something. As a reader, you must **evaluate**, or make a judgment about, the argument's accuracy and truthfulness.

Here are some questions to ask yourself when you evaluate an argument:

1. What is the author's purpose? What does the author want you to do?

2. Can you trust the author? Is the author an expert?

3. From your experience, does the information make sense?

4. What facts does the author give to support the argument?

Find a newspaper or magazine ad for a product or a service that you know little about. Study the ad. Then evaluate the ad's arguments by answering the four questions above.

The words authors choose to use help us determine whether they are writing facts or opinions. Facts include details such as dates, prices, and information that can be confirmed by a reliable source. Opinions cannot be proven.

Authors often use words such as *usually*, *probably*, *perhaps*, and *sometimes* when they are expressing an opinion.

Read the passage on this page. Circle the words and phrases that show the author is expressing an opinion.

Directions: Read the following ad. Write a brief summary of the author's purpose.

Would Your Home Be Safe in a Hurricane? Probably NOT!

If you live in an area where hurricanes are common, then your house is probably not strong enough to stand up to strong winds—not unless it's a StormStand home. StormStand homes have stood up to Hurricane Andrew in Florida and Hurricane Katrina along the Gulf Coast. Each attractive StormStand home is designed to stand up to strong winds and rain. Our trained builders combine modern engineering and design with a classic post-and-beam building system to create homes that are **strong fortresses** against dangerous storms. We raise our houses off the ground so that winds flow under, over, and around them.

Call now for more information. Our sales associates are standing by to provide you with more information and to answer all your questions. Plus, we're offering a 15% discount through the end of the month!

No home is completely stormproof, but StormStand has the best record of storm survival around. Ask anyone!

StormStand Homes

1-800-555-5555

WRITE TO LEARN

In a notebook, write a short ad for an apartment for rent, a used car for sale, or a product or service of your choice. Write several descriptive sentences about the specific product or service. Include at least two facts and two opinions. Use signal words or phrases to show that you are expressing an opinion.

THINK ABOUT READING

Directions: Answer the questions below.

1. Which information in the ad can you assume is most likely to be accurate?

    A. StormStand homes are attractive.
    B. StormStand homes have the best record of storm survival.
    C. StormStand homes are raised off the ground.
    D. Your home is probably not strong enough to stand up to strong winds.

2. What is the purpose of this statement: "Would your home be safe in a hurricane? Probably NOT!"?

    A. to convince you that your home may not be safe
    B. to persuade you not to live where there are hurricanes
    C. to convince you to leave your home during a hurricane
    D. to show that even StormStand homes are not safe

3. Is "Ask anyone!" a good way to prove that StormStand has the best record of storm survival? Why or why not?

_____

Vocabulary Review

Directions: Use these words to complete the following sentences.

advertisement   argument   fact   logo   opinion   slogan

1. A(n) _____ is a statement that can be proved.

2. The _____ convinced me to buy a new kind of ice cream.

3. The company's _____ is "Just Relax!"

4. One _____ for riding your bike is that it saves gas.

5. It's my _____ that dogs make the best pets.

6. What _____ is on your running shoes?

Skill Review

Directions: Read the ad below. Then answer the questions that follow.

A TruWhite Smile

Your smile says a lot about you. That is why you want to have the brightest, whitest teeth. The shinier your smile, the more often you'll want to use it.

TruWhite is the best, most effective tooth whitener available. It comes in a pen with a brush-on applicator. Simply brush the whitener on your teeth. The pen is convenient, mess-free, and easy to use. You don't need to rinse. You should begin seeing results in just two days. That is not a long time to wait for a movie-star smile.

TruWhite stands behind its product. If you don't see results, then send the unused portion back within 30 days, and we willl refund your money.

> "I used to never smile. Now that my smile is brighter
> and whiter, I can't stop grinning. Thanks, TruWhite!"
>
> —Betty A.

Order TruWhite today. When you order two or more whitening pens, we'll even ship your product free. Call 1-800-555-GRIN.

Remember, bright smiles equal a bright future!

Skill Review (continued)

1. Which of the following statements is a fact?

   A. "The shinier your smile, the more often you'll want to use it."
   B. "It comes in a pen with a brush-on applicator."
   C. "The pen is convenient, mess-free, and easy to use."
   D. "That is not a long time to wait for a movie-star smile."

2. How do the makers of TruWhite try to convince you to buy their product?

   A. They show a celebrity using it.
   B. They give facts and statistics to show how much whiter your teeth will be.
   C. They tell you that you will have a brighter future if you use it.
   D. They tell you that you will save money by using it.

3. Read this sentence: "TruWhite is the best, most effective tooth whitener available" (line 3). Write two words that help you recognize that this statement is an opinion.

   _____

4. Why did the makers of TruWhite include the statement from Betty A.: "I used to never smile. Now that my smile is brighter and whiter, I can't stop grinning. Thanks, TruWhite!"?

   _____

   _____

   _____

5. Evaluate the ad's argument that TruWhite is the best and most effective tooth whitener. Does the ad do a good job of supporting this claim? Why or why not?

   _____

   _____

   _____

Skill Practice

Directions: Choose the <u>one best answer</u> to each question. <u>Questions 1 through 4</u> refer to the following ad.

Easy Diet Makes It Easy

Do you enjoy your diet when you are trying to lose weight fast? On a low-carbohydrate diet, you give up bread, spaghetti, cake—all the good things in life. When following a low-protein diet, you are anemic without steak and homesick for ham. A low-fat diet means turning away from cheddar cheese and chocolate ice cream.

5   With the Easy Diet program, you can enjoy life while you peel off the pounds. You simply mix half a cup of Easy Diet Formula in a glass of water, put the mixture into the blender, and sip away your worries. Enjoy the sweet, rich flavor of a milk shake while getting all your daily nutritional requirements. Drink the formula three times a day and lose weight the Easy Diet way!

---

1. With which words does the author express an opinion?

   A. "On a low-carbohydrate diet, you give up bread"
   B. "all the good things in life"
   C. "mix half a cup of Easy Diet Formula in a glass of water"
   D. "Drink the formula three times a day"

2. Who is the intended audience for this ad?

   A. a person who likes a low-carbohydrate diet
   B. a person who likes a low-fat diet
   C. a person who wants to lose weight quickly
   D. a person who is worried

3. Allan is considering purchasing Easy Diet. What additional information would be most helpful in determining whether the product works?

   A. a list of Easy Diet Formula flavors
   B. a list of other products made by the Easy Diet company
   C. a graph created by the Easy Diet company showing how much weight customers have lost
   D. a study by the Food and Drug Administration (FDA) showing how much weight Easy Diet users have lost

4. What is the purpose of this ad?

   A. to persuade you to buy Easy Diet Formula
   B. to persuade you to go on a diet
   C. to convince you not to eat bread and spaghetti
   D. to convince you that drinking milk shakes is good for weight loss

Writing Practice

Directions: Think of a product or service that you could advertise. On another sheet of paper, write an advertisement for it that uses facts and opinions effectively. Keep your intended audience in mind, and make your advertisement as interesting and informative as you can.

Editorials

Lesson Objectives

You will be able to

- Understand the purpose and content of editorials

- Evaluate the effectiveness of arguments in excerpts

- Distinguish between conflicting viewpoints

Skills

- **Core Skill:** Compare Different Texts

- **Reading Skill:** Evaluate Support for Conclusions

Vocabulary

assumption
bias
conclusion
defend
editorial
evidence
point of view

KEY CONCEPT: Editorials express ideas and opinions from the writer's point of view.

It is election time and you are trying to decide which candidate to vote for. You have read facts about the candidates, but you want to know what others think of the candidates. Therefore, you read several editorials in the local newspaper. However, after reading the ideas of others, you still have to make up your mind about which candidate will get your vote.

Editorials

An **editorial** is an article written to express an opinion. Editorials are found in newspapers and magazines, in both print versions and online versions. An editorial expresses the author's **point of view**, or opinions, about politics, culture, or a social issue.

When you read an editorial, consider these points:

- Whose opinion is being expressed? Is the author an expert? Does the author belong to a special interest group that is trying to change people's opinions about an issue?

- What is the topic? If you know very little about the topic, you may need to do research to acquire background information.

- What is the author's point of view about the topic?

- How does the author makes his or her point? Editorial writers may use humor, logic, emotional appeals, or even cartoons.

- What are the opinions of others about this topic? When you read an editorial, think about other opinions on the topic. Ask yourself whether the arguments made would be convincing to someone who has a different opinion.

EVALUATE SUPPORT FOR CONCLUSIONS

In an editorial, a writer gives reasons and then comes to a **conclusion**. The conclusion is the final opinion reached after doing careful thinking. However, it is up to the reader to evaluate that conclusion. The reader must decide whether the conclusion makes sense based on the information presented in the editorial. A logical conclusion is based on reasons and **evidence**, or proof.

Here are some questions to ask as you evaluate a writer's conclusion:

• Does the writer give facts as evidence to **defend**, or support, the argument?

• Does the writer's reasoning, or thinking, make sense? Do the writer's points lead to the conclusion?

• Does the writer have a **bias**, or prejudice? Does the writer use certain words, facts, and descriptions to make statements that are unfair? Does the writer leave out important information because it doesn't agree with his or her opinion?

You must read critically. Sometimes the "facts" in an editorial are not true. An author with a bias might try to pass off false or misleading statements as fact. As a careful reader, you should always fact check statements that seem questionable.

Read the following paragraph. Then decide whether the conclusion makes sense.

> I know it's the law that you must wear seat belts, but I don't think I need to. Why should I be uncomfortable just because others don't drive safely? I follow the rules of the road, so I won't be in an accident. If I'm not going to be in an accident, I don't need to wear a seat belt.

The conclusion does not make sense. The author admits that "Others don't drive safely." Therefore, the author could be involved in an accident. A seat belt might save his or her life.

Research It
Find Evidence

With a partner, identify a current issue that is controversial, that is, an issue that people are debating. Use reliable sources to research two opinions on that issue. Evaluate each side of the argument. What evidence and reasoning are used to support the different opinions?

Prepare a presentation for your class in which you explain the two opinions. Tell why you think one argument is more convincing than the other.

THINK ABOUT READING

Directions: Answer this question.

Name two points that you should consider when reading editorials.

_____

_____

A conclusion must be supported with evidence. If the author makes no effort to prove a conclusion, he or she is making an **assumption**. That is, the writer is stating an idea that is not based on proven facts.

As you read the passage on this page about handgun use, circle the author's conclusions. Then underline any facts or reasons given to support these conclusions. This will help you decide whether the author has done a good job of supporting his or her ideas with evidence.

Directions: Read this editorial on handgun use. Then write a paragraph stating whether you agree with the author's conclusion and explaining why.

Ban on Handguns Robs Us of Our Rights

The city council is debating a ban on the ownership of handguns by private citizens. A ban on handguns, they say, would drastically reduce the rate of violent crime.

We believe that banning handguns won't solve our crime problem. Anyone with an ounce of common sense can see why.

Our Bill of Rights guarantees "the right of the people to keep and bear arms." Government cannot and must not violate this basic freedom. Most of our citizens keep firearms for protection against the small but dangerous minority of armed criminals among us.

If we banned handguns, the illegal buying and selling of firearms would become big business overnight on the black market.

Thousands of us already own handguns. A ban would be impractical, if not impossible, to enforce.

If someone wants to commit a crime, he will do it. If he has no handgun, he'll pick up a knife, a pipe, or a bottle. Thieves and murderers are lawbreakers by definition. If they want handguns, they'll get them on the black market or they'll steal them. When only the bad guys have guns, law-abiding citizens will be defenseless.

If the city takes away our handguns, it will be robbing us of our rights. We will be unable to meet our responsibilities to protect ourselves and our loved ones. We oppose any misguided attempts by the city to compromise our safety and jeopardize our lives.

WRITE TO LEARN

Identify an issue that affects you at home or work. Write an editorial for your local newspaper in which you state your opinion. Include evidence to defend your argument.

THINK ABOUT **READING**

Directions: Answer the following questions about the editorial on this page.

1. What does the editorial imply about banning handguns?

    A. Law-abiding citizens will be defenseless.
    B. A ban would drastically reduce the rate of violent crime.
    C. A ban would solve the crime problem once and for all.
    D. If handguns are banned, illegal buying and selling will stop.

2. The author's conclusion is "If someone wants to commit a crime, he will do it." Which statement supports this conclusion?

    A. "The city council is debating a ban on the ownership of handguns."
    B. "Thousands of us already own handguns."
    C. "If he has no handgun, he'll pick up a knife, a pipe, or a bottle."
    D. "If the city takes away our handguns, it will be robbing us of our rights."

Directions: Now read another editorial on handgun use, written from a different point of view. Write a paragraph that compares and contrasts these two points of view.

Banning a Lethal Weapon

Three days ago, Lisa Park was murdered. A masked gunman walked into her flower shop and ended her life with a bullet. Less than two weeks before, Officer Donald Smith responded to a domestic disturbance. In a scuffle with an angry husband wielding a handgun, the 31-year-old policeman and father of two was shot and killed.

Handguns were involved in 22 of the 38 murders here this year. The time has come to ban these weapons.

More than half of all murders and suicides are committed with handguns. In addition, accidental shootings occur routinely because people who do not know how to use handguns have easy access to them. Firearms training, though certainly recommended, is at best only a partial answer.

Handguns are more deadly than other weapons. There is no defense against a handgun. It doesn't matter how strong or fast you are. When crimes are committed with knives or other weapons, injury is more common than death. However, when crimes are committed with handguns, victims are more likely to die. The event is over in an instant. A handgun is small enough to conceal until the last moment, and then it is too late for all the Lisa Parks and Donald Smiths of this world.

Handguns have no real value for sport, either. Nobody needs handguns except police and security officers.

What would be the result of a handgun ban? Great Britain outlawed handguns in the 1920s. Its rate of violent crime dropped dramatically, and it is low today compared to the United States. Despite the fact that the British police are unarmed, peace and moderation are the rule in British cities and towns.

We, too, need to ban handguns to make our communities safer places to live and work.

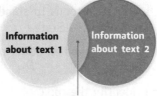

THINK ABOUT **READING**

Directions: Answer the following questions about the two editorials.

1. What is one way both editorials are alike?

   _____

2. What is the main difference between the two editorials?

   _____

Anaylze Editorial Cartoons

An editorial cartoon is a special kind of editorial. It uses humor and illustrations to make people think about an issue. Editorial cartoonists have a bias. They are not worried about presenting a balanced point of view. They are for or against something, and they want readers to agree with them.

Editorial cartoons often use symbols. A symbol is a person or thing that stands for something else. For example, Uncle Sam sometimes is used in editorial cartoons to stand for the United States.

When you read an editorial cartoon,

- identify the topic of the cartoon

- read labels or captions

- figure out what is happening

- identify the cartoonist's point of view

Find an editorial cartoon in a newspaper, magazine, or online. In a notebook, write the topic of the cartoon. Then write one or two sentences that describe the author's message or point of view.

Letters to the Editor

Letters to the editor are not written by the staff of the newspaper or magazine in which they are published. They are written by readers. Sometimes the letters are in reaction to a letter or an article that was previously published. Sometimes they are a reaction to a community event or a political issue. Although any reader can write a letter to the editor, the staff at the publication decides which letters to print.

Directions: Read these letters to the editor. Then write a paragrah describing which letter you agree with.

Should Cell Phone Use When Driving Be Banned?

Letter 1
To the Editor:

The use of cell phones while driving should be banned for the following reasons: (1) Drivers become distracted and cause accidents. A 1997 study in the *New England Journal of Medicine* found that talking on a cell phone while driving quadrupled the risk of an accident. (2) Cell phones are not a necessity—they are a convenience. (3) Cell phones may cause cancer—longtime cell phone users are 2.4 times as likely to develop a benign tumor according to a 2008 issue of the *International Journal of Oncology*, although more studies need to be done. If talking on the phone is that important, drivers should pull off the road and park.

Letter 2
To the Editor:

Cell phones represent only one of many distractions for drivers. Why penalize talking and texting when it's OK to munch on a cheeseburger, apply mascara, yell at your kids in the back seat, or even just change the radio station? Additional studies are needed to assess the real risks of talking on a cell phone while driving. Also, the National Cancer Institute reports that more research is needed before drawing conclusions about cell phones and cancer—and I agree. There are some real benefits of cell phone use, such as peace of mind in knowing you can quickly make contact if there is a problem.

THINK ABOUT READING

Directions: Answer these questions.

1. How are the letters different from other editorials you have read?

   _____

2. Which letter do you think is more persuasive?

   _____

Directions: Match these words with their definitions.

1. _____ assumption   **A.** support for an opinion or argument

2. _____ bias   **B.** an idea that cannot be supported by facts

3. _____ conclusion   **C.** an article that expresses an opinion

4. _____ editorial   **D.** an author's opinion

5. _____ evidence   **E.** a one-sided view of a topic

6. _____ point of view   **F.** an outcome based on an argument

Skill Review

Directions: Read the two editorials below and answer the questions that follow.

Is 16 Too Young to Drive?

It is the moment millions of teenagers have been waiting for. They've blown out 16 candles on the birthday cake. Now it's time to get a driver's license . . . or is it? If Highway Safety's Adrian Lund gets his way, they'll have to wait at least one more year. Lund says that car accidents are the leading cause of death among teenagers, and he wants to raise the driving age.

Lund has a point. Teenagers do get into accidents. The question is—is it age or driving experience that is causing the problem? I think it is a lack of experience. Driving is not a skill that can be mastered overnight. Instead of raising the age at which kids can get a license, why not lower the age at which kids can drive with parents? That way, young drivers will have more practice. By the time they are ready to drive on their own, they will have put in many supervised hours behind the wheel. A year won't make much difference, but several years of practice will.

It's Time to Raise the Driving Age

Eat your vegetables. Do your homework. Doing things you don't like because they are good for you is all part of being a teenager. Now teens may need to add one more item to their list of things they don't want to do: waiting another year to drive. This idea may be unpopular, but, like moms always say, it is for their own good.

The Insurance Institute for Highway Safety says that car accidents are the leading cause of death among teenagers. Adrian Lund, the group's leader, says that raising the driving age saves lives. He may be right. New Jersey is the only state that gives driver's licenses at 17 instead of 16. The number of crash-related deaths in New Jersey is 18 per 100,000 teen drivers. In Connecticut, teens can get a driver's license at age 16. The death rate is 26 per 100,000. The statistics don't lie. Raising the driving age saves lives.

Skill Review (continued)

1. Which of the following best states the author's conclusion in "Is 16 Too Young to Drive?"?

   A. Sixteen is too young to drive.
   B. The driving age should be raised to save lives.
   C. The driving age should be lowered to give kids more driving practice.

2. In "It's Time to Raise the Driving Age," how does the author support his or her conclusion?

   A. The author says that raising the driving age is unpopular.
   B. The author gives statistics that show how raising the driving age saves lives.
   C. The author gives examples of other things that teenagers have to do because those things are better for the teens.

3. What supporting facts does the writer of "Is 16 Too Young to Drive?" provide to support his or her argument?

   _____

   _____

4. What supporting facts does the writer of "It's Time to Raise the Driving Age" provide to support his or her argument?

   _____

   _____

5. How are both editorials alike?

   A. They both state that 16-year-olds are too young to drive.
   B. They both agree that drivers need more practice.
   C. They both say that teenagers get into accidents.
   D. They both agree that teenagers will like the rule.

6. In what way are the two editorials different?

   A. Only one writer thinks Adrian Lund has a point.
   B. Only one writer thinks the driving age should be raised.
   C. Only one writer thinks teenagers are safe drivers.
   D. Only one writer thinks teenagers will like the rule.

Skill Practice

Directions: Choose the <u>one best answer</u> to each question. <u>Questions 1 through 4</u> refer to the following editorial.

Margaret Palmer Begins Campaign

To kick off her campaign for re-election, Representative Margaret Palmer took a whirlwind tour of the southern farming region today. Her first stop was the Spring Agriculture Convention in Torrence, where she spoke briefly to a crowd of about a thousand farmers and agribusinessmen.

In her bright pink Chanel suit, jangling bangle bracelets, and broad-brimmed hat festooned with ribbons, Palmer was at the center of attention wherever she went. She was wooing the farm vote in a district where it is hard to find a farmer who has not had to borrow heavily just to hold on to his land.

Palmer worked the crowd with her trademark energy. When asked what she intended to do about farm problems, she airily promised to seek more federal aid for agriculture.

Later in the day, Palmer toured the 4,000-acre Powell farm. Tramping gamely through the barns in her high heels, she stopped frequently to pose for photographers. "We did not get to talk to her or even meet her," said Ed Powell, whose grandfather started the farm with just 40 acres more than half a century ago. Then Palmer got into her black limousine. Waving from the window, she promised to return soon.

---

1. How is Representative Palmer different from the farmers?

   A. She seems to have a lot of money, and the farmers don't.
   B. She is hardworking, and the farmers are not.
   C. She keeps her promises, and the farmers do not.
   D. She cares more about the future of farming than the farmers do.

2. What is the editorial biased against?

   A. farming
   B. Representative Palmer
   C. picnicking
   D. homegrown food

3. Which choice best supports the conclusion that Representative Palmer is not really concerned about farmers?

   A. She wears a pink Chanel suit.
   B. She does not meet the farmers at the Powell farm.
   C. She promises to seek more federal aid for farmers.
   D. She works the crowd with her trademark energy.

4. Who would be most likely to agree with the ideas in this editorial?

   A. Representative Palmer
   B. supporters of Palmer
   C. farmers
   D. voters in the upcoming election

Writing Practice

Directions: Choose an issue in your community that you feel strongly about. Write a letter to the editor describing the issue and your feelings about it. Include any facts or statistics that support your opinion. Be sure that any solutions you may have are presented as well.

Blogs

KEY CONCEPT: Blogs, or web logs, are personal web pages that express an author's ideas or opinions.

Do you have a favorite blog that you check regularly? Are you—or is anyone you know—a blogger? Do you like to read blogs about politics or sports or your hobby? One way to share thoughts, dreams, photos, and videos is by creating a blog. A blog is a website that you can use like a diary or journal. You can put pictures on it and share your thoughts as often as you want.

Lesson Objectives

You will be able to

- Understand how to read and evaluate blogs

- Identify an author's assumptions and beliefs

Skills

- **Core Skill:** Determine Author's Purpose

- **Reading Skill:** Draw Evidence from Text

Vocabulary

blog
connote
endorse
judgment
persuade
qualifications

Blogs

Blogs are personal web pages that are used to express the writer's ideas about a topic. Some blogs are like journals in which writers, called bloggers, post their daily thoughts and experiences. Other blogs focus on a particular topic, such as music, fashion, food, politics, or education.

When reading blogs, keep the following in mind:

- Most bloggers are not experts about their subject. They are everyday people, just like you. If a blogger suggests that he or she is an expert, look for **qualifications**, or professional experience and education.

- Some bloggers are paid by companies to **endorse**, or support, their products. Keep this in mind as you read their opinions about what they like.

- Some bloggers use words and phrases that **connote**, or suggest, emotions. Rather than using an unbiased word such as *costly*, a blogger might choose a word such as *extravagant* or *stiff*. These connotative words give strong positive or negative feelings to the blog.

- Blogs can be a convenient way to get information on technical topics. However, when you need solid facts and evidence, consider more reliable sources, such as reference books, nonfiction texts, expert interviews, and official websites of manufacturers.

USE EVIDENCE TO MAKE JUDGMENTS

Making **judgments** means forming opinions about what you have read. When you make a judgment, you should base your opinion on evidence from the text. Authors use many different techniques to **persuade**, or convince, readers to agree with their ideas and opinions. An author might provide facts, include quotes from experts or celebrities, or use words that connote strong feelings.

As you read, consider the techniques the author is using to influence you. Then combine the information you have read with your own experience to make a judgment. Judgments are neither right nor wrong, but you should be able to support them.

What I Read	My Experience	My Judgment

Read the following paragraph. Underline the evidence the author provides to help you make a judgment. Circle details the author includes that remind you of your own experience.

(1) Have you been to the movies lately? (2) If you are like many Americans, the answer is no. (3) The reason is simple. (4) Movie prices have gotten too expensive. (5) The average cost for an adult ticket is about $10. (6) Popcorn and snacks can cost as much as $6. (7) If you want a drink with your popcorn, add another $4. (8) If you're an average working person, going to the movies just cost you almost a day's take-home pay. (9) Compare that with renting a DVD and grabbing a drink and a snack from your frig, and the decision to stay home is an easy one.

You should have underlined sentences 5, 6, and 7. You may have circled sentences 8 and 9. What judgment did you make about the topic after reading this blog?

TECHNOLOGY CONNECTION

Social Media

Blogs are just one way to express your opinion online. There are many websites that offer platforms for people to express their opinions about anything they can think of.

Social media sites allow people to share ideas, pictures, and videos with friends and strangers. Some of these websites are known as "microblogs," since they allow people to post very short messages.

When you post your opinion on a blog or social media site, you are sharing it with the world. Here's a good rule to remember: Don't post anything online that you wouldn't say aloud.

In a notebook, write a blog entry telling about your day.

THINK ABOUT **READING**

Directions: Read each statement. Decide whether it is true or false. Write *T* if the statement is true. Write *F* if the statement is false.

_____ 1. Some blogs are personal journals.

_____ 2. Blogs are often based on opinions rather than facts.

_____ 3. Bloggers must be experts about their topics.

_____ 4. All bloggers are paid to endorse products.

A judgment is an opinion. Judgments are never right or wrong. They should be supported by facts. As you read, it is important to distinguish between factual statements and emotional statements.

Writers who use many words with strong connotations are appealing to your emotions. Their words may connote positive or negative feelings. When you see words that suggest emotion, be aware that the writing may not be based on fact.

Read the blog entry on this page and circle words and phrases that connote strong feelings. Mark each of these words as positive (+) or negative (–).

Directions: Read this blog entry from a member of the Y.E.S. Center. Then answer the questions that follow.

> Today, as a community, we paused to remember two of our own. Lavinia Phelps and Walter Kinski will not soon be forgotten. It was just one year ago today that Lavinia and Walter presided at the official opening of the Y.E.S. (Youth Encounter Seniors) Center. It was their dream, a place where young and old could share their lives. I am glad that they lived to see their dream come true and grateful that the center lives on after them.
>
> As many of you know, Lavinia hardly fits the stereotype of the frail old lady in a rocking chair. Dynamic and determined, she worked tirelessly for our needy youth and senior citizens. I remember with admiration and gratitude how she pried investment dollars out of our businesses, public agencies, and newspapers for the revitalization [bringing back to life] of our downtown.
>
> It was while working on the downtown project that Lavinia met Walter, a retired engineer. Something clicked. They fell in love—with an idea. They decided to help the two neediest groups downtown—aimless youth and lonely (and sometimes frightened) senior citizens. Their radical plan was to help these two groups help each other.
>
> Every day at the Y.E.S. Center, you can see young and old doing just that. Retired nurses show teenage mothers how to take care of their babies. Computer-wise teens show retirees that high tech can even be a lot of fun. Troubled and confused youth have sympathetic seniors to turn to for advice. You can see them all at the center every day—talking, walking, playing cards, strumming guitars, building furniture, and generally carrying on together across the generations. What a sight! Walter and Lavinia, thank you.

WRITE TO LEARN

In a notebook, write one judgment you made as you read the blog on this page. Explain how you came to that opinion.

THINK ABOUT **READING**

Directions: Answer the questions. Place a check next to the correct statement.

1. What evidence best supports the author's judgment that Lavinia didn't fit the stereotype of an old lady?

    _____ She was dynamic, determined, and tireless.

    _____ Lavinia met Walter, and something clicked.

    _____ Lavinia and Walter will not soon be forgotten.

2. What is the author's main purpose for writing this?

    _____ to persuade readers to join the Y.E.S. Center

    _____ to highlight the author's role at the center

    _____ to thank Lavinia and Walter for their vision for the center

Directions: Read this blog entry by the creator of Stella Marie Soaps and Scrubs. Then answer the questions that follow.

Lights Are Bright on Broadway

I love antique stores. My boyfriend and I practically live in them. I have a pretty big collection of enamelware and old glass bowls. Stuff I use regularly. Elisia Romano, the shop owner of the newest antique store in Providence, just opened her doors, and boy does she have some super cool stuff! Antiques, local artists' work and . . . Stella Marie Soaps and Scrubs!

Drop by the next time you are in the area!

Elisia's on Broadway
166 Broadway
Providence, RI

You won't be disappointed!

THINK ABOUT **READING**

Directions: Answer these questions.

1. What are some words the author uses to describe Elisia's on Broadway?

   _____

   _____

2. Which of the following best explains why the author might be biased toward Elisia's on Broadway?

   A. She has a big collection of old glass bowls.
   B. The store is new.
   C. The store sells Stella Marie Soaps and Scrubs.
   D. She lives near the store.

3. What is the author's main purpose for writing this blog entry?

   A. to persuade people to shop at a new antique shop
   B. to inform readers about antique shops
   C. to entertain readers with the story of her life
   D. to describe her recent purchases

Core Skill
Determine Author's Purpose

Authors write for a variety of purposes. As you read, it is important to figure out the reason why the author is writing. You will also want to determine who the audience is and how the author is presenting information to this audience.

Factual articles are usually written to inform. Stories, plays, and personal narratives are often written to entertain. Writing that expresses many opinions or that tries to convince you to do something is meant to persuade.

When an author's purpose is to persuade, he or she usually has a bias. A writer who expresses a preference for or against a particular person, idea, or thing has a bias. To recognize bias, ask yourself the following questions:

- Did the author leave out important facts?

- What words did the author use that suggest feelings? Do these words connote positive or negative feelings?

As you read the blog on this page, circle words that connote positive or negative feelings. Make notes about ideas you need more information about.

Vocabulary Review

Directions: Use these words to complete the following sentences.

blog   endorse   judgment   persuade   qualifications

1. The shoe company pays athletes to _____ its shoes.

2. My sister posts recipes on her cooking _____.

3. What _____ does the expert have?

4. The restaurant offered a free dessert to _____ people to eat there.

5. Use your _____ to decide if this author has a bias against the issue.

Skill Review

Directions: Read this blog entry about an announcer at a baseball game. Then answer the questions that follow.

Howie Do It

Great job by Mets announcer Howie Rose yesterday. I heard a little Mets-Yanks action on my drive from New Haven to Providence, and I heard Howie make two comments about issues that announcers are usually afraid to bring up.

1. "And the message boards are now telling the fans to make noise—as if New York fans at the Subway Series need to be told when to get rowdy."

It's about time this was brought up on a broadcast. It's ridiculous to tell fans to cheer for their own team! (Of course, as I'm always quick to point out, Yankee Stadium has been telling fans when to cheer for decades. Fenway Park, home of the Red Sox, has never needed to use this gimmick.)

2. "Tomorrow's game is the Sunday night game, the game no one wants."

Then Howie talked about how changing the Sunday game time from 1 p.m. to 7 p.m. is bad for the teams, which need to travel later that night, and bad for fans who bought tickets to an afternoon game.

Way to tell it like it is, Howie!

Skill Review (continued)

1. In the post "Howie Do It," what judgment does the blogger have about message boards that tell fans to make noise?

   A. He thinks they are a good idea.
   B. He thinks they are unnecessary.
   C. He thinks Fenway Park should use them.
   D. He likes the sound of the cheers.

2. Which words tell you that the author agrees with Howie Rose's judgments?

   A. "I heard a little Mets-Yanks action."
   B. "I heard Howie make two comments."
   C. "Way to tell it like it is!"
   D. "Tomorrow's game is the Sunday night game."

3. Which details in the blog help you to infer the author's bias toward one team?

   _____

   _____

   _____

4. What does the author mean by "as if the New York fans at the Subway Series need to be told when to get rowdy"? What does the word *rowdy* connote?

   _____

   _____

   _____

Directions: Choose the <u>one best answer</u> to each question. <u>Questions 1 through 5</u> refer to the following blog entry.

An Appeal to the Superintendent

December 10, 2014, by <u>timbailey</u>

    I requested a personal day for April 27. It was rejected—and fairly so—under the clause in my teacher contract stating that personal days cannot be used to extend school vacations. However, the superintendent reserves the right to make exceptions. Here is my plea.

    As I discussed in my earlier post, I will be traveling to Manchester to see Manchester United play Tottenham Hotspur at Old Trafford on the 25th. To be back at work on Monday, I'd have to fly out of Manchester the next day, which presents a problem. Any American who follows English football knows that the games take place on Saturdays, Sundays, Monday nights, and occasionally on Wednesdays. The schedule is released in the summer, but it is hardly in its final form at that time. No, the Premier League, much like the NFL [National Football League], employs the "flexible schedule," which allows games to be moved with only seven days' notice. That makes booking a flight home rather difficult. The game, currently scheduled for Saturday, could possibly be moved to Sunday, so if I bought a ticket for a Sunday flight, I'd be out of luck. Flights to North America tend to leave in the morning, and finding an evening flight has been impossible. If the game were guaranteed to take place on Saturday, there'd be no problem. It seems the safest way to make plans would be to fly on Monday, but that would require missing a day of work. Therefore, I put in for the personal day, which has been rejected.

    I've been planning this trip for years. I took on after-school detention duty, a job that almost no teacher wants, to help pay for its hefty cost. If I could go in the summer, I would, but the summer is the off-season for soccer. The weather would even be more pleasant in the summer months, but I'm not going for the weather.

    I started this blog as an example for my Essay Writing class, and the concluding experience is this trip to Manchester. I'd be willing to write about my trip for the school paper too. While I'm bargaining, if I'm allowed to use this one personal day, I won't use the other personal day I have left for this year.

Skill Practice (continued)

1. What does the author hope the superintendent will do?

   A. allow him to have a Monday off
   B. change the date of the game
   C. let him use both of his personal days
   D. help him book a different flight home

2. According to the blog, what judgment can you make about the author?

   A. The author does not like teaching.
   B. The author misses a lot of school days.
   C. The author wants to get a fair hearing on his plea.
   D. The author is not a careful planner.

3. Which of the following would the author most likely be biased toward?

   A. a rule that lets the superintendent decide when vacation days can be used
   B. a rule that allows the Premier League to change its schedule
   C. a rule that makes the Premier League more like the NFL
   D. a rule that lets teachers use personal days at any time

4. Which reason that the author gives for wanting a day off would be most persuasive to the superintendent?

   A. "I've been planning this trip for years."
   B. "I'd be willing to write about my trip for the school paper too."
   C. "I'm not going for the weather."
   D. "Finding an evening flight has been impossible."

5. Who is the author's intended audience?

   A. all the members of Manchester United
   B. only the superintendent
   C. only his fellow teachers
   D. anyone who reads his blog

Writing Practice

Directions: Choose a blog that interests you and read at least three entries. Then write a review of the blog. In your review, discuss the blogger's focus as well as his or her writing style. Make sure you use evidence from the text in your review and include the web address for the blog.

Reviews and Commentaries

KEY CONCEPT: A review is an evaluation, or judgment, about a product or service.

Have you ever asked friends for their opinion of a product they use? Have you ever asked someone about a recent movie? Do the opinions of others influence your decision to buy the same product or see a movie?

A review shares a writer's experiences and opinions about a product or service. The writer tells what he or she thought of something and explains why. A review can help you make a decision about whether something is worth your time and money.

Lesson Objectives

You will be able to

- Determine the author's opinion in reviews and commentaries

- Identify main ideas and essential details

Skills

- **Core Skill:** Infer

- **Reading Skill:** Interpret Words and Phrases in Text

Vocabulary

analysis
commentary
criticize
implied
review

Reviews

A **review** is a critical judgment of something. Reviews are written about books, movies, art, fashion, music, television, and restaurants. A review is more than just a summary. It is a **commentary**. In a commentary, the reviewer expresses thoughts and provides opinions about the topic.

Reviews usually have four parts: an introduction, a summary, an analysis, and a conclusion. The introduction grabs a reader's attention and tells what the review will be about. It gives the title, topic, or name of what is being reviewed. When you read a review, the introduction will usually have a positive or negative tone, or feeling. It gives you a hint about the reviewer's opinion.

Next, reviews usually summarize, or give an overview, of what is being reviewed. For example, the basic plot of a book might be outlined— though the reviewer usually does tell how the book ends. The summary helps the reader understand what is being discussed.

After the summary, the reviewer offers an **analysis**. In an analysis, a reviewer **criticizes** what was reviewed, or tells what he or she liked or disliked about it. When you read the analysis, look for the reviewer's opinions and the details used to support those opinions. This will help you decide whether you agree with the review.

Finally, reviews usually end with a conclusion. The conclusion sums up the reviewer's overall opinion and may give a recommendation about whether what is being reviewed is worth your time or money. Keep in mind, though, a review is just one person's opinion. Another reviewer may feel differently. It is up to you to evaluate the details the reviewer provides and make your own judgment.

INTERPRET AN IMPLIED MAIN IDEA

Sometimes a main idea is stated directly in a topic sentence, but sometimes the main idea is **implied**. An implied main idea is unstated. It cannot be found in the text. You must look for clues in the text to **interpret** the main idea, or figure it out.

You know that a main idea is implied when no sentence is general enough to relate to all the details in the paragraph. Use these steps to interpret the implied main idea of a text.

- Determine the topic, or subject, of the text. Ask yourself who or what the text is mostly about.

- Look at all the details. Ask yourself what they have in common. What the writer wants you to understand about these details is the main idea.

Read this review. Then identify the implied main idea.

We had heard good things about Eazy Pizza, so we couldn't wait to try out the new restaurant. It took 15 minutes before a hostess greeted us. When we finally sat down, we had to ask for menus. No one took our drink order. Finally we got the attention of a server and ordered our favorite—a large pepperoni pizza. The menu says pizzas are made to order, but when our pizza arrived almost 45 minutes later, it was barely warm. There were so few pieces of pepperoni that some slices didn't even have any. We all left hungry.

Although the reviewer never says that he or she does not like Eazy Pizza, all the details work together to imply the main idea of this review: Eazy Pizza is not a good restaurant.

Research It
Compare Reviews

You can find up-to-date reviews on any digital gadget—your smartphone, tablet, or mobile app.

Select a restaurant, movie, or entertainment event that you want to know about. Conduct an Internet search for reviews that are both positive and negative. Read the reviews, and organize them according to the reviewers' opinions.

Then write an essay that compares and contrasts the reviews. What feelings were shared by several reviewers? Do you agree or disagree with the reviewers?

When a main idea isn't stated directly in a topic sentence, you need to use clues in the text to figure out the main idea. Likewise, sometimes you need to use context clues to interpret words and phrases to understand an author's opinion.

Ask yourself these questions as you read:

- What is the author's overall message?

- Does the author have a bias toward or against the topic?

As you read the article on this page, underline details that help you understand the author's opinion.

WRITE TO LEARN

Think about the words and phrases authors use when they write a review. How do these words persuade the reader?

Write a paragraph that describes how certain words and phrases affect readers, either positively or negatively.

Directions: Read this excerpt from a review of a book by author Nikki Grimes. Then answer the questions that follow.

As author Nikki Grimes says, "I've led so many lives, sometimes I feel as though I'm a dozen different people. Is it any wonder I'm comfortable creating books in multiple voices?" One such book is *Bronx Masquerade*. *Bronx Masquerade* is a novel written in 18 voices. It tells the story of a group of students in a New York City high school who become part of a series of weekly class poetry readings, called Open Mike Fridays. They explore who they are behind the masks they wear, and they use poetry to do it.

What starts as a simple class experiment quickly becomes a means to challenge some of the ideas the students have about themselves and one another. While there is no central character, student Tyrone Bittings serves as a Greek chorus, commenting on every character in the book. There is Janelle, who is struggling with her feelings about her body image; Lupe, desperate to have a baby so she will feel loved; Raynard, hiding a secret behind his silence; and Porscha, trying to deal with her anger over troubled family dynamics. Tyrone helps the reader connect the dots from character to character and from one subplot to the next.

All of the students—black, Latino, white, male, female—talk about their sense of isolation and yearning to belong. Competent and reluctant readers alike will recognize and empathize with these students. There may be too many characters for readers to penetrate deeply into any one character, but Grimes's creative, contemporary premise will hook readers, and the poems may even inspire readers to try writing a few of their own. As always, Grimes gives young people exactly what they're looking for—real characters who show them they are not alone.

THINK ABOUT READING

Directions: Answer the questions.

1. Which sentence best expresses the main idea of paragraph 1?

    _____ Open Mike Fridays should be used in all schools.
    _____ Poetry can be a valuable tool to explore personality.
    _____ Troubled teens should read all of Nikki Grimes's books.
    _____ Using masks can add excitement to a poetry class.

2. What is the reviewer's analysis of *Bronx Masquerade*?

    _____ Readers will be hooked by Grimes's creative premise.
    _____ The use of poetry is not successful as a creative premise.
    _____ Most young readers are turned off by poetry.
    _____ All students feel isolated and yearn to belong.

3. On the line below, write one sentence in which the reviewer expresses his or her opinion of the book.

    _____

Directions: Read the following review about Latino art. Then complete the graphic organizer that follows.

The liveliness and color of Latino culture, its music, food, art, and style, lend a layer of richness to Chicago culture we often take for granted in a city already thick with ethnic diversity. The excitement generated by "Images and Objects of the Spirit," the new show at the Aldo Castillo Gallery, offers a welcome opportunity to focus clearly on the best of Latino art.

An eclectic [varied] presentation of contemporary [current] Latin American fine art mixed together with furniture, textiles, and religious artifacts from Colombia, Guatemala, Mexico, and Peru, the show offers a concentrated look into a culture steeped in religion, political conflict, and passion. . . .

Aldo Castillo describes his labor of love as a gallery with a social mission. An established Nicaraguan sculptor, Castillo left his homeland to escape civil war and received political asylum in the United States where he continued his studies at the Art Institute of Chicago. Originally intending to create a sculpture studio, he decided instead to turn his beautiful rehabbed space in Lakeview into a gallery where he could showcase his own work and that of fellow Latino artists.

The result is a glorious crash course in Latino visual arts. Contemporary work by painters Antonio Bou and Luis Fernando Uribe hang over rough-hewn cabinets. Ceremonial garments woven in bright hot colors are laid about among religious objects. . . .

Some of the most stunning pieces in the show are the humblest. Simple retablos, small carved wooden niches designed to hold images of saints, are both rough and powerful.

—Excerpted from the *Chicago Sun-Times*

Core Skill
Infer

Often authors do not directly state all their ideas. They give details and expect readers to "read between the lines" and make **inferences**. An inference is a conclusion, or judgment, based on information in the text and the reader's own experience.

Look at this example:

Kelley looked out the window. Then she went to her closet. When she returned, she had on rubber boots and was holding an umbrella.

Kelley looks outside, and then she gets out boots and an umbrella from her closet. Using these details and your own experience, you can infer that it is raining.

As you read the review on this page, underline information that helps you make an inference about Aldo Castillo.

THINK ABOUT **READING**

Directions: Complete the graphic organizer to show an inference you made about Aldo Castillo.

Text Information		What I Know		Inference
Aldo Castillo describes his labor of love as a gallery with a social mission.	+		=	

Vocabulary Review

Directions: Use these words to complete the following sentences.

analysis   commentary   criticized   implied   review

1. The review _____ the restaurant for its poor service.

2. A(n) _____ idea is an idea that is not directly stated.

3. The announcer's _____ showed his opinion of the game.

4. Before I went to the movie, I read a(n) _____ online.

5. My _____ of the situation was that it was too risky.

Skill Review

Directions: Read the two passages and answer the questions.

Rules of Thumb: 52 Truths for Winning at Business Without Losing Your Self

    Webber, entrepreneur and columnist, offers advice and inspiration with 52 practical lessons gleaned from more than 40 years of working with extraordinary leaders in a variety of endeavors. He sets out to help today's professional men and women stay focused, productive, and inspired even in our most turbulent times of change relating to
5 globalization, technology, and the knowledge economy. The author kept records of his experiences and describes them along with the lessons he learned, showing us how these lessons can be applied to our business or personal life. His rules? When the going gets tough, the tough relax; don't implement solutions, prevent problems; the difference between a crisis and an opportunity is what you learn about it; every start-up needs four
10 things: change, connections, conversation, and community; entrepreneurs choose serendipity over efficiency; knowing it ain't the same as doing it; and great leaders answer Tom Peters's great question: "How can I capture the world's imagination?" This excellent book offers valuable, thought-provoking ideas for library patrons.

—Excerpted from *Booklist*, by Mary Whaley

---

1. What can you infer about the author of *Rules of Thumb: 52 Truths for Winning at Business Without Losing Your Self*?

   A. The author is very experienced.
   B. The author does not like change.
   C. The author thinks his ideas apply only to business.
   D. The author is practical but not inspiring.

2. In line 8, the reviewer states one of the rules of the author: "Don't implement solutions, prevent problems." What do you interpret this rule to mean?

   _____

Skill Review (continued)

Talk of the Town

A Miracle in community theater is happening right now with the production of *The Miracle Worker* at our very own Bedford Community Theatre at 74 Main Street (on the corner of Church) in Bedford Hills. Community theaters are the backbone and grass roots of theater in our country, and with a production like this, they are really easy to support. Johanna Lewis and Alex Scheer are a tour de force as Helen Keller and Anne Sullivan. They absolutely channel these characters in performances that are worthy of a Broadway stage.

—Excerpted from *The Bedford Record Review*

---

3. What is the main idea of this passage?

    A. Broadway plays are better than this performance.
    B. Community theaters are unimportant.
    C. The play and the actors are excellent.
    D. Johanna Lewis gives a better performance than Alex Scheer.

4. What can you infer that the reviewer wants readers to do?

_____

_____

Skill Practice

Directions: Choose the <u>one best answer</u> to each question. <u>Questions 1 through 4</u> refer to the following article.

Barber's Carved Legacy, Finished With Rhinestones and Shoe Polish

Most artists have day jobs at one point or another, sometimes for life. A few are lucky enough to enjoy their work as well as their art. Rarely do they achieve the symbiosis [combination] of creative and occupational activity enjoyed by Ulysses Davis (1914–1990), a Savannah, Georgia, barber who whittled and carved wooden sculptures
5 in his shop when business was slow.

In the catalog for the excellent show "The Treasure of Ulysses Davis" at the American Folk Art Museum, he is quoted as saying: "I love to barber. It's something that keeps your mind together. If I had to choose between cutting hair and carving, I don't know which one I would choose, because I love to cut on wood." Art and life were inseparable and
10 interchangeable. Sometimes Davis used his hair clippers on the wood; sometimes he gave impromptu lessons in art history to his clients in Savannah.

Davis was self-taught but savvy about the ways history crowns artists. He had visited enough museums to know that his sculptures would be most impressive if they were kept together. He rarely sold a piece, turning down many collectors. After his death, his son Milton

15 arranged for the King-Tisdell Cottage Foundation in Savannah, dedicated to local African American history, to acquire most of the sculptures.

About three-quarters of the 100 or so works in this exhibition are first-time loans from the King-Tisdell. "The Treasure of Ulysses Davis," which comes from and was organized by the High Museum of Art in Atlanta, is by far the largest presentation of Davis's sculpture to be seen

20 outside Savannah.

It makes clear that he wasn't just a patriotic folk artist, or an African American artist affirming his heritage, or an inward-looking visionary artist. He was all of these, which is to say that no single cliché of "outsider" art quite fits him.

—Excerpted from *The New York Times*, by Karen Rosenberg

1. What would be the best way to use the information in this review?

   A. Learn the steps for becoming a sculptor.
   B. Decide whether to go to the Ulysses Davis show.
   C. Find out whether Ulysses Davis was a good barber.
   D. Write a report about art history.

3. If you were creating an ad for the Ulysses Davis show, which quotation from the review would be best to include?

   A. "by far the largest presentation of Davis's sculpture to be seen outside Savannah"
   B. "Art and life were inseparable and interchangeable."
   C. "his sculptures would be most impressive if they were kept together"
   D. "rarely sold a piece, turning down many collectors"

2. Which statement shows the reviewer's conclusion about Ulysses Davis?

   A. "He rarely sold a piece, turning down many collectors."
   B. "Sometimes Davis used his hair clippers on the wood."
   C. "Most artists have day jobs at one point or another."
   D. "No single cliché of 'outsider' art quite fits him."

4. Which word in the following sentence from the review shows the author's opinion?

   "In the catalog for the excellent show 'The Treasure of Ulysses Davis' at the American Folk Art Museum, he is quoted as saying: 'I love to barber.'" (lines 6–7)

   A. love
   B. Treasure
   C. excellent
   D. quoted

Directions: Find a review of a book you have read or a movie you have seen. Your review might come from a newspaper, magazine, or the Internet. Read the review, and then write a reaction to it. Note places in which you agree with the reviewer and places in which you disagree. Make sure to include any areas in which the reviewer interpreted something from the book or movie differently than you did.

_____

_____

_____

_____

_____

_____

_____

_____

_____

_____

_____

_____

_____

_____

_____

_____

_____

_____

_____

Review

Directions: Choose the <u>one best answer</u> to each question. <u>Questions 1 through 3</u> refer to the following article.

Rid Yourself of Clutter

Are you drowning in clutter? Is unfiled paperwork taking over your workspace? How about those extra items that don't quite fit in the closet. Are you constantly tripping over them? You need the Outstanding Organizers to help.

Most people don't know how to maximize the space in their homes. They end up wasting time and space. Don't let this happen to you! Call a professional. Outstanding Organizers has reorganized hundreds of spaces.

Call today and let Outstanding Organizers redo your work or storage space. Most clients find their homes are 25% more effective once Outstanding Organizers has completed the job. When Outstanding Organizers is through, the items you need will be easy to find and use. No more searching for your favorite things!

Call Outstanding Organizers today. Don't waste another minute in a disorganized home.

(800) 555-1234

---

1. What is the purpose of the first paragraph?

   A. To find out what readers needs.
   B. To make the reader think about disorganization in his or her home.
   C. To gently let the reader know that there might be better ways to organize.
   D. To serve as a tagline for the business.

2. What does the author of this ad want readers to do?

   A. Clean up their homes.
   B. Learn to become more organized.
   C. Hire Outstanding Organizers to organize their homes.
   D. Call Outstanding Organizers to learn about organization.

3. Is the phrase "Most clients find their homes are 25% more effective" a fact?

   A. Yes, because it is a statistic.
   B. Yes, because Outstanding Organizers wouldn't want to mislead readers.
   C. No, because the number does not include unhappy clients.
   D. No, because effectiveness cannot be measured in numbers.

Review

Directions: Questions 4 through 7 refer to the following article.

The Safety of Nuclear Power

The Dwight Nuclear Power Station opened yesterday in Yerba Valley. Owned and operated by CEC Electric Company, the Dwight Station is the first of three nuclear plants to be built in the Yerba Valley. The station will serve more than 1 million customers and, at full capacity, will generate almost 3 million kilowatts of electricity.

Built on 500 acres of land, the station consists of two reactors, two cooling towers, and two turbine generators. The cost of the entire project has been estimated at more than 1 billion dollars.

Stanley Novak, president of CEC, started the festivities promptly at 9:00 a.m. Standing in the control room, he activated the reactors. He then made his way to the entrance, where he addressed the crowd. He announced that the station will save customers money because nuclear power requires less energy than fossil fuel. He said that the Nuclear Regulatory Commission had certified the plant operations to be safe.

Novak's remarks, which were interrupted several times by shouts of protest, drew general applause at the end.

Citizens for a Safe Society (CSS), a protest group, displayed signs against nuclear power. CSS spokesman Bill Kerby demanded written assurances from CEC that it would follow all recommended safeguards in disposing of nuclear wastes. He also called for a meeting between Novak and CSS to discuss radiation hazards.

---

4. Does this article present a balanced view of the Dwight Nuclear Power Station opening?

   A. No, because it tells the benefits but not the costs of the project
   B. No, because it tells only what CSS thinks of the power plant
   C. Yes, because it provides quotes from Stanley Novak
   D. Yes, because it tells what both CEC and CSS think of the plant

5. A person concerned with radiation hazards would most likely agree with whom?

   A. Stanley Novak
   B. Bill Kerby
   C. CEC Electric Company
   D. the Nuclear Regulatory Commission

6. What is the most likely reason Stanley Novak supports the plant?

   A. He knows it has been certified as safe.
   B. He is an antinuclear protestor.
   C. He has written assurance that the plant will dispose of waste properly.
   D. He is president of the company that owns the plant.

7. What is the purpose of this article?

   A. to explain why the Dwight Station should not open
   B. to compare opinions about the opening of Dwight Station
   C. to persuade people to use nuclear power
   D. to describe how Consolidated Electric is helping the community

Directions: <u>Questions 8 through 11</u> refer to the following blog entry.

Advice from a Blogger

Whenever anyone asked my grandmother a personal question, she always had the same answer: "A lady never tells." I admired my grandmother and her mysterious ways, but I obviously don't follow her advice. After all, I have a blog. I put my life out there every day for the world to see. Still, sometimes I find myself wondering if I put too much of myself out there. On my blog, I post pictures of what I did, who I saw, and what I ate, even if all I did was put gas in my car and go through the drive-thru. By my grandmother's definition, I'm no lady. Not only do I tell, I tell all.

It's one thing to post the mundane details of your everyday life—that's your choice and no real harm can probably come of it. However, there are some things a lady (or a gentleman) shouldn't tell. Here are some things I think all bloggers should consider for their own safety and the safety of their friends and family members.

1. Don't post the names of children, spouses, or friends without permission.

2. Don't give too much information about where you live. Don't make it easy for others to find you unless you're sure you want to be found.

3. Before you post, consider whether you really want to share this information with the world. If your words are angry, hurtful, or argumentative, give yourself some time and reread before you post your blog.

Blogging makes me feel connected, but there's a difference between keeping secrets and keeping safe.

---

8. What is the author's main purpose for writing this?

    A. to tell a story about her grandmother
    B. to describe her blogging habits
    C. to share some thoughts about staying safe while blogging
    D. to persuade readers to share all the details of their lives

9. According to the passage, which details would the author be most likely to include on her blog if she went to her nephew's birthday party?

    A. the name and age of her nephew
    B. the address of the house where the party was
    C. the type of food and cake that was served
    D. the fact that she did not like her brother's new girlfriend

10. Which sentence best supports the author's judgment that you shouldn't give information about where you live?

    A. "A lady never tells."
    B. No real harm can come of it.
    C. Don't make it easy for others to find you unless you want to be found.
    D. Blogging makes me feel connected.

11. What is the author's overall opinion about blogging?

    A. It's mostly a way to share boring details about yourself.
    B. It's a good way to stay connected if you are careful.
    C. Blogging isn't good because you shouldn't tell your secrets.
    D. Blogging is something only young people should do.

Check Your Understanding

On the following chart, circle the number of any question you answered incorrectly. Under each content area you will see the pages you can review to learn the content covered in the question. Pay particular attention to reviewing those lessons in which you missed half or more of the questions.

Chapter 3 Review

Lesson	Item Number	Review Pages
Ads	1, 2, 3	116–123
Editorials	4, 5, 6, 7	124–131
Blogs	8, 9, 10, 11	132–139

ESSAY WRITING PRACTICE

Persuasive Texts

Directions: Write an argument to support one of the claims presented in the prompt below. Review Lesson 3.2 for help with planning, writing strategies, and text structure.

EDITORIAL

An editorial expresses an opinion about a topic. The writer presents reasons and evidence to persuade readers to agree with that opinion. The writer's argument consists of the opinion (or claim), the reasons the author has this opinion, and the supporting evidence.

Read each of the following claims, and choose one. Then write an editorial for your local newspaper. Before beginning to write, determine reasons for your opinion and gather evidence to support your claim. Be sure to use reliable, up-to-date websites for research. Sites that end in *.gov*, *.edu*, or *.org* are usually reliable. Use facts, stories, and logic when writing your editorial. Your goal is to present an argument that convinces others to agree with you.

1. Everyone should learn to play a musical instrument.

2. The United States should land a human being on Mars within the next 10 years.

3. It is time to get rid of Daylight Saving Time.

4. Violent video games should be outlawed.

UNIT 2

Literary Texts

Literary Nonfiction

What exciting real-life adventures have you experienced? Think of an event that has changed your life. How would you describe the event? How could you make sure people understand the impact this event had on your life? It seems everyone knows a story—maybe it is about a neighbor who visited Glacier National Park, a friend from work who got caught in an elevator for several hours, or a relative who has overcome great obstacles to achieve an important goal.

In this chapter, you will study the various genres of literary nonfiction that authors use to communicate their ideas. When you read an essay or a speech, a biography or an account of a true experience, you are reading literary nonfiction. The subjects of literary nonfiction are real people. They live in real places, and they face real problems.

In this chapter you will study these topics:

Lesson 4.1 Nonfiction Prose
How do you communicate your thoughts and feelings about experiences that have changed your life? Would you use a diary, a letter to a friend, or some other form of writing? Learn the various types of nonfiction that prose writers use to communicate their ideas and experiences.

Lesson 4.2 Biography
What makes a biography different from fiction? A biography is about people who really lived and events that really happened rather than people and events made up by the writer.

Lesson 4.3 Autobiography
What's an easy way to "meet" a new person? Read an autobiography! Autobiographies are personal stories—stories of the author's own experiences as seen through his or her eyes. You may feel a bond with the writer, even if the writer's life is very different from your own.

Goal Setting

Why is it important to read nonfiction prose, biographies, and autobiographies? What can you learn from them?

_____

_____

_____

Using a chart like the one below is a good way to set goals as you begin studying this chapter. What do you want to know about nonfiction prose, autobiography, and biography? In the first column, write some questions you have about these genres. Then, as you read the chapter, fill in the second column with answers you have learned.

Questions	Answers

Nonfiction Prose

KEY CONCEPT: Nonfiction prose is a form of writing about real people and real events or situations.

Have you ever kept a diary or a journal? If so, you were writing nonfiction prose. You were also writing nonfiction prose if you wrote a letter or an e-mail to a friend about what was happening in your life. Nonfiction prose is a type of writing that focuses on real people and events.

Lesson Objectives

You will be able to

- Examine various types of nonfiction prose
- Explain how individuals, events, or ideas develop and interact throughout a text

Skills

- **Core Skill:** Identify Types of Nonfiction
- **Reading Skill:** Analyze Text Connections

Vocabulary

develop
diary
essay
genre
interact
memoir
nonfiction
prose

Nonfiction Prose

Nonfiction prose is a **genre** (an artistic or literary category) that focuses on real people and real events or situations. **Prose** is written or spoken language that sounds like normal speech. Nonfiction prose includes a range of writing. In this lesson, we will focus on nonfiction prose that includes letters, diaries, memoirs, and essays.

Diary

A **diary** is a daily record of a person's thoughts, activities, and feelings. A diary reveals a lot about the person writing it. It can also give information about the time and place in which it was written.

Read the following diary entry, written in 1942 by 14-year-old Lithuanian Yitskhok Rudashevski. Notice how the writer communicates his feelings about what he is experiencing.

Sunday the 1st of November

    This is a beautiful day. Every day it has been cloudy and rainy. Today, as though suddenly, a spring day broke through between the autumn days. The sky is blue, the sun warms affectionately. And so indeed the ghetto people burst forth over the little streets to catch what are probably the very last sunbeams. Our police dressed up in their new hats. Here one of them is passing—my blood boils—in a new leather overcoat, with an insolent air, his officer's hat askew. Its peak shines in the sun. The cord of his hat dropped over his chin, he clicks his shiny little boots. Satiated, gorged with food, he struts proudly like an officer, delights—the snake—in such a life, and plays his comedy. This is the source of all my anger against them, that they are playing a comedy with their own tragedy.

—Excerpted from *Children in the Holocaust and World War II: Their Secret Diaries*, compiled by Laurel Holliday

---

ANALYZE CONNECTIONS IN TEXT

The main idea tells what a text is mostly about. Supporting details provide information about the main idea. The main idea and supporting details answer the questions who, what, when, where, why, and how.

Nonfiction means "not fiction"—that is, the story is not made up. Nonfiction texts are about real people, places, and events. They can be about anything from current events to ancient history. They can about famous people or friends and family.

Nonfiction texts usually focus on a few individuals, events, and ideas. These people, events, and ideas develop and interact with one another over the course of a text. When something **develops**, it grows or changes. For example, an author might write about how a person grew from being a bully to being the manager of a shelter for the homeless. When two or more people **interact**, they have an effect on each other. An author might write about how a person had a idea that caused many others to support an after-school program. Individuals, events, and ideas in nonfiction text often have a cause-and-effect relationship.

Read the following passage. Identify the connections in the text.

> Two years ago, Brookville Chemical Company was found guilty of dumping toxic waste directly into the Brookville River. Its pollution created an unsafe environment not only for fish but also for people who live near the river. Daniel Livingston was one of those people. He took it upon himself to organize a townwide clean-up effort, which has done wonders to make the Brookville River safe and healthy again. On Saturday the mayor of Brookville will give Mr. Livingston a special award.

There are several connections here. The actions of Brookville Chemical Company are the cause of a problem. That resulted in Livingston's cleaning up the river and receiving a special award from the mayor.

Reading Skill
Analyze Text Connections

Most—but not all—texts have individuals, events, and ideas that develop and interact with one another. As a reader, you must analyze the information the author provides and determine how everything is connected.

In the diary entry on page 156, the author describes several things, including the weather, the "ghetto people," a police officer, and his own anger.

As you read the diary entry, analyze the connections between these details. Discuss your ideas with a partner. Why is the author angry? Who or what is causing this anger? What details help you understand the author's feelings?

THINK ABOUT READING

Directions: Answer the questions about the diary entry on page 156.

1. Where does the author seem to be when writing this diary entry?

_____

2. Why does the author provide so many details about the police officer's uniform?

_____

One of the most common methods of communication in the workplace is e-mail. Often supervisors and coworkers send e-mail messages instead of making telephone calls or speaking to someone in person.

E-mails and letters function in much the same way, and they are formatted to look almost alike. The biggest difference is that the language used in e-mails tends to be more informal.

As you read the letter on this page, imagine how it might be written if it were an e-mail sent today. Rewrite the letter as an e-mail message.

Letter

A letter is a form of personal communication between two people. Today many people communicate by electronic mail (e-mail).

In letters written in 1888–1889 from Arles, France, the artist Vincent Van Gogh described his ideas, health, and work to his family and friends. While painting what has become a very famous picture of his bedroom, Van Gogh wrote the following:

> I have been and still am nearly half-dead from the past week's work. So I am forced to be quiet. I have just slept sixteen hours at a stretch, and it has restored me considerably. . . .
>
> Today I am all right again. My eyes are still tired, but then I had a new idea in my head and here is the sketch of it. This time it's just simply my bedroom, only here color is to do everything. The finished picture should suggest rest or sleep in general. In a word, looking at the picture ought to rest the brain, or rather the imagination. The walls are pale violet. The floor is of red tiles. The wood of the bed and chairs is the yellow of fresh butter, the sheets and pillows very light greenish citron [yellow]. The bedspread scarlet. The window green. The dressing table orange, the basin blue. The doors lilac. And that is all—there is nothing in this room with its closed shutters. The broad lines of the furniture again must express completed and undisturbed rest. Portraits on the walls, and a mirror and a towel and some clothes. The frame—as there is no white in the picture—will be white. I shall work on it again all day, but you see how simple the conception [idea] is. By means of all these diverse tones I have wanted to express an absolute restfulness.
>
> —Excerpted from *The Complete Letters of Vincent Van Gogh* by Vincent Van Gogh, in *Van Gogh in Arles,* by Ronald Pickvance

THINK ABOUT **READING**

Directions: Answer the questions about the letter from Vincent Van Gogh.

1. Write two phrases from Van Gogh's letter that tell something about the state of his health.

   _____

   _____

2. What can you infer about Van Gogh's character after reading this letter?

   _____

   _____

Essay

An **essay** is a piece of nonfiction writing that deals with a single subject. A personal essay usually reflects the writer's experiences, feelings, opinions, and personality.

Read the following excerpt from an essay by Judy Esway.

> Mom had come to live with us after my father-in-law died. With her came all of her huge pots and pans (she cooked for an army), her noodle machine, all her jars for canning, her pizzelle iron [a metal mold for making deep-fried desserts], her jars of roasted peppers, her superlong rolling pin. Our house was transformed—you would open a closet door and get hit with a string of garlic. Inside several drawers, seeds were growing for something that would be planted later in the garden. On the counter was always a pot of water with lupini beans soaking.
>
> And everywhere there was flour. She made noodles almost every day—just to pass the time, she would say. You would sit down and get up with flour all over your clothes. There was flour on the children, flour on the dog, flour choking all my plants, getting into all our lungs, threatening to kill us all. Sometimes I thought we were all the filling in one big pasta.
>
> —Excerpted from an article by Judy Esway,
> *New Covenant* magazine

THINK ABOUT READING

Directions: Answer the question about the excerpt above.

What details tell you this excerpt is nonfiction prose?

_____

_____

This lesson includes several types of nonfiction prose: diaries, letters, essays, and memoirs. Each genre has different qualities, or features.

For example, a memoir writer describes important events from his or her own life. Most memoirs have these features:

- Use the pronoun *I* when telling the story

- Are true accounts of actual events

- Include the writer's feelings and opinions about historical or social issues

As you read the passages in this lesson, make a list of features found in diaries, letters, essays, and memoirs.

WRITE TO LEARN

Read the excerpt by Stephen King on this page. In a notebook, list three details that tell you this excerpt is a memoir.

Memoir

A **memoir** is a story of the narrator's personal experiences. Memoir writers use plot and suspense to create a feeling of excitement so readers will be eager to find out what happens next.

The following passage relates the author's experience selling his first book.

I was still standing in the doorway. . . . Our place on Sanford Street rented for ninety dollars a month and this man I'd only met once face-to-face was telling me I'd just won the lottery. The strength ran out of my legs. I didn't fall, exactly, but I kind of whooshed down to a sitting position there in the doorway.

"Are you sure?" I asked Bill.

He said he was. I asked him to say the number again, very slowly and very clearly, so I could be sure I hadn't misunderstood. He said the number was a four followed by five zeros. "After that a decimal point with two more zeros," he added.

We talked for another half an hour, but I don't remember a single word of what we said. When the conversation was over, I tried to call Tabby at her mother's. Her youngest sister, Marcella, said Tab had already left. I walked back and forth through the apartment in my stocking feet, exploding with good news and without an ear to hear it. I was shaking all over. At last, I pulled on my shoes and walked downtown. The only store that was open on Bangor's Main Street was the LaVerdiere's Drug. I suddenly felt that I had to buy Tabby a Mother's Day present, something wild and extravagant. I tried, but here's one of life's true facts: there's nothing really wild and extravagant for sale at LaVerdiere's. I did the best I could. I got her a hair-dryer.

When I got back home she was in the kitchen. . . . I gave her the hair-dryer. She looked at it as if she'd never seen one before. "What's this for?" she asked.

I took her by the shoulders. I told her about the paperback sale. She didn't appear to understand. I told her again.

—Excerpt from *On Writing—A Memoir of the Craft*, by Stephen King

---

THINK ABOUT **READING**

Directions: Answer these questions.

1. On the basis of information in the passage, what can you infer?

   A. Before the sale of this book, Stephen King was wealthy.
   B. Stephen King's wife was upset by the sale of his book.
   C. This was the first major book Stephen King sold to a publisher.
   D. Stephen King's sister-in-law was the first to hear his news.

2. What was King's initial reaction when he heard Bill's news?

   A. horror   C. disappointment
   B. smugness   D. shock

Vocabulary Review

Directions: Use these words to complete the following sentences.

diary   essay   genre   memoir   nonfiction   prose

1. _____ writing is writing about real people and real events.

2. _____ is written language that sounds like normal speech.

3. A(n) _____ is a literary or artistic category.

4. A piece of writing that reflects the writer's feelings on an issue is a(n) _____.

5. A person writes his or her thoughts and feelings on a daily basis in a(n) _____.

6. A(n) _____ is a story of a narrator's personal experiences.

Skill Review

Directions: Read the passage below and answer the questions that follow.

> The problem of billowing skirts in windy plains country was no minor one, and though it was met and overcome, there is some evidence that the solution was the work of a male—none other than our old friend, George Armstrong Custer. When the Custers went to Fort Riley after the Civil War, Elizabeth's dresses were all "five yards around, and
> 5   gathered as full as could be into the waistband." On her first walk across the windy prairie ground, her skirt billowed like a balloon, flew out in front, then lifted over her head. His military dignity thus affronted, George immediately figured out a way to keep his wife's skirts at their proper level. He cut some leadbars into strips and ordered Elizabeth to sew them into the hems of her dresses. Thus weighted down, she was able
> 10   to outwit the elements while taking her constitutionals about the post. Other women followed her example, and a dozen years later all were wearing bar lead in their skirt hems on the windy western plains.
>
> —Excerpted from *The Gentle Tamers*, by Dee Brown

1. Lines 9–10 in the passage state: "Thus weighted down, she was able to outwit the elements while taking her constitutionals about the post." What can you infer that the word *constitutionals* means from the context of the passage?

   A. tests   **C.** rides
   B. walks   **D.** battles

2. Name two context clues that helped you determine when the events described in this passage took place.

Directions: Read the following excerpt. Then answer the questions that follow.

August 3, 1776

The Post was later than usual today, so that I had not yours of July 24 till this Evening. You have made me very happy, by the particular and favorable Account you give me of all the Family. But I don't understand how there are so many who have no Eruptions, and no Symptoms. The Inflammation in the Arm might do, but without
5 that, there is no small Pox.

I will lay a Wager, that your whole Hospital have not had so much small Pox, as Mrs. Katy Quincy. Upon my Word she has had an Abundance of it, but is finely recovered, looks as fresh as a Rose, but pitted all over, as thick as ever you saw any one. I this Evening presented your Compliments and Thanks to Mr. Hancock for his
10 polite offer of his House, and likewise your compliments to his Lady and Mrs. Katy.

—Excerpted from *My Countrymen Want Art and Address,*
John Adams to Abigail Adams
by John Adams

3. What can you infer about the meaning of the word *Post* in line 1?

   A. post office
   B. fence post
   C. mail
   D. time

4. What made John Adams very happy (lines 2–3)?

   A. his wife's letter
   B. his wife's updates on their family
   C. his visit with Mr. Hancock
   D. his wife's good health

5. This excerpt is an example of what type of nonfiction prose?

   A. a memoir
   B. a diary entry
   C. a letter
   D. an essay

Skill Practice

Directions: Choose the <u>one best answer</u> to each question. <u>Questions 1 and 2</u> refer to the following passage.

To save money while he was trying to raise funds for school, Mortenson decided not to rent an apartment. He had the storage space. And La Bamba's backseat was the size of a couch. Compared to a drafty tent on the Baltoro, it seemed like a reasonably comfortable place to sleep. He kept up his membership at City Rock, as much for access to a shower as for the climbing wall he scaled most days to stay in shape. Each night, Mortenson prowled the Berkeley Flats, a warehouse district by the bay, searching for a dark and quiet enough block so that he could sleep undisturbed. Wrapped in his sleeping bag, his legs stretched almost flat in the back of La Bamba, he'd find Marina flitting through his thoughts last thing before falling asleep.

During days he wasn't working, Mortenson hunted and pecked his way through hundreds of letters. He wrote to every U.S. senator. He haunted the public library, scanning the kind of pop culture magazines he would never otherwise read for the names of movie stars and pop singers, which he added to a list he kept folded inside a Ziploc bag. He copied down addresses from a book ranking the one hundred richest Americans. "I had no idea what I was doing," Mortenson remembers. "I just kept a list of everyone who seemed powerful or popular or important and typed them a letter. I was thirty-six years old and I didn't even know how to use a computer. That's how clueless I was."

One day Mortenson tried the door of Krishna Copy and found it unexpectedly locked. He walked to the nearest copy shop, Lazer Image on Shattuck Avenue, and asked to rent a typewriter.

"I told him, we don't have typewriters," remembers Lazer Image's owner, Kishwar Syed. "This is 1993, why don't you rent a computer? And he told me he didn't know how to use one."

—Excerpted from *Three Cups of Tea*, by Greg Mortenson and David Oliver Relin

---

1. What is the primary purpose of this excerpt?

   A. to criticize
   B. to inform
   C. to persuade
   D. to entertain

2. From the passage, what can you conclude about Greg Mortenson?

   A. He is reckless.
   B. He is determined.
   C. He is flighty.
   D. He is fearful

Writing Practice

Directions: Think about an important or interesting experience you have had. What would be the best way to write about it: a journal entry, a letter, an essay, or a memoir? Begin by writing a sentence or two explaining why you think a certain genre is the most appropriate to describe your experience. Then write about your experience in the genre you chose.

Biography

Lesson Objectives

You will be able to

- Identify the form and characteristics of a biography
- Understand how the characteristics of a genre affect an excerpt's meaning or purpose

Skills

- **Core Skill:** Gather Information from Different Media
- **Reading Skill:** Summarize Supporting Details

Vocabulary

authorized
biography
chronological
emphasize
examine
unauthorized

KEY CONCEPT: A biography is the true story of a person's life, written by another person.

Does your family have a story about a relative or family friend that has been passed down? It might be a story about how a relative came to this country for the first time. It might be a story about how people survived during difficult times. These family histories are the stories of people's lives that are told by other relatives to later generations.

Biography

A **biography** is the history of someone's life. It is written by another person. Anyone can be the subject of a biography, but most often biographies are written about famous or influential people. Most biographies have these characteristics:

- Are organized in **chronological**, or time, order
- Give information about the person's childhood or background
- List the person's significant accomplishments
- Show how the person's life has affected others

You should read biographies critically. Many biographies contain bias. The author is often writing the biography because he or she feels strongly about the subject. Think about the details the author chooses to **emphasize**, or give importance to. Why does the author highlight these events or personality traits? Does the author see the subject of the biography in a positive way or a negative way?

You should try to find out whether the biography is **authorized** or **unauthorized**. An authorized biography is a biography written with permission from the subject of the book. Often the subject of the book helps the author by supplying documents or by reviewing the manuscript. An unauthorized biography is a biography written without permission from the subject.

THINK ABOUT **READING**

Directions: Write *T* for *True* or *F* for *False* next to the following statements.

_____ 1. Biographies are made-up stories about a person.

_____ 2. Biographies are usually organized chronologically.

_____ 3. Biographies are written by the people they are about.

_____ 4. Biographies may reveal the author's feelings about the subject.

IDENTIFY AND SUMMARIZE DETAILS

Nonfiction texts are written to give information. Using the text features of nonfiction texts can help you locate factual details.

Many texts use features to highlight important details. These text features can help you locate important details as you read.

- **boldface** or *italic* type

- headings and subheadings

- bullets (·) or numbered steps

- photographs and captions

- diagrams, maps, charts, or graphs

Although nonfiction texts are about real people and real events, authors sometimes include their own opinions about these real people and events. While reading, it is important to recognize words or phrases that indicate the author's opinion. Words such as *I believe*, *always*, *never*, *best*, and *worst* signal opinions. A good summary of a nonfiction text should include factual information only.

Read the following summary of a biography about Florence Nightingale. Which sentence does not belong in the summary?

> Florence Nightingale was born in 1820 to wealthy parents. When she turned 25, she decided to become a nurse. During the Crimean War, she was called "The Lady with the Lamp." She went on to become the founder of modern nursing. I think Florence Nightingale was the best nurse ever. She continued working almost until her death at the age of 90.

The sentence "I think Florence Nightingale was the best nurse ever" is a statement of opinion. It is not fact, and it does not belong in a summary of a nonfiction text.

Research It
Read Biographies

Authors of biographies use various methods to introduce their subjects. Sometimes they begin with an anecdote, or short and interesting story. At other times they might start with a list of accomplishments that the subject is known for.

Using online or library resources, research the different ways authors introduce the subject of a biography. Find several examples, and share them with your class.

When reading a biography, it is important to distinguish between factual information and author's opinions or bias.

Dates, quotations, and numbers are details that provide factual information. As you read the biography on this page, pay attention to the dates and quotations that are included. What do they reveal about the subject, Nelson Mandela?

Write a brief summary of this passage, using factual information only. Do not include the author's personal opinions about Mandela in your summary.

WRITE TO LEARN

Reread the translation of *umuntu ngumuntu ngabantu* in the passage on this page. In a notebook, write a paragraph explaining why you agree or disagree with this idea. Be sure to use details from your own experience to support your position.

Directions: Read this passage about Nelson Mandela, president of South Africa from 1994–1999. Think about the details the author chose to emphasize, or give importance to.

A crucial part of Mandela's education lay in observing the Regent [tribal leader]. He was fascinated by Jongintaba's exercise of his kingship at the periodic tribal meetings. . . . Mandela loved to watch the tribesmen, whether laborers or landowners, as they complained candidly and often fiercely to the Regent, who listened for hours impassively and silently, until finally at sunset he tried to produce a consensus [agreement] from the contrasting views. Later, in jail, Mandela would reflect:

One of the marks of a great chief is the ability to keep together all sections of his people, the traditionalists and reformers, conservatives and liberals. . . . The Regent was able to carry the whole community because the court was representative of all shades of opinion.

As President, Mandela would seek to reach the same kind of consensus in cabinet; and he would always remember Jongintaba's advice that a leader should be like a shepherd, directing his flock from behind by skillful persuasion: "If one or two animals stray, you go out and draw them back to the flock," he would say. "That's an important lesson in politics."

Mandela was brought up with the African notion of human brotherhood, or *ubuntu*, which described a quality of mutual responsibility and compassion. He often quoted the proverb *"Umuntu ngumuntu ngabantu,"* which he would translate as "A person is a person because of other people," or "You can do nothing if you don't get the support of other people." This was a concept common to other rural communities around the world, but Africans would define it more sharply as a contrast to the individualism and restlessness of whites, and over the following decades *ubuntu* would loom large in black politics. . . .

Mandela regarded *ubuntu* as part of a general philosophy of serving one's fellowmen. From his adolescence, he recalled, he was viewed as being unusually ready to see the best in others. To him this was a natural inheritance.

—Excerpted from *Mandela, The Authorized Biography*, by Anthony Sampson

THINK ABOUT READING

Directions: Answer the question.

How do you think the author feels about Mandela?

_____

_____

Directions: Derek Jeter is a famous baseball player. Read this passage about his childhood and the big dreams he had as a young boy.

Derek was not anyone's idea of a braggart, but he had been telling classmates and teachers he would grow into a big leaguer as far back as fourth grade, inside [Shirley] Garzelloni's class in the basement of St. Augustine. Garzelloni asked her twenty students to declare their future intentions, and she heard the typical answers from most—doctor, firefighter, teacher, professional athlete.

Only Derek was not planning on being just a professional athlete; he had something far more specific in mind, a vision he shared with his parents as a child. He told Garzelloni's class he was going to be a New York Yankee, and the teacher told the student her husband—a devoted Yankee —would be happy to hear it.

Derek did not make this some grand proclamation; he just said it as if he were announcing his plans for lunch. "And if he said he was going to do something," Garzelloni said, "Derek was the kind of kid who did it."

Derek told anyone would listen that he would someday play shortstop for the Yankees, the team his father had hated in his youth. . . . The Yanks were among baseball's last all-white teams. . . .

Grandma Dot converted Derek on those summer trips to the castle and lake. She took her grandson to his first Yankee Stadium game when he was six, and years later Derek could not remember the opponent or the final score. "All I can tell you," he would say, "is everything was so big."

As big as the boy's ambition. Derek would stir his grandmother at dawn, throw on his Yankee jersey, and beg her to play catch in the yard. She always agreed, even if she knew Derek's throws would nearly knock her to the ground.

—Excerpted from *The Captain: The Journey of Derek Jeter*, by Ian O'Connor

There are many places to get information as you research a topic. When you are looking for specific information, you will need to decide what type of source to **examine**, or look closely at. Here is a short list of some common reference sources:

- Newspapers are good sources of current events and facts. Most are published both in print and online.

- Magazines have entertaining and informational articles. Many magazines are also online.

- An encyclopedia has articles about a variety of subjects. The articles are arranged alphabetically.

- Almanacs are published yearly. They have facts such as population, temperatures, and sports statistics.

- Atlases contain maps.

Pick a topic you would like to know more about, such as the New York Yankees. Make a list of what information you could find about your subject in each of the reference scources listed above.

THINK ABOUT **READING**

Directions: Answer these questions.

1. Which statement do you think the author would agree with?

   A. Derek was too nervous to play baseball as a boy.
   B. Derek was dedicated to baseball at an early age.
   C. Derek was a normal kid.
   D. Derek needed more motivation as a child.

2. Why does the author give information about Derek's childhood?

   A. to explain Derek Jeter's baseball technique
   B. to show that Derek Jeter was special from an early age
   C. to show that Derek Jeter did not enjoy baseball as a child
   D. to describe Derek Jeter's warmup routine

Vocabulary Review

Directions: Use these words to complete the following sentences.

authorized   biography   chronological   emphasize   unauthorized

1. I read a(n) _____ about my favorite actor.

2. The basketball player was upset to see a(n) _____ photo for sale.

3. If something is _____, it is allowed.

4. The author underlined the word to _____ it.

5. The news report listed the key events in _____ order.

Skill Review

Directions: Read the passage about Hillary Clinton, and answer the questions that follow. Barry Goldwater was the Republican Party's nominee for president in 1964; Lyndon Johnson was the Democratic Party's nominee for president in 1964.

POLITICS. THAT'S REALLY what she was about. When she was nine years old and trying to decide whether Dwight Eisenhower was a better president than Harry Truman. When she was fourteen and wondering why only boys could be astronauts. When she was seventeen and asking how she, a committed, banner-wearing Goldwater Girl, could possibly take the role of Lyndon Johnson in a high school debate.

"I can't do that," said Hillary Diane Rodham, balking at the assignment given by her government teachers at Maine Township High School South in Park Ridge, Illinois. "Oh, yes, you can," they told her. "You will now go to the library and you will now read about the other side of everything you have refused to look at for your entire life."

Hillary remembered that she and classmate Ellen Press Murdoch, an equally committed Lyndon Johnson girl told to play Barry Goldwater, "went ballistic" over their assignments. "With our teeth gritted," as Hillary later described the encounter, she and Murdoch squared off to argue the key issues of the 1964 presidential campaign.

Skill Review (continued)

It was the beginning of "what an education should do," she said, forcing her to read and examine opinions that weren't hers because teachers were always demanding answers to those basic and brilliant questions such as "Why do you believe this? What's the point? What's the basis?" Those same fundamental "hard questions" she said, that demanded copious research and reflective answers, provided the approach she would take throughout her life. To reach conclusions, the course would be "Don't just tell me what I should believe, don't just tell me what the correct position is. . . . Show me what it's based on. Show me why it works and will make life better."

"I firmly believe," she told a group of Maine South students on a return visit in 1992, "that the whole purpose of politics—and it's not just elective politics on a presidential or gubernatorial level but politics with a small *p*—is how people get together, how they agree upon their goals, how they move together to realize those goals, how they make the absolutely inevitable tradeoffs between deeply held beliefs that are incompatible."

—Excerpted from *Hillary Rodham Clinton: A First Lady for Our Time*, by Donnie Radcliffe

1. Write true (T) or false (F) for each of these details about Hillary Clinton.

   _____ **A.** Hillary Clinton supported Lyndon Johnson.
   _____ **B.** Hillary Clinton felt she had a good education.
   _____ **C.** Hillary Clinton believes you must support your opinions.

2. Which of the following words does the author emphasize to show what was important to Hillary Clinton?

   A. politics
   B. Goldwater
   C. education
   D. debate

3. Which reference source would you use to find out where Park Ridge, Illinois, is?

   A. an almanac
   B. an atlas
   C. an encyclopedia
   D. a magazine

4. Which of the following would be likely to feature an interview with Hillary Clinton?

   A. an almanac
   B. an atlas
   C. an encyclopedia
   D. a magazine

5. Which of the following would be the best source for information about President Lyndon Johnson?

   A. an almanac
   B. an atlas
   C. an encyclopedia
   D. a magazine

Skill Practice

Directions: Choose the one best answer to each question. Questions 1 through 5 refer to the following passage.

Late in December 1851, Harriet arrived in St. Catharines, Canada West (now Ontario), with the eleven fugitives. It had taken almost a month to complete this journey; most of the time had been spent getting out of Maryland.

The first winter in St. Catharines was a terrible one. Canada was a strange, frozen land, snow everywhere, ice everywhere, and bone-biting cold the like of which none of them had ever experienced before. Harriet rented a small frame house in the town and set to work to make a home. The fugitives boarded with her. They worked in forests, felling trees, and so did she. Sometimes she took other jobs, cooking or cleaning for people in the town. She cheered on these newly arrived fugitives, working herself, finding work for them, praying for them, sometimes begging for them.

Often she found herself thinking of the beauty of Maryland, the mellowness of the soil, the richness of the plant life there. The climate itself made for an ease of living that could never be duplicated in this bleak, barren countryside.

In spite of the severe cold, the hard work, she came to love St. Catharines and the other towns and cities in Canada where black men lived. She discovered that freedom meant more than the right to change jobs at will, more than the right to keep the money that one earned. It was the right to vote and sit on juries. It was the right to be elected to office. In Canada there were black men who were county officials and members of school boards. St. Catharines had a large colony of ex-slaves, and they owned their own homes, kept them neat and clean and in good repair. They lived in whatever part of town they chose and sent their children to the schools.

When spring came, she decided that she would make this small Canadian city her home— as much as any place could be said to be home to a woman who traveled from Canada to the Eastern Shore of Maryland as often as she did.

In the spring of 1852, she went back to May, New Jersey. She spent the summer cooking in a hotel. That fall she returned, as usual, to Dorchester County and brought out nine more slaves, conducting them all the way to St. Catharines, in Canada West, to the bone-biting cold, the snow-covered forests, and freedom.

—Excerpted from *Harriet Tubman: Conductor on the Underground Railroad*, by Ann Petry

Skill Practice (continued)

1. When Harriet Tubman was a young girl, her enslaved mother refused to give up Harriet's little brother to be sold. She hid him instead. What influence might this event in the family's history have had on Harriet?

   A. It made her afraid to leave Maryland.
   B. It caused her to fear being around enslaved persons.
   C. It influenced her belief in the possibilities of resistance.
   D. It made her determined not to return to Dorchester County.

2. The author states at the end of the passage that Harriet returned to Dorchester Country and brought nine more slaves to "the bone-biting cold, the snow-covered forests, and freedom." What qualities of Harriet Tubman are revealed in this action?

   A. her dependence on the goodwill of the Canadian people
   B. her disregard for the well-being of enslaved persons
   C. her love of the North and cold climates
   D. her determination and love for her people

3. The author states that Harriet often traveled from Canada to the Eastern Shore of Maryland. What can we infer that Harriet did on these occasions?

   A. She continued to help fugitive slaves reach freedom.
   B. She moved enslaved persons to the warmer climate of Maryland.
   C. She sat on juries and changed jobs frequently.
   D. She ran a boarding house in May, New Jersey.

4. From the passage, what can you infer about what the author thinks about Harriet Tubman?

   A. Tubman is brave but foolish to live in St. Catharines.
   B. Tubman does not fully understand freedom.
   C. Tubman is brave and hardworking.
   D. Tubman is a good county official.

Writing Practice

Directions: Choose an interesting person that you know or that you have read about. Do research to learn about that person. Then write one page of his or her biography. Choose an event or experience that was significant to the person's life or an experience that will be interesting to readers.

Autobiography

KEY CONCEPT: An autobiography is a factual account that a person writes about his or her own life.

Do you ever think of the people you knew or the events that occurred in your childhood or adolescence? Have you ever thought of writing these events down or telling a friend about them in your own words? This type of writing is called autobiography. An autobiography is a window into how someone thinks and feels about life.

Autobiography

An **autobiography** is one kind of nonfiction. It is the story of a person's life as told by that person. By understanding the **characteristics**, or qualities, of an autobiography, you will understand what an autobiography is and how it is different from a biography.

When you read an autobiography, look for these characteristics:

- Writers tell the story from their own point of view. They use pronouns such as *I*, *me*, *my*, *we*, *us*, and *our*.

- In an autobiography, events are often told in the order they happened. This is called chronological order. An autobiographical work can cover a person's lifetime, from childhood through adulthood. However, it may focus on only one part of that life, such as the person's work experience.

- Autobiographies may be based on the writer's memories, diaries, letters, and other documents. An autobiography is generally more **subjective**, or personal, than a biography because it is told from that subject's point of view. A biography is written by someone else, and it is based on research and interviews.

- Writers make their autobiographies interesting by providing descriptions of people and places and by including their private thoughts and feelings. These personal details help the reader connect to the writer's story.

POINT OF VIEW

Point of view is the perspective that a text is written from. A **perspective** is a particular way of understanding something. There are several types of point of view.

These are most common points of view in nonfiction texts:

- In the **first-person point of view**, the writer participates in the action. Readers experience events through the writer's eye—knowing only his or her thoughts and feelings. Texts written from the first-person point of view use the words *I*, *me*, and *mine*.

- In the **third-person point of view**, the narrator seems to know everything that is happening and that has happened in the past. The narrator can describe the inner thoughts, feelings, and opinions of all the characters. Biographies are written from the third-person point of view.

Read the following paragraph. In a notebook, tell what point of view the writer uses. Explain how you know that.

> As a boy, Norberto had had little formal education. What schooling he did have was poor. As he grew up, it became increasingly difficult for him to admit that he could not read. Instead, he just pretended to understand. But when he met Carmen, he did not try to keep the secret from her. She understood his problem, and she did not judge him. She urged him to see a specialist at the reading clinic.

This paragraph is written in the third-person point of view. The author describes two people—Norberto and Carmen—and tells what they are thinking. The author is not part of the action.

TECHNOLOGY CONNECTION

Media Literacy

Watch an excerpt from a movie that is based on an autobiography. Analyze the difference between reading about someone's life and seeing it acted out in a movie.

How does the medium (motion picture) affect the way the subject of the film is presented? In what way are your opinions of the subject influenced by the actors rather than the facts?

Write a paragraph about the differences between autobiography and film. Consider the importance of point of view in the two media presentations.

To understand the events of a nonfiction text, it is important to recognize and analyze various relationships within the text.

This is especially true in autobiographies. When you understand the relationships between people in the story, you will have a better understanding of the subject of the autobiography.

As you read the passages in this lesson, ask yourself these questions:

- How are these events important to the person's life?

- How are these people, ideas, or events connected?

- What **patterns** (repeated actions) occur in the events?

- How do these events relate to the author's main idea?

- Is the author's perspective apparent?

Directions: Read this passage about Booker T. Washington, who was born into slavery and became free after the Civil War.

> The first thing I ever learned in the way of book knowledge was while working in this salt-furnace. Each salt-packer had his barrels marked with a certain number. The number allotted to my stepfather was "18." At the close of the day's work the boss of the packers would come around and put "18" on each of our barrels, and I soon learned to recognize that figure wherever I saw it, and after a while got to the point where I could make that figure, though I knew nothing about any other figures or letters.
>
> From the time that I can remember having any thoughts about anything, I recall that I had an intense longing to learn to read. I determined, when quite a small child, that, if I accomplished nothing else in life, I would in some way get enough education to enable me to read common books and newspapers. Soon after we got settled in some manner in our new cabin in West Virginia, I induced my mother to get hold of a book for me. How or where she got it I do not know, but in some way she procured an old copy of Webster's "blue-back" spelling-book, which contained the alphabet, followed by such meaningless words as "ab," "ba," "ca," "da." I began at once to devour this book, and I think that it was the first one I ever had in my hands.
>
> —Excerpted from *Up from Slavery*, by Booker T. Washington

THINK ABOUT READING

Directions: Answer the questions below in the space provided.

1. Which words in the first paragraph offer clues that this is an autobiography?

   _____

2. Name two characteristics of an autobiography found in this passage.

   _____

Directions: Read this passage about the comedian John Leguizamo. Think about what techniques the author **applies**, or uses, to help you connect to his story.

> When you're a poor kid at a poor school, you worry a lot about how you look all the time, how much money you're spending on clothes and all that. I had problems, man. I wore high waters [pants that were too short]. And my shoes? Forget about it. I had fake sneakers—you know, the kind your mother finds in those big wire bins.

"Hey, John, here's one I like! Go find the one that matches!"

"I found it, Ma, but it's only a three and a half."

"Don't worry. We'll cut out the toes."

So there I am, pants too high, sneakers too tight, underwear without leg holes. I was the Quasimodo of Jackson Heights. Then it hits me: this is no way to get girls. So I had my mission then: become cool.

I totally changed. I hung out with the gangsters. Cut class. By the time I got to high school, I was getting in trouble all the time.

What I loved most was cracking jokes in school. I liked keeping the kids laughing. Even the teachers laughed sometimes, which was the best part. See, I was still so out of it in a way—too cool to hang with the nerds, not cool enough to be with the real cool guys—I figured my only value was to be funny. I enjoyed people enjoying me.

Anyway, one day during my junior year, I was walking down the hallway, making jokes as usual, when Mr. Zufa, my math teacher, pulled me aside. I got collared by the teachers all the time, so I didn't think much about it. Mr. Zufa looked at me and started talking.

"Listen," he says, "instead of being so obnoxious all the time— instead of wasting all that energy in class—why don't you rechannel your hostility and humor into something productive? Have you ever thought about being a comedian?"

I didn't talk back to Mr. Zufa like I usually would have. I was quiet. I probably said something like "Yeah, cool, man," but for the rest of the day, I couldn't get what he said out of my head.

It started to hit me, like, "Wow, I'm going to be a loser all my life." And I really didn't want to be a loser. I wanted to be somebody.

But that one moment Mr. Zufa collared me was the turning point in my life. Everything kind of converged, you know? The planets aligned.

—Excerpted from *The Right Words at the Right Time*,
by John Leguizamo

Reading Skill
Identify Point of View

Autobiographies are written in the first-person point of view. The author is writing about himself or herself.

Reread the passages on these two pages and underline the details that only the author could have known.

The write one paragraph explaining how these details make the autobiographies more interesting.

WRITE TO LEARN

John Leguizamo tells about a teacher who influenced him. Think about a person in your life who has influenced you. In a notebook, write one paragraph describing what that person did and what effect that person has had on you.

THINK ABOUT READING

Directions: Use a graphic organizer like the one shown here to answer the following question.

In his autobiography, Leguizamo talks about his feelings and attitudes as a teenager. What does this tell you about him?

What the Character Does	What This Shows about the Character

Autobiographies can be more accurate than biographies because the writer knows details that a biographer may not know. However, autobiographies are subjective. Writers may hide or alter unpleasant details to present themselves in the best possible light. They may also be so close to the information that they cannot see the patterns in their actions.

Directions: Read the excerpt below about Suze Orman, a well-known financial advisor.

> I was supposed to graduate in 1973, but my degree was withheld because I hadn't fulfilled the language requirement. Once again, it was the shame of my grade-school years holding me back. If I had trouble with English, what made me think I could learn a foreign language? I decided to leave school without my degree. I wanted to see America. I wanted to see what a hill looked like . . . a mountain . . . the Grand Canyon!
>
> I borrowed $1,500 from my brother to buy a Ford Econoline van and, with the help of my friend Mary Corlin (a great friend to this day), converted the van into a place I could sleep during the drive across country. I convinced three friends—Laurie, Sherry, and Vicky—to come with me; I was way too scared to try this on my own. With $300 and a converted van to my name, we set out to see America. Sherry and Vicky jumped out in Los Angeles, but Laurie and I continued on to Berkeley, California. As we drove through the hills on the day of our arrival, we were stopped by a man with a red flag who held up traffic so trees that had been cut down could be cleared. That year a frost in the Berkeley Hills killed many of the eucalyptus trees. I got out of the van to watch and walked up to the man with the red flag and asked him if they needed any help. He pointed me to the boss, and before we knew it Laurie and I had landed our first jobs—working for Coley Tree Service for $3.50 an hour. We worked as tree clearers for two months, living out of the van and using a friend's home nearby to shower.
>
> When it was time to move on, I applied for a job as a waitress at the Buttercup Bakery, a great little place where we used to get our coffee. To my delight, I got the job. While I worked at the Buttercup, I faced up to my shame of not having finished college and took Spanish classes at Hayward State University. Finally, in 1976, I got my degree from the University of Illinois. I was an official college graduate, working as a waitress. I stayed at the Buttercup Bakery, where I made about $400 a month, until 1980, when I was twenty-nine years old.
>
> —Excerpted from *Women & Money*, by Suze Orman

THINK ABOUT **READING**

Directions: Answer the question.

Describe one personal trait Orman revealed about herself that another writer might have tried to hide.

_____

_____

_____

_____

Vocabulary Review

Directions: Use these words to compete the following sentences.

autobiography   characteristics   pattern   perspective   subjective

1. Something that occurs in a repeated arrangement or order has a _____.

2. The president brings a unique _____ to historical events that everyone thought they already understood.

3. An autobiography is more _____ than a biography.

4. One of the _____ of an autobiography is the use of the pronouns *I* and *me*.

5. A(n) _____ is the story of a person's life written by that person.

Skill Review

Directions: Read the passage below and answer the questions that follow.

My parents wanted my brother Minh and me to have freedom and arranged for us to escape out of Vietnam to a free country. It was 1982, and I had just finished seventh grade. One morning at approximately 4:00 a.m., my parents told us to get out of bed. I was very sleepy, and I asked my father why we had to get up so early. He told me that my brother and I had to go away for a long time. Minh was glad that we were going on a trip because most of the time we never went anywhere except around the city. The early morning was cloudy and dreary, much like my feeling about leaving my family—probably forever. Our parents told us to act as natural as possible, so that neighbors and police would never suspect this was our great escape. Our parents had been planning this day for many months. Nothing could now interfere with the plans.

Our father took us to the bus station, which was the first part of our long trip to freedom. At about 5:30 a.m. that morning, my nine-year-old brother and I got off our father's motorcycle with just a small package that contained a change of clothing. We waited while our father bought the tickets. Then with my hat in hand, I boarded the old, light-colored bus. My brother looked for a seat for us, but I looked elsewhere. Outside, I saw my father near his motorcycle staring at the bus and his two children. I saw the sparkling in his eyes, and he tried to hide his feelings. I had never seen my father emotional before. I was thinking, "Dad, don't worry about us; we'll see you again, but I don't know when." His tall stature against the early morning light brought a sick feeling to my stomach. I tried so hard to hide my tears. So sadly, I took the seat. As the bus slowly moved on, my father grew smaller and smaller and smaller and finally disappeared. His gradual vanishing is a moment that I know I will never forget.

—Excerpted from *A Personal Narrative*,
by Kim-Hue Phan

Skill Review (continued)

1. What is the main idea of this passage?

_____

_____

2. Putting things in chronological, or time, order can help you summarize a passage. Use the sequence chain diagram below to record the important events of this passage in order.

SEQUENCE CHAIN

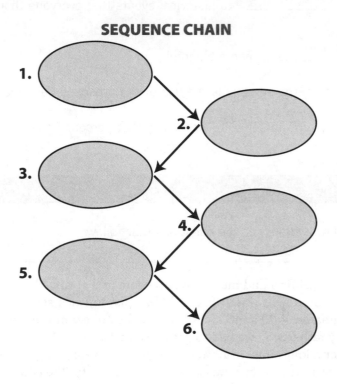

3. Use your answers to questions 1 and 2 to write a summary of the passage.

_____

_____

_____

_____

_____

4. How might this story have been different if it had been written as a biography rather than as an autobiography?

_____

_____

_____

Skill Practice

Directions: Choose the <u>one best answer</u> to each question. <u>Questions 1 and 2</u> refer to the following passage.

> Sunday afternoons we'd climb into our rust-spackled 1963 T-Bird, which sounded like a Civil War cannon, and go for a drive. We'd start on Shore Drive, the finest street in Manhasset, where the white-columned houses were bigger than Town Hall, and several had Long Island Sound as their front lawns. "Imagine living in one of these showplaces," my mother would say.
> 5 She'd park in front of the grandest house, the one with the golden yellow shutters and the wraparound porch. "Imagine lying in bed on a summer morning," she'd say, "with the windows open, and a warm breeze off the water blowing the curtains in and out."
>
> It always seemed as if a misty rain was falling during our drives, so my mother and I couldn't get out of the car for a closer look. We'd sit with the engine and heater running and the
> 10 windshield wipers slinging back and forth. My mother would study the house and I would study my mother. She had lustrous auburn hair, which she wore to her shoulders, and green-brown eyes that turned a shade greener whenever she smiled. Her most common facial expression, however, was one of enormous self-command, like a young aristocrat posing for her coming-out portrait. It was the look of a woman who could be gentle and fragile, but who would assuredly
> 15 be fierce when protecting those she loved.
>
> —Excerpted from *The Tender Bar, A Memoir*
> by J. R. Moehringer

1. From the information in this excerpt, how would you describe the relationship between the author and his mother?

   A. cold and indifferent
   B. sad and unhappy
   C. concerned and anxious
   D. close and affectionate

2. The author says the family's car was "rust-spackled" and "sounded like a Civil War cannon" (lines 1 and 2). How could the car best be described?

   A. The car was brown and shiny.
   B. The car was old and loud.
   C. The car was built during the Civil War.
   D. The car was a brand new car.

Writing Practice

Directions: If you were writing your autobiography, what would you focus on? Would you tell your whole life story, or would you focus on a particular time period? Write the first two pages of your autobiography. Include details that an outside biographer wouldn't know.

Directions: Questions 1–3 refer to the following passage.

Back at Yale for her senior year, Maya Lin enrolled in Professor Andrus Burr's course in funerary [burial] architecture. The Vietnam Veterans Memorial competition had recently been announced, and although the memorial would be a cenotaph—a monument in honor of persons buried someplace else—Professor Burr thought that having his students prepare a design of the
5 memorial would be a worthwhile course assignment.

Surely, no classroom exercise ever had such spectacular results.

After receiving the assignment, Maya Lin and two of her classmates decided to make the day's journey from New Haven, Connecticut, to Washington to look at the site where the memorial would be built. On the day of their visit, Maya Lin remembers, Constitution Gardens
10 was awash with late November sun; the park was full of light, alive with joggers and people walking beside the lake.

"It was while I was at the site that I designed it," Maya Lin said later in an interview about the memorial with *Washington Post* writer Phil McCombs. "I just sort of visualized it. It just popped into my head. Some people were playing Frisbee. It was a beautiful park. I didn't want
15 to destroy a living park. You use the landscape. You don't fight with it. You absorb the landscape. . . . When I looked at the site I just knew I wanted something horizontal that took you in, that made you feel safe within the park, yet at the same time reminding you of the dead. So I just imagined opening up the earth. . . ."

When Maya Lin returned to Yale, she made a clay model of the vision that had come to her
20 in Constitution Gardens. She showed it to Professor Burr; he liked her conception and encouraged her to enter the memorial competition. She put her design on paper, a task that took six weeks, and mailed it to Washington barely in time to meet the March 31 deadline.

A month and a day later, Maya Lin was attending class. Her roommate slipped into the classroom and handed her a note. Washington was calling and would call back in fifteen
25 minutes. Maya Lin hurried to her room. The call came. She had won the memorial competition.

—Excerpted from *The Vision of Maya Ying Lin*,
by Brent Ashabranner

1. Maya Lin says, "You use the landscape. You don't fight with it" (line 15). What does she mean?

    A. You should ignore the landscape.
    B. The landscape is an important element in the design.
    C. It was not a living park, so the landscape didn't matter.
    D. You need people and joggers to visualize the landscape.

2. What is Lin's most important success?

    A. putting her design on paper
    B. making a clay model of her vision
    C. winning the design contest
    D. being interviewed by the *Post*

3. What is the likely effect Lin's design has had on people who view it?

    A. Viewers remember the dead.
    B. Viewers can play in the park.
    C. Viewers can use the landscape.
    D. Viewers overcome racism.

Review

Directions: Questions 4 and 5 refer to the following passage.

The earliest memory is of sounds. In a place of all-encompassing silence, any sound is something to be noted and remembered. When the wind is not blowing, it is so quiet you can hear a beetle scurrying across the ground or a fly landing on a bush. Occasionally an airplane flies overhead—a high-tech intrusion penetrating the agrarian [agricultural] peace.

When the wind blows, as it often does, there are no trees to rustle and moan. But the wind whistles through any loose siding on the barn and causes any loose gate to bang into the fence post. It starts the windmills moving, turning, creaking.

At night the sounds are magnified. Coyotes wail on the hillside, calling to each other or to the moon—a sound that sends chills up the spine. We snuggle deeper in our beds. What prey have the coyotes spotted? Why are they howling? What are they doing? Just before dawn the doves begin to call, with a soft cooing sound, starting the day with their endless search for food. The cattle nearby walk along their trail near the house, their hooves crunching on the gravel. An occasional *moo* to a calf or to another cow can be heard, or the urgent bawl of a calf that has lost contact with its mother, or the low insistent grunt, almost a growl, of a bull as it walks steadily along to the watering trough or back out to the pasture. The two huge windmills turn in the wind, creaking as they revolve to face the breeze, and producing the clank of the sucker rods as they rise and fall with each turn of the huge fan of the mill.

The Lazy B Ranch straddles the border of Arizona and New Mexico along the Gila River. It is high desert country—dry, windswept, clear, often cloudless. Along the Gila the canyons are choked with cottonwoods and willows. The cliffs rise up sharply and are smooth beige sandstone. The water flowing down the riverbed from the Gila Wilderness to the northeast is usually only a trickle. But sometimes, after summer rains or a winter thaw in the mountains, the river becomes an angry, rushing, mud-colored flood, carrying trees, brush, rocks, and everything else in its path. Scraped into the sandstone bluffs are petroglyphs of the Anasazi of centuries past. Their lives and hardships left these visible traces for us to find, and we marvel at their ability to survive as long as they did in this harsh environment.

—Excerpted from *Lazy B: Growing Up on a Cattle Ranch in the American Southwest*, by Sandra Day O'Connor

4. Why does the author include words such as *howl, moo, creaking,* and *bang?*

   A. to show what the ranch looks like
   B. to show how the author feels
   C. to show what the ranch sounds like
   D. to show how the ranch has changed over time

5. What is the author's primary purpose for writing this selection?

   A. to describe a special place
   B. to explain what life is like on a ranch
   C. to help readers locate the Lazy B Ranch
   D. to persuade people to visit the Lazy B Ranch

Directions: Questions 6–9 refer to the following passage.

I talked to my children, even when they were very small, about the ways of the Ojibway people. They were good children and they listened, but I had a feeling that they listened the same as when I read a story about the Bobbsey twins or Marco Polo. I was speaking of another people, removed from them by rock and roll, juvenile singers, and the bobbing movement of the new American dance.

My two, born and raised in Minneapolis, are of the generation of Ojibway who do not know what the reservation [a place set aside for Native Americans to live] means, or the Bureau of Indian Affairs, or the tangled treaties and federal—so called—Indian laws which have spun their webs for a full century around the Native People, the First People of this land.

Now my children are urging me to recall all the stories and bits of information that I ever heard my grandparents or any of the older Ojibway tell. It is important, they say, because now their children are asking them. Others are saying the same thing. It is well that they are asking, for the Ojibway young must learn their cycle.

I have been abroad in this society, the dominating society, for two-thirds of my life, and yet I am a link in a chain to the past. Because of this, I shall do as they ask. I can close my eyes and I am back in the past.

—Excerpted from *The Forest Cries*, by Ignatia Broker

6. According to this passage, which is a value held by the author?

   A. an appreciation of her culture and traditions
   B. a belief that the reservation system is good
   C. a belief in the importance of rock and roll music
   D. a disregard for the influence of stories and storytelling

7. Which statement would the author be most likely to agree with?

   A. It is dangerous to live in the past.
   B. Children are not interested in the past.
   C. The Ojibway think the present is more important than the past.
   D. It is important to have knowledge of the past.

8. What will the author of this selection most likely do next?

   A. tell stories about the past to her grandchildren
   B. become familiar with modern American culture
   C. decide to live in the present and move on from the past
   D. make her children tell stories about the past

9. The author compares herself to a link in a chain. What does this reveal about the author?

   A. The author is a prisoner of the past.
   B. The author is connected to the past.
   C. The author is free from the past.
   D. The author travels back to the past.

Review

Check Your Understanding

On the following chart, circle the number of any question you answered incorrectly. Under each content area you will see the pages you can review to learn the content covered in the question. Pay particular attention to reviewing those lessons in which you missed half or more of the questions.

Chapter 4 Review

Lesson	Item Number	Review Pages
Nonfiction Prose	6, 7, 8, 9	156–163
Biography	1, 2, 3	164–171
Autobiography	4, 5	172–179

ESSAY WRITING PRACTICE

Literary Nonfiction

Directions: Using the prompt below, write a biography about someone you know. Review Lesson 4.2 for help with planning, writing strategies, and text structure.

BIOGRAPHY

A biography tells the true story of someone's life. Usually it highlights significant accomplishments so that others can learn from those accomplishments. An autobiography is a form of biography. The story is told by the person who is the subject.

Think about people you know who have affected your life in a meaningful way: your relatives, neighbors, coworkers, employers, and friends. Choose one person and write a brief biography of that person. As you plan the biography, first make a list of the important events of that person's life. You can use that list to structure, or organize, your text. Open with an engaging story that will show others why this person's life is important to you.

As an alternative, you can choose to write an autobiography. List the important events in your own life, and use the list to organize your text. In your opening, present a story that will make others interested in reading about your life.

Review

ESSAY WRITING PRACTICE

Fiction

Chances are that wherever you go, you'll hear someone tell a story. Conversations, TV programs, jokes, and even some songs tell stories. Some of the best stories—mysteries, romances, ghost stories, thrillers—are found in novels and short stories.

Why read fiction? Most people read fiction for enjoyment, but a good story also makes you think about important ideas in your own life. A story might introduce you to a different part of the world or to a time in the distant past. A good story might teach you something about yourself or others. It might stir up your imagination, challenge your beliefs, or give you a new way of looking at the world.

In this chapter you will study these topics:

Lesson 5.1 Plot and Setting
This lesson helps you understand what a plot is and how the author moves the plot forward in a story. You will learn to identify the story's conflict and recognize how the conflict is resolved. You will also see why the location and the time of a story are important.

Lesson 5.2 Character
If you were in a character's place, would you act as that character does? In this lesson you will learn to find out information about a character by what the character says and does. The lesson helps you understand what motivates a character's actions and feelings.

Lesson 5.3 Point of View
When an event occurs, everyone participating in the event or watching the event understands what happens in a slightly different way. This is because everyone has his or her own point of view. This lesson helps you figure out who is telling the story and what the point of view of the storyteller is.

Lesson 5.4 Literal and Figurative Language
Have you ever heard the expression "a picture is worth a thousand words"? This lesson shows you how authors use literal and figurative language to help you "see" details about the characters and the setting of a story.

Lesson 5.5 Theme
How can you identify the theme of a story? What connection does the theme have to the setting, characters, and plot? This lesson helps you look for the theme, or message, in fiction.

Lesson 5.6 Text Structure
This lesson helps you identify how an author organizes a piece of writing. Different genres require different forms, or structures. You will learn to recognize the text structures used in fiction.

Goal Setting

What would you like to learn in this chapter about reading fiction?

_____

_____

_____

How will you use what you learn? In what ways will this information help you become a better reader?

_____

_____

_____

To help you set goals for learning as you study this chapter, use this checklist as you read the passages in each lesson.

☐ Where and when does this story take place? How do I picture the scene?

☐ What characters are in the story?

☐ Who is telling the story?

☐ What events are taking place? How are the events connected?

☐ What is the main message, or theme?

☐ What figurative and literal language is used? Does the language change the way I feel about the story?

☐ What structure does the author use to tell the story?

Plot and Setting

Lesson Objectives

You will be able to

• Analyze how incidents in a story propel the action

• Analyze the development of plot and setting

Skills

• **Core Skill:** Analyze the Relationship between Plot and Setting

• **Reading Skill:** Sequence Events

Vocabulary

climax
conflict
diagram
propel
resolution
sensory details
sequence
setting

KEY CONCEPT: The plot is the action of a story. The setting is the time and place of the action.

Have you ever told a friend about an exciting movie you just saw? You most likely told details of the plot (the events of the story). You probably also mentioned the setting (where and when the story took place). Was the story set in a long-ago castle or on a spaceship in the future? Often a story's setting determines how a plot unfolds.

Plot Development

The **plot** is the basic action of a story. A plot moves ahead in a series of events. Most plots develop in five stages, which are shown on the **diagram**, or drawing, below.

Exposition

The **exposition** introduces the characters and the setting. It presents the problem, or **conflict**, that the main character faces. The main character may struggle with other characters, with society, with nature, or with his or her own emotions.

Rising Action

During the **rising action**, tension increases. Each action that occurs and each decision that is made should **propel**, or drive, the story forward. The story becomes more suspenseful and more complicated.

Climax and Resolution

The **climax** is the high point of the story. Tension is at its peak. The action is the most exciting.

Falling Action

The **falling action** moves the story toward its conclusion. Events that occur after the climax help tie up the loose ends of the story. The conflict is being settled.

Resolution

The **resolution** is the conclusion of the story. The problem is solved.

PLOT DEVELOPMENT

Directions: Read the following story. Notice how the author develops the plot and how one event leads to the next. Then use the plot development diagram on the previous page to determine which parts of the story are the exposition, rising action, climax, falling action, and resolution.

Reading Skill
Sequence Events

The **sequence** of events is the order in which events occur. In Langston Hughes's story, some of the action takes place in the past, and some of the action takes place in the present. In addition, the characters speak about a possible future event.

As you read the story, notice the sequence of events. In a notebook, draw a graphic organizer such as the one below. Fill in the organizer to show the sequence of past and present events. Also add the event that might take place in the future.

Then write a note that explains how past and present events make it unlikely the future event will take place.

Past
Present
Future

Early Autumn

When Bill was very young, they had been in love. . . . Then something not very important had come between them, and they didn't speak. Impulsively [without much thought], she had married a man she thought she loved. Bill went away, bitter about women.

Yesterday, walking across Washington Square [a park in New York City], she saw him for the first time in years.

"Bill Walker," she said.

He stopped. At first he did not recognize her, to him she looked so old.

"Mary!" Where did you come from?"

Unconsciously [without thinking], she lifted her face as though wanting a kiss, but he held out his hand. She took it.

"I live in New York now," she said.

"Oh"—smiling politely. Then a little frown came quickly between his eyes.

"Always wondered what happened to you, Bill."

"I'm a lawyer. Nice firm, way downtown."

"Married yet?"

"Sure. Two kids." . . .

A great many people went past them through the park. People they didn't know. It was late afternoon. Nearly sunset. Cold.

"And your husband?" he asked her.

"We have three children. . . . We live on Central Park West," she said. "Come and see us sometime."

"Sure," he replied. "You and your husband must have dinner with my family some night. Any night. Lucille and I'd love to have you."

Use Quotations

Quotations repeat the words that people speak. These words are enclosed in quotation marks. In a story, characters often reveal information about themselves when they speak.

Reread this dialogue, or conversation, between Mary and Bill. It reveals that Mary has kept Bill in her thoughts over the years.

"Always wondered what happened to you, Bill."

"I'm a lawyer. Nice firm, way downtown."

"Married yet?"

"Sure. Two kids."

In the workplace, quotations are most often used when people are quoted in reports or other workplace documents. The quotations usually support important points. For instance, in a memo about a new company wellness program, the company president might include a quotation from a well-known health and wellness expert.

Go online and locate two workplace documents that include quotations. In a notebook, record the quotations you find. Explain why the writers included the quotations. Tell what point each quotation supports.

The leaves fell slowly from the trees in the Square. Fell without wind. Autumn dusk. She felt a little sick.

"We'd love it," she answered.

"You ought to see my kids." He grinned.

Suddenly the lights came on up the whole length of Fifth Avenue, chains of misty brilliance in the blue air.

"There's my bus," she said.

He held out his hand, "Good-bye."

"When . . ." she wanted to say, but the bus was ready to pull off. . . . She was afraid to open her mouth. . . . Afraid it would be impossible to utter a word.

Suddenly she shrieked very loudly, "Good-bye!" But the bus door had closed.

The bus started. . . . She lost sight of Bill. Then she remembered she had forgotten to give him her address—or to ask him for his—or tell him that her youngest boy was named Bill too.

—Excerpted from "Early Autumn," by Langston Hughes

THINK ABOUT **READING**

Directions: After reading "Early Autumn," answer the following questions.

1. What setting and characters are introduced in the exposition?

   _____

   _____

2. What is the conflict in the story?

   _____

   _____

3. What is the climax?

   _____

   _____

4. What is the story's resolution?

   _____

   _____

Setting

The **setting** is the place and time of a story. It tells where and when a story occurs. A story may be set in a real place or an imaginary place. The action may occur in the past, present, or future.

Place

Place refers to the physical setting. A nineteenth-century castle, a high-rise office building, a city bus, someone's living room—these are all examples of place. The plot, or action of a story, can be confined to one place, or it can move from one place to another. The movie *Jaws* is set in a small resort community on the fictional Amity Island. In Amy Tan's novel *The Joy Luck Club*, the action takes place in two countries—China and the United States. Occasionally you must use details provided by the author and your own experience to figure out the physical setting of a story.

Time

The second element of setting is time. Every plot takes place at some point in time—in the past, the present, or the future. Some stories are set in a particular time period. Stacy Cohen's *The Last Train from Paris* unfolds during World War II. Jane Austen's novel *Pride and Prejudice* is set in the mid-nineteenth century.

How much time can pass in a story? James Joyce's novel *Ulysses*, which is hundreds of pages long, covers only one day in 1904. In *Roots*, a popular historical novel about slavery written by Alex Haley, the action takes place over centuries.

Mood

Mood refers to the general feeling of a story. The setting, the plot, and the writer's word choice help develop the mood of a story. The mood throughout most of *The Wizard of Oz* is bright, colorful, and happy. The mood of Suzanne Collins's novel *The Hunger Games* is extremely tense. The quirky Hogwarts School of Witchcraft and Wizardry helps create the mysterious and magical mood of the Harry Potter series.

Core Skill
Analyze Relationship between Plot and Setting

There is a close relationship between the plot and the setting of a story. Often the setting determines what action will take place.

For example, in "Early Autumn," the bus stop is an important part of the setting. Mary is waiting at the bus stop. This setting propels the plot—the bus comes, and Mary must board the bus. Because the bus departs quickly, Mary's encounter with Bill is shortened and her conversation with Bill remains unfinished.

Now, consider this passage:

Old Jacoba Cochran was a gold miner. One night, while searching for gold in the high mountains of Canada, she made her camp by a stream. Near the stream she saw large tracks. Not wanting to attract a wild animal into her camp, she hung her food from a tree several yards from her tent and campfire.

In a notebook, respond to this question: Why is the setting important to the event that occurs at the end of the passage?

Authors often use **sensory details**, or language that appeals to the reader's five senses, when describing the setting of a story.

Reread the excerpt from *Chesapeake*. In a notebook, identify one example from the passage for each sense: sight, sound, smell, taste, and touch.

Then explain how these details help you **visualize**, or see in your mind's eye, the setting of the story.

Directions: Read the story below. Then list two events that occur because of the story's setting.

Knowing that there would be ample food, if he could but catch it, Pentaquod pulled his canoe farther inland, hiding it among the oaks and maples which lined the shore, for he knew that he must explore this island quickly. And as he moved among the trees and came to a meadow, he heard the comforting cry so familiar in his days along the great river: "Bob-white! Bob-white!" Now the call came from his left, then from a clump of grass to his right, and sometimes from a spot almost under his feet, but always it was as clear and distinct as if an uncle who could whistle had been standing at his side.

"Bob-white!" It was the call of the quail, that sly bird with the brown-and-white head. Of all the birds that flew, this was the best eating, and if this island held a multitude, Pentaquod could not only survive on his fish but eat like a chieftain with his quail.

With extreme caution he started inland, noticing everything, aware that his life might depend upon the carefulness of his observation. With every step he found only reassurance and never a sight of danger: nut trees laden with midsummer shells not yet ripe; droppings of rabbits, and the signs that foxes lived here, and the location of brambled berry bushes, and the woody nests of eagles, and the honeysuckle twisting among the lower branches of cedar trees.

—Excerpted from *Chesapeake*, by James A. Michener

THINK ABOUT READING

Directions: Read the passage from *Chesapeake*. Then answer these questions. Cite evidence from the text to support your responses.

1. Where does the story take place?

    _____

    _____

2. What is the time of the story?

    _____

    _____

3. What is the mood of the story?

    _____

    _____

Vocabulary Review

Directions: Match each vocabulary word with its definition.

1. _____ climax   **A.** solution of the conflict

2. _____ conflict   **B.** drive forward

3. _____ propel   **C.** high point of a story

4. _____ resolution   **D.** order

5. _____ sequence   **E.** problem in a story

Directions: Read the passage below. Then answer the questions that follow.

"TOM!"

No answer.

"TOM!"

No answer.

"What's gone with that boy, I wonder? You TOM!"

No answer.

The old lady pulled her spectacles down and looked over them about the room; then she put them up and looked out under them. She seldom or never looked THROUGH them for so small a thing as a boy; they were her state pair, the pride of her heart, and were built for "style," not service—she could have seen through a pair of stove-lids just as well. She looked perplexed for a moment, and then said, not fiercely, but still loud enough for the furniture to hear:

"Well, I lay if I get hold of you I'll—"

She did not finish, for by this time she was bending down and punching under the bed with a broom, and so she needed breath to punctuate the punches with. She resurrected nothing but the cat.

"I never did see the beat of that boy!"

She went to the open door and stood in it and looked out among the tomato vines and "jimpson" weeds that constituted the garden. No Tom. So she lifted up her voice at an angle calculated for distance and shouted:

"Y-o-u-u TOM!"

There was a slight noise behind her and she turned just in time to seize a small boy by the slack of his roundabout and arrest his flight.

"There! I might 'a' thought of that closet. What you been doing in there?"

"Nothing."

"Nothing! Look at your hands. And look at your mouth. What IS that truck?"

"I don't know, aunt."

"Well, I know. It's jam—that's what it is. Forty times I've said if you didn't let that jam alone I'd skin you. Hand me that switch."

The switch hovered in the air—and the peril was desperate—

"My! Look behind you, aunt!"

The old lady whirled round, and snatched her skirts out of danger. The lad fled on the instant, scrambled up the high board-fence, and disappeared over it.

His aunt Polly stood surprised a moment, and then broke into a gentle laugh.

—Excerpted from *The Adventures of Tom Sawyer*, by Mark Twain

Skill Review (continued)

1. What information is in the exposition?
   - **A.** An old lady is in a bedroom looking for Tom.
   - **B.** Tom is found in the closet.
   - **C.** Tom's aunt turns in reaction to Tom's warning.
   - **D.** Aunt Polly laughs about Tom's escape.

2. When does the climax of the plot occur?
   - **A.** when Aunt Polly adjusts her spectacles
   - **B.** when Tom runs away from Aunt Polly
   - **C.** when Tom is seen with jam on his face
   - **D.** when Aunt Polly searches for Tom under the bed

3. Where does MOST of the story take place?
   - **A.** tomato garden
   - **B.** Aunt Polly's house
   - **C.** jam closet
   - **D.** bedroom

4. What is the mood of the story?
   - **A.** scary
   - **B.** angry
   - **C.** humorous
   - **D.** mysterious

5. Which detail described in the setting is important because it allows Tom to escape the switch?
   - **A.** tomato vines
   - **B.** "jimpson" weeds
   - **C.** cat under the bed
   - **D.** high board-fence

Directions: Read the passage below. Then complete the activity that follows.

Someone thrust a mask at the young man near Gwen, who had been wounded. Though swaying, and scarcely aware of what was happening, he managed to hold it to his face.

Even so, barely half of the passengers were on oxygen at the end of fifteen seconds—the critical time. By then, those not breathing oxygen were lapsing into a drowsy stupor; in another fifteen seconds, most were unconscious.

Gwen Meighen received no oxygen, nor immediate help. The unconsciousness, caused by her injuries, deepened.

Then, on the flight deck, Anson Harris, accepting the risk of further structural damage and possible total destruction of the aircraft, made his decision for a high-speed dive, saving Gwen and others from asphyxiation [unconsciousness].

The dive began at twenty-eight thousand feet altitude; it ended, two and a half minutes later, at ten thousand feet.

A human being can survive without oxygen for three to four minutes without damage to the brain.

For the first half of the dive—for a minute and a quarter, down to nineteen thousand feet—the air continued to be rarefied and insufficient to support life. Below that point, increasing amounts of oxygen were present and breathable.

At twelve thousand feet regular breathing was possible. By ten—with little time to spare, but enough—consciousness returned to all aboard Flight Two who had lost it, excepting Gwen. Many were unaware of having been unconscious at all.

—Excerpted from *Airport*, by Arthur Hailey

Skill Practice (continued)

Directions: Refer to the passage from the novel *Airport* on the previous page. On the plot diagram below, tell what information is in the exposition, describe the rising action, tell where the climax occurs, and describe the resolution of the passage. Then answer the questions that follow.

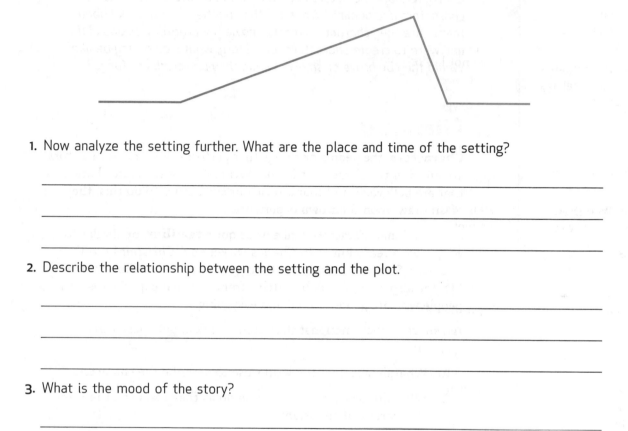

1. Now analyze the setting further. What are the place and time of the setting?

   _____

   _____

   _____

2. Describe the relationship between the setting and the plot.

   _____

   _____

   _____

3. What is the mood of the story?

   _____

Writing Practice

Directions: Write a one-page story about an event (real or imagined) in which a conflict developed and was later resolved. Begin with an exposition that introduces the characters, the setting, and the conflict. Use dialogue, description, and sensory language to develop the characters, plot, and mood.

Organize the sequence of events so the action rises to a climax and then falls. Be sure your resolution follows logically from the sequence of events.

Character

KEY CONCEPT: Characters—people, animals, robots, or whatever the writer chooses—perform the action in a story.

Characters are the actors in a story. Do you have some favorite characters you admire? What are the qualities that you like about them? Are they characters from a movie, TV program, or book? If you were to create characters for a story, what would they be like? Would they be brave or smart? Would they be serious or funny?

Lesson Objectives

You will be able to

• Recognize how characters are used in stories

• Interpret the actions, thoughts, and feelings of characters

Skills

• **Core Skill:** Compare and Contrast

• **Reading Skill:** Draw Evidence from Text

Vocabulary

adjust
characters
familiar
motivation
prediction
reasonable

Character

Characters, the people or things that perform the actions in a story, are an essential element of fiction. Writers strive to create characters that are believable and that arouse our sympathy. To do this, they often draw upon their own experiences.

Some fictional characters strike us as quite **familiar**, or similar to people we already know. In Charles Dickens's *A Christmas Carol*, Ebenezer Scrooge reminds us of stingy people we have met in real life. We also recognize Bob Cratchit from our own experiences with people who are good-natured and easygoing.

As you read about fictional characters, think about these three questions:

1. What details does the writer use to describe the characters?

2. What do the characters say and do as they react to others and to a variety of situations?

3. What do the characters reveal about themselves in their thoughts and feelings?

When you study a character, it may help you to think of the three questions as sides of a triangle. Each side represents one category of information about a character.

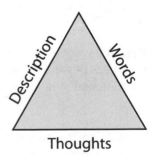

DRAW EVIDENCE FROM THE TEXT

A **prediction** is an attempt to answer the question *What will happen next?* You can also predict how characters will act by asking *What will this character do next?* Predicting keeps you involved in a story, and it can add interest to your reading. To make a prediction, readers use evidence and clues in the text, along with their prior knowledge and experience, to make guesses that are **reasonable**, or that make sense, about how characters will act.

Here are some key points to consider when making predictions.

- Make predictions before reading and while you read. Predicting while you read means thinking ahead about how characters might act and how events might turn out.

- Use your prior knowledge and experience as you predict. Ask yourself: *Have I been in a similar situation? What decisions did I make? How would I act if I were this character?*

- **Adjust**, or change, your prediction as you read. Predictions should make sense, but they do not always turn out to be correct.

Read the following passage. What do you think Miguel and Sonrisa might do next?

> The storm clouds gathered as Miguel and Sonrisa listened to the news on their local radio station. They heard the wind howling outside, and already there were reports of trees down and flooded highways. People were advised by the police to leave town on Highway 601 rather than on local roads. Although Miguel's car was in the garage, Sonrisa didn't want to leave the apartment. Suddenly they heard a loud clap of thunder, and a large object hit the roof.

If you predicted that Miguel and Sonrisa will get in their car and do as the police are advising, that is a good prediction. It is based on the evidence and clues in the passage, which tell you that a big storm is coming and that the police are advising people to leave town. To know whether your prediction was accurate, you would have to read on.

There is as much variety among the characters you read about in fiction as there is variety among people in the world. Perhaps there is more, since the only limit to characters is the writer's imagination.

Writers usually include many details that describe their characters: what they look like, how old they are, where they come from, what kind of experiences they've had. All of these details let the reader visualize the characters and understand them better. They also let the reader understand why characters act the way they do.

In a notebook, use a Venn diagram to compare and contrast the characters of Estella and Pip in this passage from *Great Expectations*. Be sure to include evidence from the text and details the writer includes that describe each character's appearance, thoughts, and emotions.

Compare and Contrast Characters

Writers compare two or more characters to show similarities, and they contrast characters to show differences. They compare and contrast characters' appearance, actions, and **motivations**, or their reasons for doing something.

Some passages use only comparison or only contrast. Other passages compare and contrast. Look for direct statements of comparison and contrast such as *They are alike because* or *One major difference is.*

You can also look for certain words and phrases that signal comparison, such as *also, both, similar, the same as,* and *in the same way.* For contrasts, look for words or phrases such as *however, but, different from, better than,* and *on the other hand.*

A Venn diagram can help you compare and contrast two people, events, or things. Similarities are placed in the overlapping area, and differences are placed in the outside areas.

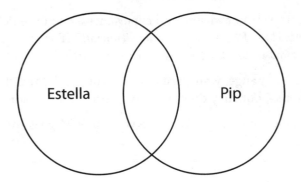

Directions: Read the passage below, which is from a story by Charles Dickens. One of the characters is Estella. The other character is Pip. He is the narrator in the passage, which means he is telling the story from his point of view. As you read, try to imagine what both characters are like.

The garden was too overgrown and rank for walking in with ease, and after we had made the round of it twice or thrice, we came out again into the brewery yard [a place where they make beer]. I showed her to a nicety where I had seen her walking on the casks, that first old day, and she said with a cold and careless look in that direction, "Did I?" I reminded her where she had come out of the house, and given me my meat and drink, and she said, "I don't remember." "Not remember that you made me cry?" said I. "No," said she, and shook her head and looked about her. I verily [truly] believe that her not remembering and not minding in the least, made me cry again, inwardly—and that is the sharpest crying of all.

"You must know," said Estella, condescending [acting superior] to me as a brilliant and beautiful woman might, "that I have no heart—if that has anything to do with my memory."

I got through some jargon [language] to the effect that I took the liberty of doubting that. That I knew better. That there could be no such beauty without it.

"Oh! I have a heart to be stabbed in or shot in, I have no doubt," said Estella, "and, of course, if it ceased to beat I should cease to be. But you know what I mean. I have no softness there, no—sympathy—sentiment—nonsense."

—Excerpted from *Great Expectations*, by Charles Dickens

THINK ABOUT **READING**

Directions: Answer these questions.

1. According to the passage, which of these descriptions best matches the narrator?

   A. a character in the story who has no part of the action
   B. the elderly father of Estella
   C. a speaker who is observing the actions of Estella and the other characters but who is not taking part in the action
   D. a young man who is part of the story

2. According to the narrator, what effect did Estella's behavior have on him when they first met?

   A. Her behavior caused him to cry.
   B. Her behavior gave him joy.
   C. Her behavior had no effect on him.
   D. He cannot remember meeting Estella.

3. Which of the following words best describe the character of Estella?

   A. warm and tenderhearted
   B. unfeeling and distant
   C. easygoing and friendly
   D. bitter and angry

4. Estella describes herself in the last paragraph of the excerpt. How does she seem to feel about the type of person she is?

   _____

   _____

   _____

   _____

As you read, combine evidence in the text with what you already know to make predictions about what the characters will do.

The passage on this page is taken from the story "A Worn Path." When reading, ask yourself how the title can help you understand what the story is about.

"A Worn Path" suggests that the main character, Phoenix Jackson, often walks the same road. The title also suggests that the path may be long, hard, and difficult.

To understand Phoenix Jackson, discuss these questions with a partner:

- How would you feel if you often had to walk a difficult road?

- Do you think Phoenix Jackson feels the same way?

- Why?

WRITE TO LEARN

In a notebook, use a Venn diagram to compare and contrast Estella (on pages 200–201) and Phoenix Jackson (on this page). How are they similar? How are they different?

Then write a short essay comparing and contrasting the characters.

Directions: Read the passage below. Then answer the questions about the character in this story.

> It was December—a bright frozen day in the early morning. Far out in the country there was an old Negro woman with her head tied in a red rag, coming along a path through the pinewoods. Her name was Phoenix Jackson. She was very old and small and she walked slowly in the dark pine shadows, moving a little from side to side in her steps, with the balanced heaviness and lightness of a pendulum in a grandfather clock. She carried a thin, small cane made from an umbrella, and with this she kept tapping the frozen earth in front of her. This made a grave and persistent noise in the still air that seemed meditative [thoughtful] like the chirping of a solitary little bird.
>
> She wore a dark striped dress reaching down to her shoe tops, and an equally long apron of bleached sugar sacks, with a full pocket: all neat and tidy, but every time she took a step she might have fallen over her shoelaces, which dragged from her unlaced shoes. She looked straight ahead. Her eyes were blue with age. Her skin had a pattern all its own of numberless branching wrinkles and as though a whole little tree stood in the middle of her forehead, but a golden color ran underneath, and the two knobs of her cheeks were illuminated [lit] by a yellow burning under the dark. Under the red rag her hair came down on her neck in the frailest of ringlets, still black, and with an odor like copper.
>
> —Excerpted from "A Worn Path," by Eudora Welty

THINK ABOUT READING

Directions: Answer the questions below.

1. What does Phoenix Jackson look like?

   _____

   _____

2. How would you describe Phoenix Jackson's character?

   _____

   _____

3. The narrator says, "She wore a dark striped dress reaching down to her shoe tops, and an equally long apron of bleached sugar sacks, with a full pocket: all neat and tidy . . ."

   What does this description suggest about Phoenix Jackson?

   _____

   _____

Directions: Use these words to complete the following sentences.

adjust   characters   familiar   prediction   reasonable

1. You can _____ your ideas about what you are reading as you continue to read.

2. You make a(n) _____ when you try to determine what will happen next in a story.

3. A _____ guess is a guess that makes sense based on the information you have.

4. When something is _____, you have seen it or heard it before.

5. The _____ perform the actions in a story.

Directions: Read the passage below and answer the questions that follow.

When he was ready and mounted before the door, mounted on his father's saddle that was so old that the oaken frame showed through torn leather in many places, then Mama brought out the round black hat with the tooled leather band, and she reached up and knotted the green silk handkerchief about his neck. Pepé's blue denim coat was much darker than his jeans, for it had been washed much less often.

Mama handed up the big medicine bottle and the silver coins. "That for the medicine," she said, "and that for the salt. That for a candle to burn for papa. That for dulces [candy] for the little ones. Our friend Mrs. Rodriguez will give you dinner and maybe a bed for the night. When you go to the church say only ten Paternosters [the "Our Father" prayer] and only twenty-five Ave Marias [prayers to Mary]. Oh! I know, big coyote. You would sit there flapping your mouth over Aves all day while you looked at the candles and the holy pictures. That is not good devotion to stare at the pretty things."

The black hat, covering the high pointed head and black thatched hair of Pepé, gave him dignity and age. He sat the rangy horse well. Mama thought how handsome he was, dark and lean and tall. "I would not send thee now alone, thou little one, except for the medicine," she said softly. "It is not good to have no medicine, for who knows when the toothache will come, or the sadness of the stomach. These things are."

"Adios, Mama," Pepé cried. "I will come back soon. You may send me often alone. I am a man."

—Excerpted from "Flight" (*The Long Valley*), by John Steinbeck

Skill Review (continued)

1. Do you think Mama will send Pepé to get medicine the next time medicine is needed? Explain your prediction.

_____

_____

_____

2. Write two predictions about what might happen to Pepé after he leaves his mother on his trip to get the medicine.

_____

_____

_____

3. Use a Venn diagram to compare and contrast the feelings of Pepé and Mama about the upcoming trip for medicine. How does Pepé feel? How does Mama feel? Are any of their feelings the same?

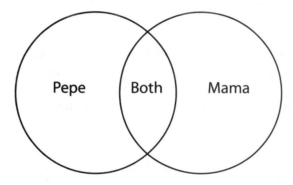

Skill Practice

Directions: Read the passage. Then choose the one best answer to each question.

A Struggle at Sea

After a while the fish stopped beating at the wire and started circling slowly again. The old man was gaining line steadily now. But he felt faint again. He lifted some sea water with his left hand and put it on his head. Then he put more on and rubbed the back of his neck.

"I have no cramps," he said. "He'll be up soon and I can last. You have to last. Don't even speak of it."

> He kneeled against the bow [forward part of a boat] and, for a moment, slipped the line over his back again. I'll rest now while he goes out on the circle and then stand up and work on him when he comes in, he decided.
>
> 10 It was a great temptation to rest in the bow and let the fish make one circle by himself without recovering any line. But when the strain showed the fish had turned to come toward the boat, the old man rose to his feet and started the pivoting [turning] and the weaving pulling that brought in all the line he gained.
>
> —Excerpted from *The Old Man and the Sea*, by Ernest Hemingway

1. Which of Ernest Hemingway's techniques listed below is the most effective for showing the character's thoughts and feelings?

   A. describing the setting of the story
   B. having another character explain what he is feeling
   C. describing the character's actions
   D. having the character speak about his feelings

2. Why does the old man pour sea water on his head?

   A. to cool and revive himself
   B. to scare the fish in the water
   C. to alert others fishing nearby
   D. to stop the boat from drifting

3. The old man says, "He'll be up soon and I can last. You have to last. Don't even speak of it." (lines 4–5)

   What does this tell you about his character?

   A. He is tired and faint.
   B. He is determined and focused.
   C. He is angry and upset.
   D. He is sad and gloomy.

4. In the last line of the story, the old man rises to his feet and pivots. What does this suggest that the old man is doing?

   A. turning the boat around to head to land
   B. catching the fish and reeling it in
   C. overturning the boat
   D. letting the fish get away

Writing Practice

Directions: Choose a character from one of the passages in this lesson or from a book or story you have read. On a sheet of paper, write a description of the character. Provide evidence from the text—from how the character is described, how the character acts and speaks, and what the character is thinking—that demonstrates the character's traits.

Point of View

Lesson Objectives

You will be able to

- Understand point of view
- Identify how point of view affects a story

Skills

- **Core Skill:** Draw Conclusions
- **Reading Skill:** Make inferences

Vocabulary

first-person point of view
identify
inference
logical
perspective
third-person point of view

KEY CONCEPT: Point of view is the way of looking at an issue. In literature, it is the attitude, or outlook, of the person telling the story.

Have you been at a gathering of friends or family where something unusual happened? How do you remember the event? Would others who were there remember the event in the same way, or would they describe it differently? Are you surprised by how people can describe one event in many diffent ways?

Point of View

Point of view refers to how someone understands an event or an idea. When two people describe an event that they both have witnessed, the descriptions might differ because each person speaks from his or her **perspective**, or point of view. Each person's viewpoint is unique. Past experiences influence your perspective on many issues.

In a story, the person telling the story is the narrator. When a story is told in the **first-person point of view**, the narrator is a character in the story. The narrator explains everything in his or her own words and from his or her perspective. The narrator uses the pronouns *I*, *me*, and *we*.

When a story is told in the **third-person point of view**, the narrator is someone outside the story. The story is told by someone who observes what is going on. The narrator describes the action but doesn't take part in it. The pronouns *he, she,* and *they* are used. Occasionally, an author may use more than one narrator, telling a story from several different points of view.

MAKE INFERENCES

Every time you use bits of **evidence**, or information, to figure things out, you are making an **inference**. An inference is a **logical**, or reasonable, guess about something that is not directly stated but is strongly hinted at or implied. Making inferences allows you to learn more about the people, places, or events that you encounter in your reading.

Here is how to practice making inferences:

- Pay attention to what the characters do and say. Notice what other characters say about them.

- Look for words that describe the action or the characters.

- Watch for clues about the author's message. Ask yourself, *What is the author really saying here?*

- Think about what you already know. What personal experiences can you use to make inferences about what you are reading? Ask yourself, *What do I know about this topic from real life?*

Read the passage below. The main idea of the paragraph below is unstated. Use the details to **identify**, or point out, the main idea. What kind of event is this?

> Some drove up in beat-up station wagons and dusty pickup trucks. Other, more citified types arrived in shiny convertibles or new campers. Cousin Otis Barnett, who owned half of the county, brought his family to the occasion in a private jet. Last, but not least, came Jack and Marge Barnett, oldest living members of the clan. They gladly volunteered details about their 22 great-grandchildren.

The main idea of this passage: family members have gathered for a **reunion**, or get together. Did you infer this? Four generations of a family—young and old, rich and poor—have gathered for a special occasion. You simply put the details together to come up with the main idea. Even the vocabulary helps you—*cousin, clan, great-grandchildren.*

Research It
Learn about the Author

The narrator is the person telling the story. The narrator can tell a story from the first-person point of view or from third-person point of view. In a work of fiction, the narrator is not a real person.

The author is the real person who wrote the story. The author is not a participant in the story.

Remember: the author writes the story; the narrator tells it.

Use the Internet to look up biographical information about one author whose work appears in this lesson. Write a paragraph telling how the life experiences of the author might have affected his or her perspective when writing the story.

When you draw a conclusion, you combine details to come up with an new idea. Be sure to consider the point of view that the story is being told from when you draw a conclusion from a passage in a book.

If the story is told from the first-person point of view, ask yourself whether the narrator is honest or whether the narrator is exaggerating or lying. A third-person narrator is more likely to tell describe events objectively.

Read through the passages on this page. Choose one of the narratives. What conclusions can you draw from the passage? Keep the narrator in mind as you think about the passage.

Write a paragraph in a notebook stating your conclusions and providing evidence for them.

WRITE TO LEARN

In a notebook, answer this question: What conclusion can you make about what is happening in passage 3 on this page?

Use details from the story and your own experiences to support your conclusion.

Directions: Read the short passages below. Use details in the excerpts to determine whether the story is written from the first-person point of view or the third-person point of view. If the story is told in the first person, identify the narrator.

1. Mrs. Pocket was sitting on a garden chair under a tree, reading, with her legs upon another garden chair; and Mrs. Pocket's two nursemaids were looking about them while the children played. "Mamma," said Herbert, "this is young Mr. Pip." Upon which Mrs. Pocket received me with an appearance of amiable dignity.

   —Excerpted from *Great Expectations*, by Charles Dickens

2. Albert went away regretfully, but the drayman [the driver of a dray, a type of wagon] and some of the Methodist ladies were in Mr. Holliday's yard, packing chairs and tables and ice-cream freezers into the wagon, and the twins forgot the sick cat in their excitement. By noon they had picked up the last paper napkin, raked over the gravel walks where the salt from the freezers had left white patches, and hung the hammock in which Vickie did her studying back in place.

   —Excerpted from *Old Mrs. Harris*, by Willa Cather

3. And right there he'd stay, watching that door like a hawk until I came through it again. Well he'd just have to watch it for a while; I was doing the best I could.

   —Excerpted from *The Sound and the Fury*, by William Faulkner

4. And she told her sister, as well as she could remember them, all these strange Adventures of hers that you have just been reading about; and, when she had finished, her sister kissed her, and said "It was a curious dream, dear, certainly; but now run in to your tea; it's getting late." So Alice got up and ran off, thinking while she ran, as well as she might, what a wonderful dream it had been.

   —Excerpted from *Alice's Adventures in Wonderland*, by Lewis Carroll

5. We were there for many hours. I remember the search boats and the sunset when dusk came. I had never seen a sunset like that: a bright orange flame touching the water's edge and then fanning out, warming the sea.

   —Excerpted from *The Joy Luck Club*, by Amy Tan

THINK ABOUT **READING**

Directions: For the five passages above, determine who is telling the story. Write an *O* in the blank if an outside narrator is telling the story. Write a *P* if the narrator is a participant in the story.

_____ Passage 1   _____ Passage 3   _____ Passage 5

_____ Passage 2   _____ Passage 4

Directions: Read about the characters and the action that is taking place in this excerpt from *The War of the Worlds*. Circle words that help you draw a conclusion about who is telling the story.

As I drew nearer I heard Stent's voice: "Keep back! Keep back!"

A boy came running toward me.

"It's a-movin'," he said to me as he passed—"a-screwin' and a-screwin' out. I don't like it, I'm a-goin' 'ome, I am."

I went to the crowd. There were really, I should think, two or three hundred people elbowing and jostling one another, the one or two ladies there being by no means the least active.

"He's falling in the pit!" cried someone.

"Keep back!" said several.

The crowd swayed a little, and I elbowed my way through. Everyone seemed greatly excited. I heard a peculiar humming sound from the pit.

"I say," said Ogilvy, "help keep the idiots back. We don't know what's in the confounded [strange] thing, you know."

I saw a young man, a shop assistant in Woking I believe he was, standing on the cylinder and trying to scramble out of the hole again. The crowd had pushed him in.

The end of the cylinder was being screwed out from within. Nearly two feet of shining screw projected. Somebody had blundered against me, and I narrowly missed being pitched on the top of the screw. I turned, and as I did so the screw must have come out, for the lid of the cylinder fell upon the gravel with a ringing concussion. I struck my elbow into the person behind me, and turned my head towards the Thing again. For a moment that circular cavity seemed perfectly black. I had the sunset in my eyes.

—Excerpted from *The War of the Worlds*, by H. G. Wells

THINK ABOUT **READING**

Directions: Answer the following question.

Is this excerpt told from the first-person or third-person point of view? How do you know?

_____

_____

_____

Authors directly state some facts and ideas, but often they leave other things unsaid. Then you have to make an inference, or combine what you know from your own experiences with the details in the story to figure out what is going on.

When a story is written in the first-person point of view, you may be given details about what the narrator is thinking.

In this excerpt from *Adventures of Huckleberry Finn*, we are not told directly what might happen to Huck. Instead, we are given indirect information about what is taking place. Since Huck himself is the one giving the information, we are learning only what Huck understands and what he wants us to know.

In a notebook, make an inference about the relationships between Huck and Pap and between Huck and the widow. Ask yourself: *Is Huck afraid of Pap? What is Pap trying to do? Does Huck want to go to the widow? Why or why not?*

Directions: Read the passage below. Pay attention to who the narrator is and what the narrator's relationship is to Pap. Then answer the questions.

Pap wasn't in a good humor—so he was his natural self. He said he was down to town, and everything was going wrong. His lawyer said he reckoned he would win his lawsuit and get the money, if they ever got started on the trial; but then there was ways to put it off a long time
5   and Judge Thatcher knowed how to do it. And he said people allowed there'd be another trial to get me away from him and give me back to the widow for my guardian, and they guessed it would win, this time. This shook me up considerable, because I didn't want to go back to the widow's any more and be so cramped up and sivilized, as they called it.
10 Then the old man got to cussing and cussed everything and everybody he could think of, and then cussed them all over again to make sure he hadn't skipped any, and after that he polished off with a kind of a general cuss all round, including a considerable parcel of people which he didn't know the names of, and so called them what's-his-name, when
15 he got to them, and went right along with his cussing.

He said he would like to see the widow get me. He said he would watch out, and if they tried to come any such game on him he knowed of a place six or seven mile off, to stow me in, where they might hunt till they dropped and they couldn't find me. That made me pretty uneasy
20 again, but only for a minute; I reckoned I wouldn't stay on hand till he got that chance.

—Excerpted from *Adventures of Huckleberry Finn*,
by Mark Twain

THINK ABOUT **READING**

Directions: Answer these questions.

1. From which point of view is this story told?

    A. first-person point of view
    B. third-person point of view
    C. several points of view
    D. Pap's point of view

2. How does the narrator seem to feel toward Pap?

    A. affectionate and loving
    B. amused and comfortable
    C. afraid and anxious
    D. surprised and delighted

3. The narrator says, "This shook me up considerable, because I didn't want to go back to the widow's any more and be so cramped up and sivilized, as they called it." (lines 8–9)

    What does this tell you about the narrator?

    _____

    _____

Vocabulary Review

Directions: Use these words to complete the following sentences.

first-person   logical   perspective   third-person

1. A narrator who is a participant in a story tells that story in the _____ point of view.

2. You should make _____ conclusions based on details and your own experiences.

3. An outside narrator tells stories in the _____ point of view.

4. The story is told from the _____ of one of the supporting characters.

Skill Review

Directions: Read the following passage and answer the questions that follow.

Anger Management

"Anger is just hurt covered over," Aunt Rosie had said. "If you want to solve the problem, stay in touch with the hurt. Don't let the anger take over or you'll never get anything worked out. The ego uses anger to build a fence around itself so it won't get hurt again."

I heard the click of the door. "Stay in touch with the hurt," I told myself. I thought about her advice. Les was late again. He'd said he'd be home by six. It was nearly 8:30.

Les stood hesitantly, as if I were going to throw something.

"Sorry I'm late," he said softly. He had tired lines around his eyes and mouth. His shoulders drooped.

"I felt really hurt that you weren't here when you said you would be. I fixed a really nice dinner, but it's all cold now," I said.

"I'm sorry. I couldn't even call. The boss insisted I go out to that new construction site and settle the change of plans with the foreman. I couldn't even get to a phone to call you. . . . Thanks for not being mad."

Aunt Rosie was right, I thought. If I had hit him full tilt with anger, we'd have just had a big fight. I smiled at him.

"Well, it can't be undone now, I guess," I told him. I wasn't feeling angry anymore.

Les put down his briefcase and drew me into his arms. "Tell you what," he said, "how 'bout Friday night, we'll go out to eat—just to make up for tonight's ruined dinner?"

"OK," I agreed. Then to myself I said, "Thanks, Aunt Rosie, you were right. If you want to solve the problem, don't let anger take over. Stay in touch with the hurt."

Skill Review (continued)

1. Which statement best states the main idea of the passage?

   A. Inconsiderate behavior can destroy a marriage.
   B. Aunt Rosie can't resist interfering.
   C. Anger is pain in disguise.
   D. Les is overworked.

2. Which is a logical inference based on the passage?

   A. Aunt Rosie is a busybody.
   B. Aunt Rosie is a wise woman.
   C. Les intended to make his wife angry.
   D. Adults are not able to change their patterns of behavior.

3. Suppose a neighbor carelessly trampled some flowers you had just planted. What would Aunt Rosie most likely advise you to do?

   A. Say nothing and plant new flowers.
   B. Confront the neighbor and demand to know how a person could be so careless.
   C. Insist that the neighbor repay you what the flowers cost.
   D. Quietly tell the neighbor how this carelessness has upset you.

4. Do you think the narrator will change her mind about Aunt Rosie's advice? Explain why or why not.

   _____

   _____

   _____

   _____

5. Draw two conclusions about the importance of Aunt Rosie's advice. Use details in the passage and your own experience to support your conclusions.

   _____

   _____

   _____

   _____

   _____

Skill Practice

Directions: Read the passage. Then answer the questions.

> The night was not so pleasant as the evening, for it got chilly; and being put between two gentlemen (the rough-faced one and another) to prevent my tumbling off the coach [a carriage pulled by horses], I was nearly smothered by their falling asleep, and completely blocking me up. They squeezed me so hard sometimes, that I could not help crying out, "Oh, if you please!" which they didn't like at all, because it woke them. Opposite me was an elderly lady in a great fur cloak, who looked in the dark more like a haystack than a lady, she was wrapped up to such a degree. This lady had a basket with her, and she hadn't known what to do with it, for a long time, until she found that, on account of my legs being short, it could go underneath me. It cramped and hurt me so, that it made me perfectly miserable; but if I moved in the least, and made a glass that was in the basket rattle against something else (as it was sure to do), she gave me the cruelest poke with her foot, and said, "Come, don't you fidget. Your bones are young enough, I'm sure!"
>
> —Excerpted from *David Copperfield*, by Charles Dickens

1. From which point of view is this story told?
   A. third-person point of view
   B. first-person point of view
   C. point of view of the gentlemen in the coach
   D. point of view of the lady in the coach

2. Which statement describes the use of first-person point of view?
   A. It is told from the point of view of all the characters in a story.
   B. The narrator does not tell his or her own views.
   C. The story is told by someone who is not a character in the story.
   D. The narrator uses the pronouns *I, me,* and *we* to tell the story.

3. Which statement about the coach ride would the narrator most likely make?
   A. My ride in the coach was comfortable.
   B. My companions were friendly.
   C. My coach ride was uncomfortable and upsetting.
   D. The lady treated me in a kind, reassuring way.

4. If the story were told from the elderly lady's point of view, which thoughts and feelings would be described?
   A. only the thoughts and feelings of the coach driver
   B. only the thoughts and feelings of the two gentlemen
   C. the thoughts and feelings of all the people in the coach
   D. only the thoughts and feelings of the elderly lady

Writing Practice

Directions: Write a short scene from the first-person point of view about a tense encounter between two characters. Then write the same scene from the point of view of the other character. Compare your two scenes. Finally, write a few sentences describing how the change in point of view changed the scene.

Literal and Figurative Language

Lesson Objectives

You will be able to
- Recognize effective word choice and sentence structure
- Identify how the use of language affects writing

Skills

- **Core Skill:** Analyze Word Choice
- **Reading Skill:** Analyze Text Structure

Vocabulary

connotation
denotation
emotion
figurative
literal

KEY CONCEPT: Literal and figurative language helps create effective and expressive word choices in writing.

What do you mean when you say "KNOCK IT OFF!" to a friend? You want your friend to stop joking around. "Knock it off" gets your point across. Your friends know what you mean. This is an example of figurative language. To express the same idea using literal language, you would say, "Stop it." Authors use literal or figurative language depending on the tone they want to create.

Literal and Figurative Language

In the following conversation, a group of students talk about taking an important test. Joe and Antonio use **figurative** language to express their feelings. Figurative language is used to create pictures in our minds.

JOE: I'm on pins and needles about this test. Aren't you worried, Janelle?

JANELLE: Of course not. I've been studying.

ANTONIO: Janelle, you are always as cool as a cucumber. But not me. I'm shaking like a leaf.

Joe is not sitting "on pins and needles," and he is not "shaking like a leaf." Janelle's temperature is not really "as cool as a cucumber."

If Joe and Antonio were saying exactly what they meant, they would be using **literal** language. However, saying "I am nervous" and "You are relaxed" is not as interesting as the words the boys chose. Figurative speech is often a powerful way to show **emotion**, or feelings.

THINK ABOUT **READING**

Directions: Match each figurative expression with its meaning.

Figurative Expressions
_____ 1. raining cats and dogs
_____ 2. head in the clouds
_____ 3. with hair standing on end
_____ 4. like death warmed over
_____ 5. hit the jackpot
_____ 6. like two peas in a pod
_____ 7. beat around the bush
_____ 8. keep your shirt on

Meanings
A. visibly afraid
B. sickly in appearance
C. alike in every way
D. downpour
E. give unclear answers
F. a great achievement or success
G. not practical
H. stay calm

MAKE CONNECTIONS TO TEXTS

Characters, setting, and plot are the elements that make up a work of fiction. When you read, try to connect these elements to your own life or to people, places, and events that you know about. By making these connections, you can often visualize a scene in your mind. This not only helps you understand the text, it will also helps you understand the figurative language.

Here are three important types of connections.

- **Text-to-self connection:** a connection between what you are reading and something that has occurred in your life. Thinking about something that has happened to you can help you understand what the characters are doing, thinking, and feeling.

- **Text-to-text connection:** a connection between what you are reading and another selection you are familiar with. This might be a reading passage, but it can be a film, a song, or TV show. The connection could be a similar theme or setting, or it could be something similar in the characters' actions or feelings.

- **Text-to-world connection:** a connection between what you are reading and something that is happening in the world. What you know of real places or events can help you interpret events in the story.

Read the following passage. Think of what connections you can make to the text. Visualize what the author is describing so you understand the figurative language.

A shoe by the side of the road is an untold story. Where is the mate? How did it get there? People are curious about a shoe lying on the side of a road. Sometimes they come up with explanations for why the shoe is where it is. But no one knows about the shoe for sure. These single roadside shoes are silent. They don't share their secrets.

Did you make a connection to a personal experience? Did you find a connection to another story you have read? What figurative language does the author use?

Core Skill
Analyze Word Choice

The **denotation** of a word expresses the word's meaning, as found in a dictionary. For example, literally, a weasel is a small mammal. Here is the dictionary definition of the word *weasel*:

wea•sel \wēzəl\ *n* A small animal that has a slender body, short legs, a long neck, and soft, thick fur. *pl* **weasels**

The **connotation** of a word is its suggested meaning. A word's connotation can be positive or negative. In the following paragraph, *weasel* is used figuratively. The word has a negative connotation.

Johnny can be a weasel at times. He's sneaky, and I don't trust him.

Write two sentences for each of the following words. In the first sentence, use the word literally; in the second, use the word figuratively.

- gold

- star

- chicken

The passage on this page describes an event that took place during the Great Depression, which occurred in the 1930s. Many farmers lost their jobs because new machines could do their work. In addition, drought was destroying the farmland.

As you read, think about connections that you can make in order to understand the selection.

- Do the characters remind me of people I know or have read about?

- What other historical event can I make a connection to?

- Do I know of something happening in the world today that is similar?

Share your answers with a partner. Discuss the connections you were each able to make.

WRITE TO LEARN

In a notebook, use ideas from your conversation above to write a paragraph about a specific connection you made to this passage.

Directions: As you read the passage below, underline (or highlight) examples of figurative language.

Tractors Take Over

The tractors came over the roads and into the fields, great crawlers moving like insects, having the incredible strength of insects. They crawled over the ground, laying the track and rolling on it and picking it up. Diesel tractors, puttering while they stood idle; they thundered
5 when they moved, and then settled down to a droning roar. Snubnosed monsters, raising the dust and sticking their snouts into it, straight down the country, across the country, through fences, through dooryards, in and out of gullies [valleys] in straight lines. They did not run on the ground, but on their own roadbeds. They ignored
10 hills and gulches, water courses, fences, houses.

The man sitting in the iron seat did not look like a man; gloved, goggled, rubber dust mask over nose and mouth, he was a part of the monster, a robot in the seat. The thunder of the cylinder sounded through the country, became one with the air and the
15 earth, so that earth and air muttered in sympathetic [shared] vibration. The driver could not control it—straight across country it went, cutting through a dozen farms and straight back.

—Excerpted from *The Grapes of Wrath*, by John Steinbeck

THINK ABOUT **READING**

Directions: Answer the following questions.

1. What does the first paragraph describe?
   - A. monsters
   - B. tractors
   - C. insects
   - D. robots

2. In the first sentence, what does the phrase "moving like insects" indicate about the machines?
   - A. They flew over the ground.
   - B. They kicked up dust.
   - C. They crawled across the ground.
   - D. They moved quickly.

3. The author describes the driver of the traffic as "a part of the monster, a robot in the seat" (lines 12–13). How does the author feel about the driver?
   - A. He is cold and uncaring.
   - B. He is doing a good job.
   - C. He is smart to use the tractor to plant more crops.
   - D. He is a robotic machine.

4. The author writes, "they thundered when they moved" (lines 4–5). Is this literal or figurative language? Explain your response.

_____

_____

Vocabulary Review

Directions: Use these words to complete the following sentences.

connotation denotation emotion figurative literal

1. When you feel strongly about something, you show _____.

2. You are using _____ language when you choose words that create a mental image.

3. _____ is the suggested meaning of a word, not its actual meaning.

4. _____ is the description of a word that you would find in the dictionary.

5. When you use _____ language, you say exactly what you mean.

Skill Review

Directions: Read this passage from *The Wind in the Willows* and answer the questions that follow.

> There was nothing to alarm him at first entry. Twigs crackled under his feet, logs tripped him, funguses on stumps resembled caricatures, and startled him for the moment by their likeness to something familiar and far away; but that was all fun, and exciting.
> 5 It led him on, and he penetrated [forced his way] to where the light was less, and trees crouched nearer and nearer, and holes made ugly mouths at him on either side.
>
> Everything was very still now. The dusk advanced on him steadily, rapidly, gathering in behind and before; and the light seemed to be
> 10 draining away like floodwater.
>
> Then the faces began.
>
> It was over his shoulder, and indistinctly [not clearly], that he first thought he saw a face: a little evil wedge-shaped face, looking out at him from a hole. When he turned and confronted it, the thing had vanished.
>
> 15 He quickened his pace, telling himself cheerfully not to begin imagining things, or there would be simply no end to it. He passed another hole, and another, and another; and then—yes! no!—yes! certainly a little narrow face, with hard eyes, had flashed up for an instant from a hole, and was gone. He hesitated—braced himself up
> 20 for an effort, and strode on. Then suddenly, and as if it had been so all the time, every hole, far and near, and there were hundreds of them, seemed to possess its face, coming and going rapidly, all fixing on him glances of malice and hatred: all hard-eyed and evil and sharp.

TECHNOLOGY CONNECTION

Internet Resources

Figurative language is one of the most difficult aspects of any language. Knowing the literal meaning of the individual words does not not help you understand a figure of speech like *raining cats and dogs*.

Luckily, there are many resources available. To find the meaning of a figure of speech, type the phrase into an Internet search engine.

Also on the Internet you can find websites that list examples of figurative language.

Try for yourself! Look up three examples of figurative language from this lesson. Write the meanings of these phrases in a notebook.

25   If he could only get away from the holes in the banks, he thought, there would be no more faces. He swung off the pace and plunged into the untrodden [not walked on] places of the wood.

     Then the whistling began.

30   Very faint and shrill it was, and far behind him, when first he heard it; but somehow it made him hurry forward. Then, still very faint and shrill, it sounded far ahead of him, and made him hesitate and want to go back. As he halted in indecision it broke out on either side, and seemed to be caught up and passed on through out the whole length of the woods to its furthest limit. They were up and alert and ready, evidently, whoever they were! And he—he was alone, and unarmed, and far from any help; and the night was closing in.

35   Then the pattering began.

    —Excerpted from *The Wind in the Willows*, by Kenneth Grahame

1. Is the phrase "the night was closing in" (line 34) an example of literal or figurative language? Describe what the author means by this phrase.

_____

2. How does the author's use of literal and figurative language enhance the description of what the character is feeling?

_____

3. In this passage, the character experiences an increasing sense of fear as he continues walking. Have you ever felt scared by a dark night, a strange noise, or an odd shape? Connect this passage to an event in your life when you felt scared.

_____

_____

4. If you were the character in this passage, would you have responded to your fears in the same way? Explain why or why not.

_____

_____

Directions: Choose the one best answer to the question.

5. In paragraph 5 of the passage, the author writes, "yes! certainly a little narrow face, with hard eyes, had flashed up for an instant from a hole, and was gone" (lines 17–19).

What connotation does the word *hard* have in this sentence?

A. a positive connotation
B. a negative connotation
C. something that has a hard surface
D. something that is soft and yielding

Skill Practice

Directions: Read the passage and answer the questions.

> Meme has a dog with gray eyes, a sheepdog with two names, one in English and one in Spanish. The dog is big, like a man dressed in a dog suit, and runs the same way its owner does, clumsy and wild and with the limbs flopping all over the place like untied shoes.
>
> Cathy's father built the house Meme moved into. It is wooden. Inside the floors slant. Some
> 5 rooms uphill. Some down. And there are no closets. Out from there are twenty-one steps, all lopsided and jutting like crooked teeth (made that way on purpose, Cathy said, so the rain will slide off), and when Meme's mama calls from the doorway, Meme goes scrambling up the twenty-one wooden stairs with the dog with two names scrambling after him.
>
> Around the back is a yard, mostly dirt, and a greasy bunch of boards that used to be a
> 10 garage. But what you remember most is this tree, huge, with fat arms and mighty families of squirrels in the higher branches. All around, the neighborhood of roofs, black-tarred and A-framed, and in their gutters, the balls that never came back down to earth. Down at the base of the tree, the dog with two names barks into the empty air, and there at the end of the block, looking smaller still, our house with its feet tucked under like a cat.
>
> —Excerpted from *The House on Mango Street*, by Sandra Cisneros

1. Which phrase is an example of figurative language?

   A. "Cathy's father built the house"
   B. "Meme has a dog with gray eyes"
   C. "Inside the floors slant."
   D. "this tree, huge, with fat arms"

2. What is the writer saying about the dog when she says that he was "like a man dressed in a dog suit" (line 2)?

   A. The dog is small.
   B. The dog is funny.
   C. The dog is large.
   D. The dog is playful.

3. Which phrase is an example of literal language?

   A. "with the limbs flopping all over the place like untied shoes"
   B. "twenty-one steps, all lopsided and jutting like crooked teeth"
   C. "a sheepdog with two names, one in English and one in Spanish"
   D. "Inside the floors slant. Some rooms uphill. Some down."

4. Which of the author's techniques is most effective for developing the character of Meme?

   A. using figurative language
   B. using literal language
   C. using long, complex sentences
   D. using references to animal

Writing Practice

Directions: Write a description of something you experienced recently. Use figurative language to enhance the mood of your description.

Lesson Objectives

You will be able to

• Identify and interpret themes

• Understand a theme's connection to setting, character, and plot

Skills

• **Core Skill:** Determine Theme

• **Reading Skill:** Compare Themes in Different Genres

Vocabulary

conclusion
motivate
relationship
strategy
universal

KEY CONCEPT: The theme is the central idea or message in a work of fiction.

Have you ever learned something important about life from watching a movie or reading a book? Do you remember the message from a story that taught you a life lesson? This was the author's message, or theme, in the story. Authors often have a message they want readers to think about as they read.

Theme

The **theme** of a work of fiction is the message about life that the author wants the reader to understand. Some stories have a stated theme. More often, a story has a theme that is not directly stated. Instead, it is revealed through plot, character, setting, or point of view.

Certain themes are **universal**. They are relevant to everyone, in all times and in all places. These universal themes appear over and over in literature and in films. Here are some of the most common universal themes.

Example	Theme
Huckleberry Finn	Life is a struggle between right and wrong.
Lord of the Rings	Good will defeat evil.
Gone with the Wind	Difficult situations can be overcome by determination.

There are, of course, many other themes as well. Writers sometimes combine several themes in a single novel or short story. These suggestions can help you figure out a story's theme.

• Think about the story's title. Does it help you understand the writer's message?

• Review what happens to the main character. Does the character change during the story? What does the character learn about life?

• Skim for key phrases that say something in general about life or people.

UNDERSTAND RELATIONSHIPS BETWEEN IDEAS

When you read, it is important to identify connections between ideas. Making connections is a helpful **strategy**, or a skill, that you can use when reading new material.

As you read, think about the **relationships**, or connections, between ideas. Here are examples of relationships you can find as you read:

- The main idea is supported by details. This connection between the main idea and the details ties together parts of the the text.

- One event may cause another event to occur. This is called a cause-and-effect relationship.

- Comparisons and contrasts may connect ideas. Knowing how people, places, or things are similar or different helps you understand what the author thinks is important.

- Similar ideas are found throughout life. Make connections between what you are reading and what you already have learned or what you have experienced. Ask yourself how ideas are the same and how they are different.

To figure out the author's message, ask yourself, *What does one idea have to do with another?* Understanding how ideas are connected can help you determine a story's theme, or message.

Read the following paragraph. Think about the relationships between ideas. What connections can you make?

All his life, Antonio had to work hard to make a living. He knew only one person who didn't seem to have to work—the storekeeper who owned the shop where Antonio worked. When Antonio learned how much money he would need to open a shop of his own, he became obsessed with saving money. In fact, he became quite stingy and miserly. Even when his own siblings needed his help, he resented their requests and refused to help them.

In this passage, there is a cause-and-effect relationship. Antonio wants to open up a store—that is the cause. Antonio becomes stingy and miserly—that is the effect. What do you think is the theme of this passage?

Media Literacy
Compare Themes

Like books, multimedia works such as movies and TV programs have themes. The writer has a message about life that viewers should understand. Viewers use visual and aural elements—that is, sights and sounds—to identify the theme.

For example, the movie adaptations of J. R. R. Tolkien's *Lord of the Rings* books have a theme of "good overcomes evil."

In a notebook, name a favorite movie or TV program. Then write one sentence stating its theme. What message about life does the writer want you to understand?

Presently he proceeded again on his forward way. The battle was like the grinding of an immense and terrible machine to him. Its complexities and powers, its grim processes, fascinated him. He must go close and see it produce corpses.

He came to a fence and clambered over it. On the far side, the ground was littered with clothes and guns. A newspaper, folded up, lay in the dirt. A dead soldier was stretched with face hidden in his arm. Farther off there was a group of four or five corpses keeping mournful company. A hot sun had blazed upon the spot.

In this place the youth felt that he was an invader. This forgotten part of the battle ground was owned by the dead men, and he hurried, in the vague apprehension [fear] that one of the swollen forms would rise and tell him to begone.

He came finally to a road from which he could see in the distance dark and agitated bodies of troops, smoke-fringed. In the lane was a blood-stained crowd streaming to the rear. The wounded men were cursing, groaning, and wailing. In the air, always, was a mighty swell of sound that it seemed could sway the earth. With the courageous words of the artillery and the spiteful sentences of the musketry mingled red cheers. And from this region of noises came the steady current of the maimed [wounded].

One of the wounded men had a shoeful of blood. He hopped like a schoolboy in a game. He was laughing hysterically.

One was swearing that he had been shot in the arm through the commanding general's mismanagement of the army. One was marching with an air imitative of some sublime drum major. Upon his features was an unholy mixture of merriment and agony.

—Excerpted from *The Red Badge of Courage*, by Stephen Crane

THINK ABOUT **READING**

Directions: Circle the best answer to the question.

Which of the following best states the theme of this passage?

A. If you are not prepared for battle, you will be gravely injured.
B. Victory brings honor and glory.
C. War brings pain and misery.
D. One victory does not decide a war.

Directions: As you read this story, think about the theme, or the message the author is trying to communicate to readers.

Estara walked carefully between the yawning craters of Novos. Moments before, her bubble rocket had crash-landed on a ridge of soft volcanic sand. Little was left of the vast meteor shower that had carried her off course, hurling the rocket into this strange place.

She stared into the black void of space. Somewhere out there was a burning cinder or perhaps a swirl of smoky debris. That was all one would find of planet Earth. Because of the Great A-War, she and thousands like her had sought a way out of the annihilation [sudden death]. The famous bubble rockets were the answer, but only a few people had been able to secure them. She was sure the rest had perished.

Where were the others, she wondered? Did they reach the earthlike planet Geos, or did they too lose their way?

Ahead of her, Estara saw rocks of many colors, and they glowed. She heard an odd sound like water rushing over rocks. She listened more closely for other sounds. Suddenly there was a noise like a squeal, perhaps human but possibly an animal. She was not sure. She pulled out her laser gun, stopped, and listened again. Was she safe, or was she about to confront an alien? Estara did not know, but she was not going to take any chances.

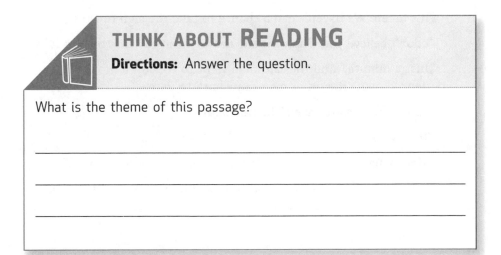

THINK ABOUT **READING**

Directions: Answer the question.

What is the theme of this passage?

_____

_____

_____

Core Skill
Determine Theme

The theme of a book or story usually isn't stated outright. It is the message you understand by reading "between the lines." Different people may find different themes in the same book.

To determine the theme, you must draw **conclusions**, that is, make general statements about the people, places, events, and ideas of the story.

Active readers often draw conclusions about what characters are doing or thinking. They ask themselves what **motivates** (encourages) the characters to behave in a certain way. For example, drawing a conclusion about why a character is unhappy may help you discover the theme of a story.

As you read the passage on this page, note places where you find yourself drawing conclusions that help you understand the overall message. *What has happened to Estara? Where is she? What has happened to the others? What might happen next?*

In a notebook, record the conclusions you draw about Estara as you read.

The passages on pages
223 and 224 represent
different genres. The
passage on page 223
is science fiction. The
passage on this page is
realistic fiction.

Sometimes two texts
have similar characters
or settings. Sometimes
they have similar
themes—even when the
texts are very different.

In a notebook, compare
or contrast the themes
of these two passages.
If they are different,
why are they different?
If they are the same or
similar, explain how such
different stories could
have similar themes.

Directions: As you read the passage below, note the setting, plot, and characters. These elements will help you identify the theme.

He could just see himself in a new home with a nice back yard, nice trees and lawn, a patio with a barbecue—these things he'd never had, never missed. But why not? A nice garage with a little workshop, like the gringo magazines show all the time. It would be fun.

The more he thought about it, the more he liked the idea. What he enjoyed most was the ability he now had—the freedom due to his financial success—that allowed him to make a decision to move where he wanted. This was a luxury little known in his environment. And on the way home from his various out-of-town jobs he began dropping in to look at houses in new tract developments.

It was an old story, but new to Pete. The ghetto protects as well as imprisons. As he drove along in the burgeoning [growing] suburbs, he saw tract after tract, with signs advertising the homes for miles in all directions.

Pete almost believed it when the salesman at the first office where he stopped told him there were no homes available. He didn't want to argue. But a few days later, when he'd stopped at the fifth or sixth tract office, he was a little better prepared. Not much, but a little.

"No, I'm sorry, Mr. Sandoval. The houses are all taken."

"Well, that one on the corner, it has a for sale sign on it. I want that one."

"It's taken. We haven't had a chance to take the sign down yet."

"I don't believe you. Show me the name of the guy that bought it."

"Just a minute," and the salesman went to consult a more experienced man. The other man came back to Pete.

"All our homes are taken," he said simply.

"Then why . . . "

"Make what you want of it, sir, but we have none to sell you."

—Excerpted from *Chicano*, by Richard Vasquez

THINK ABOUT **READING**

Directions: Answer to these questions.

1. What is Pete doing?

   A. mowing his lawn
   B. looking for a house
   C. applying for a job as a salesman
   D. exploring a new town

2. What does Pete expect at first?

   A. The good houses will all be gone.
   B. The salesmen will try to sell him something.
   C. His money will buy him whatever he wants.
   D. His wife will not like his choice.

3. What is the salesmen's attitude toward Pete?

   A. avoidance
   B. fear
   C. helpfulness
   D. hostility

4. Which of the following statements best expresses the theme of this passage?

   A. Everyone dreams about a better life.
   B. Prejudices are easily overcome.
   C. Financial success is no guarantee against discrimination.
   D. You just have to work for what you want and you will get it.

5. What details in the story help you figure out the theme?

   _____

   _____

   _____

WRITE TO **LEARN**

Write three paragraphs about your favorite work of fiction—either a novel or a short story.

In the first paragraph, describe the setting. In the second, summarize the plot. In the third, identify the theme.

Be sure to give at least one specific example of how the setting, plot, or characterization helps you determine the theme.

Comparing Theme across Genres

Every work of fiction, regardless of its genre, has a theme. Realistic fiction, historical fiction, science fiction, fairy tales, plays, and short stories all have at least one theme. Some themes are universal, or so common that they appear in almost every genre and culture. Because the most powerful themes reflect our own experiences, it makes sense that some themes appear again and again.

The method for determining theme is the same in any genre. Use details and clues the author provides about character, setting, and plot to draw conclusions about the author's message.

Since "theme" means the same thing in every genre, it is possible to compare and contrast themes across genres. Look for similarities and differences in the messages of different stories. Different genres might have more in common with each other than you think!

Directions: As you read the passage below, think about its genre and theme. Write a paragraph that describes both, using evidence from the text to support your ideas.

I hear America singing, the varied carols I hear,
Those of mechanics, each one singing his as it should be blithe and
    strong,
The carpenter singing his as he measures his plank or beam,
The mason singing his as he makes ready for work, or leaves off work,
The boatman singing what belongs to him in his boat, the deckhand
    singing on the steamboat deck,
The shoemaker singing as he sits on his bench, the hatter singing
    as he stands,
The wood-cutter's song, the ploughboy's on his way in the morning,
    or at noon intermission or at sundown,
The delicious singing of the mother, or of the young wife at work,
    or of the girl sewing or washing,
Each singing what belongs to him or her and to none else,
The day what belongs to the day—at night the party of young
    fellows, robust, friendly,
Singing with open mouths their strong melodious songs.

—"I Hear America Singing," by Walt Whitman

Directions: As you read the passage below, think about its genre and theme. Identify how the passage is similar to the passage on the previous page and how it is different.

WALTER *(Gathering Travis up in his arms)* You know what, Travis? In seven years you going to be seventeen years old. And things is going to be very different with us in seven years, Travis. . . . One day when you are seventeen I'll come home—home from my office downtown somewhere—

TRAVIS You don't work in no office, Daddy.

WALTER No—but after tonight. After what your daddy gonna do tonight, there's going to be offices—a whole lot of offices. . . .

TRAVIS What you gonna do tonight, Daddy?

WALTER You wouldn't understand yet, son, but your daddy's gonna make a transaction . . . a business transaction that's going to change our lives. . . . That's how come one day when you 'bout seventeen years old I'll come home and I'll be pretty tired, you know what I mean, after a day of conferences and secretaries getting things wrong the way they do . . . 'cause an executive's life is hell, man—*(The more he talks the farther away he gets)* And I'll pull the car up on the driveway . . . just a plain black Chrysler, I think, with whitewalls—no—black tires. More elegant. Rich people don't have to be flashy . . . though I'll have to get something a little sportier for Ruth— maybe a Cadillac convertible to do her shopping in. . . . And I'll come up the steps to the house and the gardener will be clipping away at the hedges and he'll say, "Good evening, Mr. Younger." And I'll say, "Hello, Jefferson, how are you this evening?" And I'll go inside and Ruth will come downstairs and meet me at the door and we'll kiss each other and she'll take my arm and we'll go up to your room to see you sitting on the floor with the catalogues of all the great schools in America around you. . . . All the great schools in the world! And—and I'll say, all right son—it's your seventeenth birthday, what is it you've decided? . . . Just tell me where you want to go to school and you'll go. Just tell me, what it is you want to be—and you'll be it. . . . Whatever you want to be—Yessir! *(He holds his arms open fot TRAVIS)* You just name it, son . . . *(TRAVIS leaps into them)* and I hand you the world!

(WALTER's voice has risen in pitch and hysterical promise and on the last line he lifts TRAVIS high)

(Blackout)

—Excerpted from *A Raisin in the Sun*, by Lorraine Hansberry

THINK ABOUT **READING**

Directions: Answer the questions.

1. What are the genres of the passages on these two pages?

   _____

2. These two passages share a theme. In one sentence, identify the theme of these two passages.

   _____

3. What details from the passages did you use to determine the theme?

   _____

   _____

Vocabulary Review

Directions: Match each vocabulary word with its definition.

1. _____ conclusion **A.** connection between ideas or people

2. _____ motivate **B.** general statement about ideas or people

3. _____ relationship **C.** common throughout the world

4. _____ universal **D.** encourage someone to act in a certain way

Skill Review

Directions: Read the passage below. Then answer the questions that follow.

Most of these people didn't have any real idea of what it was like to be rich. Benny Briggs just couldn't understand that anybody could own a whole pond. Something like a pond would just be *there*, and wouldn't belong to anybody any more than the Atlantic Ocean belonged to anybody. Oh, he knew he wasn't supposed to swim in it. For people like the Briggses, there were a lot of things they weren't supposed to do. But they did them anyway, if they figured they could get away with it.

I knew about that, too, because when I was little and first came to live in the gatehouse on the Winchester estate, I was scared of doing nearly everything. I figured I wasn't allowed to ride my bike on the driveway or play ball on the grass, and I wouldn't go into the big house unless somebody told me to, and wouldn't go in by the front door, either, but always went in through the laundry room.

I'd got over a lot of that from hanging around with Ernest, who could do what he pleased and go wherever he wanted. He rode his bike on the driveway and played ball on the grass, and I went along with him. But I still wouldn't go into the big house unless I had a reason for it, and I still always went in through the laundry room, unless it was Christmas or Thanksgiving and I went up with Mom and the twins, all dressed up in a suit and a tie. Then we went in through the front door.

So I knew how Benny Briggs felt. But Ernest didn't. He didn't have any idea of what Benny Briggs was like at all. Ernest knew that some people had more money than other people, but he couldn't imagine what it was really like. He couldn't imagine that some kids never had their own room, but had to share with brothers and sisters. He couldn't imagine that some kids had never been in a powerboat or gone water skiing. So it wasn't just meanness that made him want to get Benny and the other guys out of the pond. He couldn't imagine that they didn't have a decent place to swim.

Excerpted from *The Winchesters*, by James Lincoln Collier

Skill Review (continued)

1. How does the narrator describe the relationship between the idea of being rich and not being rich?

_____

_____

_____

2. What is the relationship between the characters of the narrator and Ernest? How are they similar? How are they different?

_____

_____

_____

3. Fill in this idea web with ideas that come to mind when you think of the word *rich*.

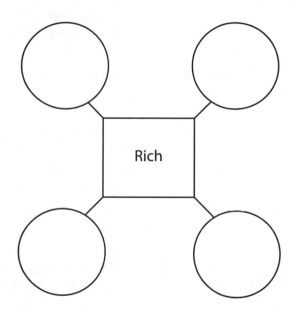

4. What conclusion can you draw about the character Benny Briggs from the information in the passage?

_____

_____

_____

Skill Practice

Directions: Read the passage and answer the questions.

He plunged in among the big spruce trees. The trail was faint. A foot of snow had fallen since the last sled had passed over, and he was glad he was without a sled, travelling light. In fact, he carried nothing but the lunch wrapped in the handkerchief. He was surprised, however, at the cold. It certainly was cold, he concluded, as he rubbed his numb nose and cheekbones with his mittened hand. He was a warm-whiskered man. But the hair on his face did not protect the high cheekbones and the eager nose that thrust itself aggressively into the frosty air.

At the man's heels trotted a dog, a big native husky, the proper wolf dog. It was gray-coated and without any visible or temperamental difference from its brother, the wild wolf. The animal was depressed by the tremendous cold. It knew that it was no time for travelling. Its instinct told it a truer tale than was told to the man by the man's judgment. In reality, it was not merely colder than fifty below zero; it was colder than sixty below, than seventy below. It was seventy-five below zero. The dog did not know anything about thermometers. Possibly in its brain there was no sharp consciousness of a condition of very cold such as was in the man's brain. But the brute had its instinct.

—Excerpted from "To Build a Fire," by Jack London

1. From the passage, which of the following can you logically conclude?

   A. Human judgment is always better than animal instinct.
   B. Humans are better equipped to deal with the cold than dogs.
   C. The man and the dog are in danger because of the extreme weather.
   D. The man and the dog will safely reach their destination.

2. Which is the most accurate characterization of the man?

   A. bold
   B. cautious
   C. cruel
   D. misguided

3. Which states the theme of the passage?

   A. Humans and animals are sensitive to nature in different ways.
   B. Humans are better able to survive in the wilderness than animals.
   C. Fire cannot help anyone survive in cold weather.
   D. Extreme cold can cause depression.

4. In lines 5–7, the author says that "the hair on the his face did not protect the high cheekbones and the eager nose that thrust itself aggressively into the frosty air."

   What does this reveal about the man's personality?

   A. his unusual intelligence
   B. his vivid imagination
   C. his fear of the unknown
   D. his adventurous spirit

5. What is the author's purpose in this excerpt?

   A. to show that a man is smarter than an animal
   B. to show that a wolf is smarter than a dog
   C. to show that an animal's instincts can be more accurate than a man's judgment
   D. to show that an animal cannot be trusted

Directions: Sometimes writers choose what themes they want to include in their writing, and sometimes themes emerge without planning. Choose a theme that interests you. Write a story that has that message. Ask a partner to read your work and identify your theme. Keep in mind that different people sometimes find different messages in the same text.

_____

_____

_____

_____

_____

_____

_____

_____

_____

_____

_____

_____

_____

_____

_____

_____

_____

_____

Text Structure

KEY CONCEPT: Information in a text can be organized in a variety of ways. The pattern of organization that an author chooses is the structure of the text.

How do boldfaced headings and numbered items help you read reference texts? What special features are you apt to find in an instruction manual? Just as nonfiction writers organize, or structure, their texts in certain ways, so do the writers of fiction who create poems, stories, and plays.

Text Structure

The term **text structure** refers to the organizational pattern that an author uses to present information in a text. Authors choose text structures that best fit their **genre**, or type of writing.

Works of fiction can be organized in different ways. For example, short stories are divided into paragraphs. Longer works may be divided into sections, with each section having a new heading. Novels and some long stories are divided into **chapters**. Plays are divided into **acts** and **scenes**. Many poems are divided into **stanzas**. This division into small sections helps the author organize ideas and events clearly. It also makes long texts easier to read and understand.

Fiction writing has fewer rules than nonfiction writing. However, fiction—whether it is a novel, a play, a poem, or a short story— usually follows a basic **narrative**, or storytelling, structure. Each work of fiction has a beginning, a middle, and an end. The plot, setting, character, point of view, and theme all help determine a text's structure.

Tone

Another important element of fiction is **tone**, or the author's attitude toward the topic. The tone of a story can be serious, humorous, formal, or sad. The tone of the story, poem, or novel usually brings an emotional response from the reader. This response is called **mood**. If the tone of a text is uplifting, you may feel happy reading it. If the tone is humorous, you may find yourself chuckling as you read. Authors establish tone—and influence your mood—by their choice of setting, vocabulary, and other details.

COMPARE TEXT STRUCTURES

Different genres of fiction are structured differently. Novels are divided into chapters. Authors may focus individual chapters on specific characters or events. Chapters usually follow chronological order. Together, the chapters combine to form the whole story. In a novel, the author is free to use dialogue, narration, and descriptive language to convey ideas and emotions. The author can describe what a character is thinking about and how the character feels.

Like the chapters of a novel, the acts and scenes of a play help to organize the events and action. You can think of the acts of a play as the "chapters," while the scenes are the smaller "sub-chapters" that make up the acts. Often a new act or scene indicates that the time or place of the action has changed.

A play is meant to be performed and seen by an audience, not simply read. Therefore, the playwright must put the message of the play and its emotion into **dialogue**, or conversation between characters. Occasionally an actor gives information to the audience by "thinking aloud," that is, by speaking directly to the audience rather than to another character. Descriptions of how a character should move or speak are often written in italics.

Action in a play is limited to the movement that can take place on the stage. When a play is developed into a movie, action scenes are often written into the screenplay because the film director and actors are not confined to the space inside a theater.

In a poem, stanzas are groups of lines that are read together. You can think of stanzas as the "paragraphs" of a poem. Poems are usually much shorter than novels and plays. Because they are shorter, authors use figurative language rather than long descriptions to create images in the reader's mind.

Chapters, stanzas, and acts are the building blocks of fictional texts. Writers join one chapter, stanza, or act to the next, constructing the text that has a message or story.

21st Century Skills
Media Literacy

Play scripts and movie scripts are structured differently. By comparing a play script and a movie script, you can see at a glance that a play director and a film director have different tasks to accomplish.

Research online to find a play script and a movie script. Notice how each script is structured. Look at the font (type of print) used for the setting, stage directions, and dialogue.

In a notebook, answer these questions:

- What are some key similarities and differences between the two types of scripts?

- What conclusions can you draw about the reasons for the differences?

Compare the first four lines of Morris's poem "Woodman, Spare That Tree!" to the following excerpt from Walt Whitman's poem "Song of the Open Road."

Whitman's poem is free verse; that is, the lines of poetry do not rhyme and do not have a steady rhythm.

Why are there trees I never walk under but large and melodious thoughts descend upon me?

(I think they hang there winter and summer on those trees, and always drop fruit as I pass;)

What is it I interchange so suddenly with strangers?

What with some driver as I ride on the seat by his side?

In a notebook, compare and contrast the excerpts of the poems by Whitman and Morris. List the similarities and differences you find in the structure. Also explain how the meaning of the poems is similar or different.

Directions: As you read the two texts that follow, notice how the texts look. Then make a list of features the writers have used to structure their texts.

Woodman, Spare That Tree!
by George Pope Morris

Woodman, spare that tree!
    Touch not a single bough!
In youth it sheltered me,
    And I'll protect it now.
'Twas my forefather's hand
    That placed it near his cot;
There, woodman, let it stand,
    Thy axe shall harm it not.

That old familiar tree
    Whose glory and renown
Are spread o'er land and sea—
    And wouldst thou hew it down?
Woodman, forbear thy stroke!
    Cut not its earth-bound ties;
O, spare that aged oak
    Now towering to the skies!

When but an idle boy,
    I sought its grateful shade;
In all their gushing joy
    Here too my sisters played.
My mother kissed me here;
    My father pressed my hand—
Forgive this foolish tear,
    But let that old oak stand.

My heart-strings round thee cling,
    Close as thy bark, old friend!
Here shall the wild-bird sing,
    And still thy branches bend.
Old tree! the storm still brave!
    And, woodman, leave the spot;
While I've a hand to save,
    Thy axe shall hurt it not.

An Enemy of the People
by Henrik Ibsen

CAST
Dr. Thomas Stockmann, Medical Officer of the Municipal Baths
Mrs. Stockmann, his wife
Petra (their daughter), a teacher
Hovstad, editor of the "People's Messenger"
Billing, sub-editor

(DR. STOCKMANN comes in from his room with an open letter in his hand.)

DR. STOCKMANN: *(waving the letter)* Well, now the town will have something new to talk about, I can tell you!

BILLING: Something new?

MRS. STOCKMANN: What is this?

DR. STOCKMANN: A great discovery, Katherine.

PETRA: But, father, tell us what it is.

DR. STOCKMANN: Yes, yes—only give me time, and you shall know all about it. If only I had Peter here now! It just shows how we men can go about forming our judgments, when in reality we are as blind as any moles—

HOVSTAD: What are you driving at, Doctor?

DR. STOCKMANN: (*standing still by the table*) Isn't it the universal opinion that our town is a healthy spot?

HOVSTAD: Certainly.

DR. STOCKMANN: Quite an unusually healthy spot, in fact—a place that deserves to be recommended in the warmest possible manner either for invalids or for people who are well—

MRS. STOCKMANN: Yes, but my dear Thomas—

DR. STOCKMANN: And we have been recommending it and praising it—I have written and written, both in the "Messenger" and in pamphlets . . .

HOVSTAD: Well, what then?

DR. STOCKMANN: And the Baths—we have called them the "main artery of the town's life-blood," the "nerve-centre of our town," and the devil knows what else—

BILLING: "The town's pulsating heart" was the expression I once used on an important occasion.

DR. STOCKMANN: Quite so. Well, do you know what they really are, these great, splendid, much praised Baths, that have cost so much money—do you know what they are?

HOVSTAD: No, what are they?

MRS. STOCKMANN: Yes, what are they?

DR. STOCKMANN: The whole place is a pest-house!

THINK ABOUT **READING**

Directions: Write the answer to each question.

1. What genre of fiction is "Woodman, Spare That Tree!"? How is the text arranged?

   _____

   _____

2. What genre of fiction is *An Enemy of the People*? How is the text organized?

   _____

   _____

3. Imagine one of these texts presented as a novel. How would the author organize the information and describe the events? How would the novel be similar to the original text? How would it be different?

   _____

   _____

Reading Skill
Identify Tone

Tone is the author's attitude toward the topic. To set the tone of a text, authors select words that convey emotion. For example, in "Woodman, Spare That Tree!" the speaker shows his passion by addressing the woodman directly. He uses commands such as *spare*, *touch not*, and *leave the spot*.

The punctuation also suggests that the writer is deeply moved by the topic. Notice how many exclamation points are in the poem.

Read the excerpt from *An Enemy of the People*. In a notebook, answer these questions: What emotion is conveyed by the author's tone? Which words help the author convey that tone? How does the punctuation help you interpret, or understand, the tone?

Use Key Words

Many literary works are available on Internet sites. You can find complete texts of books, poems, and plays online.

Look for the complete texts of "An Occurrence at Owl Creek Bridge" and "The Raven" on the Internet. As key words in your search, use the title and author of the work and the term "full text."

Directions: As you read, list words that describe the tone of the text.

An Occurrence at Owl Creek Bridge
by Ambrose Bierce

A man stood upon a railroad bridge in northern Alabama, looking down into the swift water twenty feet below. The man's hands were behind his back, the wrists bound with a cord. A rope closely encircled his neck. It was attached to a stout cross-timber above his head and the slack fell to the level of his knees. Some loose boards laid upon the ties supporting the rails of the railway supplied a footing for him and his executioners—two private soldiers of the Federal army, directed by a sergeant who in civil life may have been a deputy sheriff. . . .

The man who was engaged in being hanged was apparently about thirty-five years of age. He was a civilian, if one might judge from his habit [his clothes], which was that of a planter. . . .

He closed his eyes in order to fix his last thoughts upon his wife and children. . . .

He unclosed his eyes and saw again the water below him. "If I could free my hands," he thought, "I might throw off the noose and spring into the stream. By diving I could evade the bullets and, swimming vigorously, reach the bank, take to the woods and get away home. . . ."

As these thoughts, which have here to be set down in words, were flashed into the doomed man's brain . . . the captain nodded to the sergeant. The sergeant stepped aside. . . .

As Peyton Farquhar fell straight downward through the bridge he lost consciousness and was as one already dead. . . . Then all at once, with terrible suddenness, the light about him shot upward with the noise of a loud splash; a frightful roaring was in his ears, and all was cold and dark. The power of thought was restored; he knew that the rope had broken and he had fallen into the stream. . . .

He felt the ripples upon his face and heard their separate sounds as they struck. He looked at the forest on the bank of the stream, saw the individual trees, the leaves and the veining of each leaf—he saw the very insects upon them: the locusts, the brilliant bodied flies, the gray spiders stretching their webs from twig to twig. He noted the prismatic [rainbow] colors in all the dewdrops upon a million blades of grass. . . .

Suddenly he felt himself whirled round and round—spinning like a top. . . . In few moments he was flung upon the gravel at the foot of the left bank of the stream—the southern bank—and behind a projecting point which concealed him from his enemies. . . .

He sprang to his feet, rushed up the sloping bank, and plunged into the forest. . . .

Doubtless, despite his suffering, he had fallen asleep while walking, for now he sees another scene—perhaps he has merely recovered from a delirium. He stands at the gate of his own home. All is as he left it, and all bright and beautiful in the morning sunshine. He must have traveled the entire night. As he pushes open the gate and passes up the wide white walk, . . . his wife, looking fresh and cool and sweet, steps down from the veranda to meet him. . . . Ah, how beautiful she is! He springs forwards with extended arms. As he is about to clasp her he feels a stunning blow upon the back of the neck; a blinding white light blazes all about him with a sound like the shock of a cannon—then all is darkness and silence!

Peyton Farquhar was dead; his body, with a broken neck, swung gently from side to side beneath the timbers of the Owl Creek Bridge.

The Raven
by Edgar Allan Poe

Once upon a midnight dreary, while I pondered, weak and weary,
Over many a quaint and curious volume of forgotten lore,
While I nodded, nearly napping, suddenly there came a tapping,
As of some one gently rapping, rapping at my chamber door.
"'Tis some visitor," I muttered, "tapping at my chamber door—
                    Only this, and nothing more."

Ah, distinctly I remember it was in the bleak December,
And each separate dying ember wrought its ghost upon the floor.
Eagerly I wished the morrow; —vainly I had tried to borrow
From my books surcease of sorrow—sorrow for the lost Lenore—
For the rare and radiant maiden whom the angels name Lenore—
                    Nameless here for evermore. . . .

WRITE TO LEARN

Choose a story or novel you enjoy. Select a page that has two or more people talking, and rewrite that page as a poem. Include figurative language. Use stanzas to divide the poem into sections.

Share both passages with a friend. Discuss which version was more enjoyable to read.

THINK ABOUT READING

Directions: Answer these questions.

1. How is the short story "An Occurrence at Owl Creek Bridge" organized?

    A. stanzas
    B. paragraphs
    C. chapters
    D. scenes

2. What is the author's tone in "The Raven"? Which words in the poem help the author convey this tone?

    _____

    _____

    _____

Directions: Match each vocabulary word with its definition.

1. _____ chapter   **A.** pattern of organization

2. _____ text structure   **B.** section of a novel

3. _____ tone   **C.** section of a play

4. _____ scene   **D.** author's attitude toward a topic

5. _____ stanza   **E.** section of a poem

Skill Practice

Directions: Read the following play. Then answer the questions that follow.

Peter Pan *or* The Boy Who Would Not Grow Up
by J. M. Barrie

PETER (*in a whisper*): Tinker Bell, Tink, are you there? (*A jug lights up.*) Oh, do come out of that jug. (*TINK flashes hither and thither.*) Do you know where they put it? (*The answer comes as of a tinkle of bells . . .*) Which big box? This one? But which drawer? Yes, do show me. (*TINK pops into the drawer where the shadow is. . . . In his joy at finding his shadow, . . . PETER sits on the floor with the shadow . . . [and] tries to stick it on with soap from the bathroom . . . This wakens WENDY, who sits up, and is pleasantly interested to see a stranger.*)

WENDY (*courteously*): Boy, why are you crying?

(*PETER jumps up, and crossing to the foot of the bed bows to her. WENDY, impressed, bows to him from the bed.*)

PETER: What is your name?

WENDY (*well satisfied*): Wendy Moira Angela Darling. What is yours?

PETER (*finding it lamentably brief*): Peter Pan.

WENDY: Is that all?

PETER (*biting his lip*): Yes.

WENDY (*politely*): I am so sorry.

PETER: It doesn't matter.

WENDY: Where do you live?

PETER: Second to the right and then straight on till morning.

WENDY: What a funny address!

PETER: No, it isn't.

WENDY: I mean, is that what they put on the letters?

PETER: Don't get any letters.

WENDY: But your mother gets letters?

PETER: Don't have a mother.

WENDY: Peter!

(She leaps out of bed to put her arms round him, but he draws back; he does not know why, but he knows he must draw back.)

PETER: You mustn't touch me.

WENDY: Why?

PETER: No one must ever touch me.

WENDY: Why?

PETER: I don't know.

---

1. What genre of fiction is *Peter Pan or The Boy Who Would Not Grow Up?* What text structure does the writer use to organize the text?

   _____

   _____

2. This passage is part of a longer work. How would that work be organized?

   A. stanzas
   B. paragraphs
   C. chapters
   D. scenes

3. From the events and the dialogue you have just read, do you think this passage probably takes place at the beginning, middle, or end of the longer work? What evidence supports your opinion?

   _____

   _____

   _____

   _____

4. Imagine this same dialogue between Peter and Wendy were presented in a novel. How would the author organize the information? What would be similar? What would be different?

   _____

   _____

   _____

   _____

   _____

Directions: Read the following passage. Then answer the questions that follow.

Peter Pan
by J. M. Barrie

"Tinker Bell," he called softly, after making sure that the children were asleep, "Tink, where are you?" She was in a jug for the moment, and liking it extremely; she had never been in a jug before.

"Oh, do come out of that jug, and tell me, do you know where they put my shadow?"

The loveliest tinkle as of golden bells answered him. It is the fairy language. You ordinary children can never hear it, but if you were to hear it you would know that you had heard it once before.

Tink said that the shadow was in the big box. . . . In a moment he had recovered his shadow, and in his delight he forgot that he had shut Tinker Bell up in the drawer.

If he thought at all, but I don't believe he ever thought, it was that he and his shadow, when brought near each other, would join like drops of water, and when they did not he was appalled. He tried to stick it on with soap from the bathroom, but that also failed. A shudder passed through Peter, and he sat on the floor and cried.

His sobs woke Wendy, and she sat up in bed. She was not alarmed to see a stranger crying on the nursery floor; she was only pleasantly interested.

"Boy," she said courteously, "why are you crying?"

Peter could be exceeding polite also, having learned the grand manner at fairy ceremonies, and he rose and bowed to her beautifully. She was much pleased, and bowed beautifully to him from the bed.

"What's your name?" he asked.

"Wendy Moira Angela Darling," she replied with some satisfaction. "What is your name?"

"Peter Pan."

She was already sure that he must be Peter, but it did seem a comparatively short name.

"Is that all?"

"Yes," he said rather sharply. He felt for the first time that it was a shortish name.

"I'm so sorry," said Wendy Moira Angela.

"It doesn't matter," Peter gulped.

She asked where he lived.

"Second to the right," said Peter, "and then straight on till morning."

"What a funny address!"

Peter had a sinking. For the first time he felt that perhaps it was a funny address.

"No, it isn't," he said.

Skill Practice (continued)

1. What genre of fiction is this second *Peter Pan* passage? What text structure does the writer use?

_____

_____

2. Use a Venn diagram to compare and contrast this passage with the *Peter Pan* play on pages 238-239.

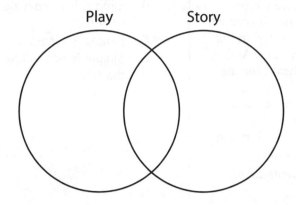

Play   Story

3. How do the different text structures affect the tone in the two versions of *Peter Pan*?

_____

_____

_____

_____

4. Which text structure for *Peter Pan* do you prefer? Explain your answer.

_____

_____

_____

_____

Writing Practice

Directions: Reread the poem "Woodman, Spare That Tree!" Then write a scene from a play, using the characters, setting, and events described in the poem. Use dialogue and stage directions to convey the emotion and action of the scene.

Directions: Questions 1 through 3 refer to the following passage.

"I have had so many hardships in this life," said Simple, "that it is a wonder I'll live until I die. I was born young, black, voteless, poor, and hungry, in a state where white folks did not even put Negroes on the census. My daddy said he were never counted in his life by the United States government. And nobody could find a birth certificate for me nowhere. It were not until I come to Harlem that one day a census taker dropped around to my house and asked where were I born and why, also my age and if I was still living. I said, 'Yes, I am here, in spite of all.'"

"'All of what?' asked the census taker. 'Give me the data.'"

"'All of my corns and bunions, for one,' I said. 'I were borned with corns. Most colored peoples get corns so young, they must be inherited. As for bunions, they seem to come natural, we stands on our feet so much. These feet of mine have stood in everything from soup lines to the draft board. They have supported everything from a packing trunk to a hungry woman. My feet have walked ten thousand miles running errands for white folks and another ten thousand trying to keep up with colored. My feet have stood before altars, at crap tables, bars, graves, kitchen doors, welfare windows, and social security railings. Be sure and include my feet on that census you are taking,' I told that man."

"Then I went on to tell him how my feet have helped to keep the American shoe industry going, due to the money I have spent on my feet. 'I have wore out seven hundred pairs of shoes, eighty-nine tennis shoes, forty-four summer sandals, and two hundred and two loafers. The socks my feet have bought could build a knitting mill. The razor blades I have used cutting away corns could pay for a razor plant. Oh, my feet have helped to make America rich, and I am still standing on them.'"

—Excerpted from "Census" in *Simple's Uncle Sam*, by Langston Hughes

1. What is one main theme of this passage?
   A. Simple has spent a lot of money on shoes.
   B. Simple, like most people in Harlem, has sore feet.
   C. Simple is long-suffering.
   D. Simple is not telling the census taker the truth.

2. What sentiment toward Simple does the author convey in this excerpt?
   A. sympathy
   B. embarrassment
   C. disdain
   D. affection

3. Simple says, "The socks my feet have bought could build a knitting mill" (lines 39–40). What does Simple mean?
   A. Simple once worked in a knitting mill.
   B. Simple had to buy special socks.
   C. Simple has lived a long, hard life.
   D. Simple is helping build a knitting mill.

Directions: Questions 4 through 6 refer to the following passage.

On Sunday, at breakfast, his grandmother asks, "What time did you get in?"

He knows that she knows. The light was on in their bedroom when he pulled into the drive; off, as he came up the stairs.

5

"I don't know. Twelve? Twelve-thirty?"

"One-thirty," she says.

"One-thirty, then." He nods amiably [cheerfully], helping himself to the toast she has kept warm for him in the oven. The small breakfast nook is washed in sunlight. Sun glints off the jar of honey sitting on the table, filtering through the pale yellow curtains at the window. His head sings with an intricate, melodic line—Telemann? Marais? John Bull? He cannot remember, but he loves those fresh and unfamiliar instruments, the recorder, the harpsichord; their simple statements of truth. He wonders what the weather is like in Dallas. Sunny, he hopes. Warm.

10

15

20

"How can you expect to get a decent night's sleep, coming in at that hour?" She is frowning across the table at him.

25

"I give up. How can I?"

She sighs. "Everything's a joke with you, isn't it?"

"Grandmother, you know something, I'm nuts about you," he says cheerfully.

30

"You're always agitating. I think it's great. You oughta run for President. No kidding."

He gets to his feet, pushing the chair back.

"Where are you going?"

35

"Outside to wash my car."

"Well, don't get chilled. It's not summer, you know."

"I know, I know!"

—Excerpted from *Ordinary People*, by Judith Guest

4. Around what does the action of this passage center?
   A. a breakfast conversation
   B. a shared interest in music
   C. an election
   D. washing a car

5. What do the words and actions of the young man reveal about his character?
   A. He is depressed.
   B. He is angry.
   C. He is sarcastic.
   D. He is affectionate.

6. From information in the passage, what can you conclude about the grandmother's feelings toward her grandson?
   A. She dislikes him.
   B. She cares about him.
   C. She is uninterested in him.
   D. She thinks he is very funny.

Directions: Questions 7 through 9 refer to the following passage.

According to Auntie Francine, Alex was badly spoiled by them all. "If you asked for the moon," said Francine, "Grandpa Paul would hang it shining around your neck in a minute. But we've all spoiled you. We're to blame for lavishing all this love on you so that you've come to expect it, like royalty."

"Don't be ridiculous, Auntie."

"It's true," said Francine, grabbing her close, kissing her hair. "You've always been marked for something special. Just don't let it go to your head."

Three nights after Grandpa called about the dark, Alex was out with Serena Fitzpatrick and Andrea Larkin and Jeremy Huntinghawk in the snowy park down the street. It was the only place nearby where she could find the solace of the country in the middle of the city. On this prairie winter night, deep in the sleeping heart of January, it was twenty-six below zero. The only light was the moon, dazzling down on the snow.

They played tag all through the cathedral of frozen trees. And then Jeremy said, "Okay, now, on the count of three, everybody howl."

They threw back their heads and counted, and then they howled. Like feral [wild] creatures. Like heartsick lonely wolves. And it felt so good as they ran through the snow crying, "A-wooo!" at the flying moon. "A-wah-wah-woooo!"

She stopped to watch the others howling and leaping. And it was at this moment that she knew her grandfather had just moved, without saying good-bye, far beyond reach. With absolute certainty, her heart thudding against her chest, she knew that he had slipped past her, past them all, past the dark of winter and midnight and consciousness and eating and sleeping and caring. Then she watched as her own breath rose in front of her astonished eyes, took form, and floated like a spirit hand on the crystal air.

—Excerpted from *Bone Dance*,
by Martha Brooks

7. Which of the following phrases is an example of figurative language?

   A. "Alex was badly spoiled by them all."
   B. "They played tag all through the cathedral of frozen trees."
   C. "They threw back their heads and counted."
   D. "Then she watched as her own breath rose in front of her."

8. Auntie Francine says, "You've always been marked for something special. Just don't let it go to your head" (lines 10–12). What does this sentence tell you about her feelings for Alex?

   A. They are dismissive and uncaring.
   B. They are angry and upset.
   C. They are concerned and wary.
   D. They are affectionate and caring.

9. How is Bone Dance organized?

   A. chapters
   B. paragraphs
   C. stanzas
   D. scenes

Check Your Understanding

On the following chart, circle the number of any question you answered incorrectly. Under each content area you will see the pages you can review to learn the content covered in the question. Pay particular attention to reviewing those lessons in which you missed half or more of the questions.

Chapter 5 Review

Lesson	Item Number	Review Pages
Plot and Setting	4	188–197
Character	5, 6, 8	198–205
Point of View	2	206–213
Literal and Figurative Language	3, 7	214–219
Theme	1	220–231
Text Structure	9	232–241

ESSAY WRITING PRACTICE

Fiction

Directions: Write a passage of fiction in response to the prompt below. Review Lessons 5.1, 5.2, and 5.4 for help with plot, setting, character, and literal and figurative language.

FICTION

Everyone in your class is writing a fiction passage that will be included in the yearbook. The writing may be in the form of a poem, a dramatic scene, or a three-paragraph short story.

Choose one of these topics, or create one of your own.

- Something happens during the morning commute that prevents the main character from reaching his or her workplace.

- The main character takes a wrong turn that changes the course of history.

- Retell Aesop's fable "The Boy Who Cried, 'Wolf!'" from the point of view of the wolf. You will find "The Boy Who Cried, 'Wolf!'" at this website. Use "Find" to search for the story.

  http://www.gutenberg.org/files/21/21-h/21-h.htm#link2H_4_0075

Include literal and figurative language in your writing.

Review

ESSAY WRITING PRACTICE

_____

_____

_____

_____

_____

_____

_____

_____

_____

_____

_____

_____

_____

_____

_____

_____

_____

_____

_____

_____

_____

_____

_____

_____

_____

_____

_____

_____

Reading

This Posttest will help you evaluate whether you are ready to move up to the next level of test preparation. The Posttest consists of 40 multiple-choice questions that test your ability to understand informational texts and literary texts.

Directions: Read each question carefully. Then choose the <u>one best answer</u> to the question.

When you have completed the Posttest, check your work with the answers and explanations on pages 261–262. Use the Evaluation Chart on page 263 to determine which areas you need to review.

Reading

Directions: Questions 1–5 refer to the following passage.

> He stopped the car and studied the opening with his field glasses. Then he motioned to the driver to go on and the car moved slowly along, the driver avoiding wart-
> 5 hog holes and driving around the mud castles ants had built. Then, looking across the opening, Wilson suddenly turned and said,
>
> "By God, there they are!"
>
> And looking where he pointed, while the
> 10 car jumped forward and Wilson spoke in rapid Swahili to the driver, Macomber saw three huge, black animals looking almost cylindrical in their long heaviness, like big black tank cars, moving at a gallop across the
> 15 far edge of the open prairie. They moved at a stiff-necked, stiff-bodied gallop and he could see the upswept wide black horns on their heads as they galloped heads out; the heads not moving.
>
> 20 "They're three old bulls," Wilson said. "We'll cut them off before they get to the swamp."
>
> —Excerpted from "The Short Happy Life of Francis Macomber," by Ernest Hemingway

1. In lines 1–2, the author says, "He stopped the car and studied the **opening** with his field glasses." Which definition of **opening** is intended in those sentences?

A. a large crack or hole in the road
B. an opportunity to begin something
C. the beginning of a performance
D. area of grassy land with few trees

2. What does the author compare the three bulls to?

A. stiff-bodied horses
B. big black tank cars
C. round barrels
D. muddy castles

3. Which of the author's techniques is most effective in helping the reader imagine the road?

A. sharing what the driver thinks as he drives
B. comparing the road and the prairie
C. telling what the driver avoids on the road
D. including dialogue between two characters

4. "Wilson suddenly turned and said, 'By God, there they are!'" (lines 7–8)

Which word best describes how Wilson feels?

A. worried
B. excited
C. energetic
D. curious

5. What is the author's purpose in the paragraph beginning with "And looking where he pointed . . ."? (lines 9–19)

A. to help readers visualize the bulls
B. to describe Macomber's reaction to bulls
C. to give facts about animals on the prairie
D. to explain what Wilson said to the driver

Reading

Directions: Questions 6–12 refer to the following passage.

Statistics form the spine of the legend of Babe Didrikson Zaharias. This is true of nearly all athletes: the results of sporting events are finite [measurable], almost never abstract. In most other human pursuits, in art, music, literature, and so forth, greatness is a matter of intangibles. But in sports there are winners and losers; the results are unmistakable; the statistics are immutable [unchangeable]. In the case of Babe, the statistics that define her greatness are so impressive they seem almost too good to be true.

Between 1930 and 1932 she held American, Olympic, or world records in five different track and field events. During the A.A.U. national meet of 1932, she entered as the sole member of the Golden Cyclones, a team sponsored by the Employers Casualty Company of Dallas; Babe scored thirty points in the meet. The next best team, the Illinois Women's Athletic Club, had twenty-two members who scored a total of twenty-two points.

In the Olympics at Los Angeles, she won gold medals and set world records in the 80-meter hurdles and the javelin—breaking the javelin record by an astounding eleven feet. She tied for first place in the high jump, setting another world record; officials ruled, however, that she had dived illegally during her last successful jump and she was awarded the silver medal instead of the gold.

—Excerpted from *Whatta Gal: The Babe Didrickson Story*, by William O. Johnson and Nancy P. Williamson

6. Which title best expresses the main idea of the passage?
   A. Los Angeles Olympics: Winning the Gold
   B. Babe Didrikson's Greatest Accomplishment
   C. Babe Didrikson: Statistical Wonder
   D. How to Define Greatness with Statistics

7. In lines 5–7, the authors say "in art, music, literature, and so forth, greatness is a matter of intangibles."

   Which words define **intangibles** as it is used in the sentence above?

   A. things that are measurable
   B. things that are not easily measured
   C. unbelievable events
   D. winners and losers in sports

8. In the high jump at the Los Angeles Olympics, why did Babe Didrikson win a silver medal instead of a gold?
   A. She had the second-highest jump in the event.
   B. She set a world record with her successful jump.
   C. The officials ruled that she had dived illegally.
   D. She tied for first place in the event.

Reading

9. On the basis of the excerpt, which word best describes Babe Didrikson?

A. insecure
B. lazy
C. intelligent
D. competitive

11. Babe Didrikson went on to become the first female golf celebrity in the United States. Which of the following facts about Babe Didrikson might the authors have used to support the main idea of this article?

A. She was born on June 26, 1914, in Port Arthur, Texas.
B. She won 82 golf championships, including 17 in a row.
C. She bought a golf course in Tampa, Florida.
D. She played many sports, including baseball and golf.

10. Which technique is the most effective for reinforcing the assertion that "statistics form the spine of the legend of Babe Didrikson" (lines 1–2)?

A. describing her victories

B. including her personal thoughts and feelings

C. comparing and contrasting her with other athletes

D. recording other people's opinions about her

12. On the basis of this excerpt, which statement would the authors most likely agree with?

A. Sports are more important than arts and literature.
B. The results of sporting events are often misunderstood.
C. It is easier to excel in the arts than in athletics.
D. Greatness is easier to measure in sports than in the arts.

Reading

Directions: Questions 13–17 refer to the following form.

GRANT MANUFACTURING COMPANY PERFORMANCE ASSESSMENT AND EMPLOYEE DEVELOPMENT FORM

Employee Name _____

ID # _____ Date of Review _____

Job Title _____

Performance Assessment Period from _____ to _____

Manager _____

The assessment of your on-the-job performance is based on the ratings assigned to you by your manager (or supervisor), who compares your performance to the responsibilities and duties stated in your job description. The purpose of a performance assessment is to provide workers and supervisors with a clear and permanent record of the worker's job performance on an annual basis.

The Grant Manufacturing Company performance assessment system uses the following rating system to assess each employee.

EXEMPLARY	Worker's job performance exceeds expectations and goals every day.
GOOD	Worker's job performance meets and frequently exceeds expectations and goals.
AVERAGE	Worker's job performance is average and occasionally exceeds expectations and goals.
BELOW AVERAGE	Worker's job performance is insufficient and does not meet the expectations of the company.

Employee's Performance Assessment

(Manager: Check one box in each category.)

	EXEMPLARY	GOOD	AVERAGE	BELOW AVERAGE
PRODUCTIVITY				
TEAMWORK				
CREATIVITY				
ATTITUDE				
PROFESSIONALISM				
ATTENDANCE				

Reading

13. Why does the company use the performance assessment form?

    A. to provide evidence of a worker's poor performance so he or she can be fired
    B. to simplify the manager's job of helping employees
    C. to reward good workers with financial incentives
    D. to have a yearly record of a worker's job performance

14. What is meant by "worker's job performance exceeds expectations and goals every day"?

    A. The worker does what is stated in the job description, no more and no less.
    B. The worker expects the company to perform well every day of every year.
    C. The worker works longer, harder, and more productively than asked to.
    D. The worker has goals that he or she expects the company to meet.

15. According to the rating scale, what rating would workers get if they usually do only the work expected of them?

    A. Exemplary
    B. Good
    C. Average
    D. Below average

16. Which consequence might a worker expect if he or she is continually rated Below Average in Productivity, Attitude, and Attendance?

    A. If the company needs to reduce staff, he or she will be fired.
    B. At bonus time, the worker will get a large bonus.
    C. After three years, the worker will be promoted to manager.
    D. The worker will work on an important, high-priority project.

17. Which additional category might be added to the employee's performance assessment form?

    A. AGE OF EMPLOYEE
    B. QUALITY OF WORK
    C. HIRE DATE
    D. PERSONALITY

Reading

Directions: Questions 18–23 refer to the following passage.

"Where do they get vegetables like this?" Minnie asked. She saw other women feeling the tomatoes, sampling the lush bunches of grapes. "The prices are the same as we pay,
5 but what a difference."

Mrs. Jameson laughed a little. "It's worth driving over here, isn't it?" she said. "We used to live not far from here. That's how I happen to know about it." But Mariana suspected
10 this store was not unique, that in the gringo neighborhoods everything was a little better.

At the meat counter, Minnie was even more impressed. She examined carefully all the meat behind the glass, and then asked
15 the butcher to cut some filet mignon. Mariana couldn't ever recall hearing her mother order that, and she noticed it was the most expensive meat. She thought she understood why her mother ordered it.

20 On the way back to East Los Angeles, Mariana sensed her mother felt defensive and perhaps a little offended because the gringa had shown her a better way to do something, had shown that shopping near
25 home was not good enough for someone with taste.

She heard her mother say, "Next week Pete's buying me a new Cadillac. Then I'll take you shopping with me," and Mariana had
30 never seen such a forced smile on her mother's face.

"Oh, that'll be nice," Mrs. Jameson said.

—Excerpted from *Chicano*, by Richard Vasquez

18. Minnie, Mariana, and Mrs. Jameson are at a store. According to the passage, which statement about the store is true?

A. The store is in East Los Angeles.
B. The store is where Minnie often shops.
C. The store is owned by Mrs. Jameson.
D. The store is in a gringo neighborhood.

19. Why does Minnie say, ". . . but what a difference"? (line 5)

A. The store has a new meat counter.
B. The shoppers feel the tomatoes.
C. The fruit and vegetables are fresher.
D. The food prices are more expensive.

Reading

20. How do the women get to the store?

    A. They take a bus from their neighborhood.
    B. Minnie drives everyone in her Cadillac.
    C. Mrs. Jameson drives Minnie and Mariana.
    D. They walk together across town.

22. According to this excerpt, why does Minnie feel defensive and offended?

    A. She realizes that a Cadillac is an expensive car to use for shopping.
    B. She realizes that people with taste shop at stores that have better food.
    C. She realizes that the filet mignon, tomatoes, and grapes are all very expensive.
    D. She realizes that Mariana does not want to go shopping with her next week.

21. On the basis of this excerpt, why does Minnie decide to order filet mignon?

    A. Minnie wants to impress Mrs. Jameson.
    B. Filet mignon is Mariana's favorite food.
    C. Minnie often buys expensive meat.
    D. The butcher says that it is the tastiest cut.

23. Which of the author's techniques is the most effective for developing Minnie's character?

    A. using the store as a setting for the passage
    B. including a dialogue between Mariana and Minnie
    C. having the narrator share Mariana's thoughts
    D. comparing and contrasting Mariana and Mrs. Jameson

Reading

Directions: Questions 24–29 refer to the following excerpts from two editorials.

Editorial 1

Bicycles Are the Way to Go

Traffic congestion in Hancock City has doubled over the past five years. This is due, in part, to development in the inner city. Construction of high-rise buildings brought jobs, as well as workers for those jobs, into the city. Then the new buildings filled with offices, stores, and companies. Now there are commuters and shoppers flooding into the city on a daily basis and traffic jams have become a common sight.

Studies have shown that there are fewer traffic problems in a city when bicycles are used as a means of transportation. For that reason, Hancock City should encourage commuters to ride bicycles instead of driving cars. This solution will decrease the number of cars in the city; therefore, there will be less congestion. This solution will also encourage commuters to live a healthy life style. While commuting to work, people will get their daily exercise.

To encourage safe bicycle traffic, the city should install bicycle lanes. Bicycle lanes define the road space. The lanes also remind motorists that bicycles have a right to be on the road. In addition, bicycle lanes promote safe bicycling habits. Cyclists are more likely to follow the rules of the road when they are riding in bike lanes.

Editorial 2

Too Much Traffic

Hancock City needs to decrease its traffic. The roads into and out of the city, especially at commuting times, are snarled with cars. The streets inside the city are crawling with bumper-to-bumper traffic as well. All the traffic causes pollution—not only air pollution but noise pollution too.

Some people believe that bike lanes are the solution to this problem. If the city installs bike lanes, these people say, automobile traffic will be reduced. Bike lanes may be one answer, but they are not a satisfactory answer! Bike lanes might encourage more cyclists but this will not reduce automobile traffic in any substantial way. The city streets will have not only cars, trucks, and buses but also bikes going in every direction. Drivers will have a hard time avoiding all the bikes. Accidents are just waiting to happen!

The best solution to the traffic problem is better public transportation. With additional bus and train service at a lower cost, more commuters will leave their cars—and bikes—at home and use public transportation to get to work. I, for one, would rather see our tax dollars spent on public transportation than on bike lanes.

24 Who is the intended audience for Editorial 1, "Bicycles Are the Way to Go"?

A. shoppers
B. city residents
C. motorists
D. office workers

25. What additional information might the writer of Editorial 1, "Bicycles Are the Way to Go," add to support the argument?

A. statistics from a report about bicycles as a means of transportation
B. facts and figures about the cost of buying a new bicycle
C. instructions for how to install bicycle lanes on city streets
D. a list of rules of the road that motorists and cyclists should follow

26. Hancock City is having a meeting to discuss the pros and cons of bike lanes. What would the writer of Editorial 2, "Too Much Traffic," probably do?

A. plan a presentation on city tax expenditures and tax savings
B. write a report detailing the failing public transportation system
C. stay home because he has no opinion about bike lanes in the city
D. attend the meeting and give reasons against creating bike lanes

27 The writer of Editorial 2, "Too Much Traffic," says, "Accidents are just waiting to happen" (paragraph 2). What does the writer mean?

A. As a result of all the congestion, automobile accidents will be on the rise.
B. Having bike lanes will increase the number of accidents in Hancock City.
C. Commuters will accidentally leave their bicycles in the bike lane.
D. It will be dangerous when cyclists do not follow the rules of the road.

28. Which statement describes both editorials?

A. The writer's purpose is to persuade.
B. The tone of the editorial is humorous.
C. The writer believes in using tax money for public transportation.
D. Bike paths are promoted as a way of reducing traffic problems.

29. Which statement describes a difference between the editorials?

A. One writer thinks traffic congestion is a problem in Hancock City; the other writer does not agree.
B. One writer thinks commuters should not drive to work daily; the other thinks driving is the best way to commute into the city.
C. One writer thinks public transportation is the best solution; the other writer thinks more commuters should ride their bikes.
D. One writer promotes walking as a healthy way to commute to work; the other promotes cycling as a healthy way to commute.

Reading

Directions: Questions 30–35 refer to the following newspaper article.

Tracking the Storm

June 1 starts the hurricane season for the East Coast of the United States. Now, at the end of August, the season is half over. Until recently, it has been a quiet season. In fact, up until last week, there were no named storms. None of the storms had strong enough winds to be classified as either tropical storms or hurricanes. Since last week, however, there have been three named
5   storms. Two have dissipated, but the third, with winds of up to 105 miles per hour, qualifies as a Category 2 hurricane.

As recently as yesterday, Friday, Bermuda was preparing itself to be hit by the full brunt of the storm. Last night the hurricane skipped past Bermuda but not before heavy winds and rain caused massive damage throughout the island. Even so, Bermudians feel lucky to have been
10   missed by the eye of the hurricane. "It could have been much worse," said one local hurricane observer, "had we been hit by the eye. We narrowly avoided a disaster."

Meanwhile, the hurricane is traveling over the open seas off the East Coast of the United States and Canada. Even though the storm is expected to stay out to sea, the National Hurricane Center has said that hurricane-force winds can extend 85 miles outward from the eye of the
15   storm. Tropical-storm winds can extend 275 miles outward.

The National Weather Service is warning beach goers and boaters from North Carolina to
20   Maine to be prepared for the effects from the storm, such as heavy surf, rip currents, and high swell. Fifteen-foot waves are expected at beaches along the National Seashore in
25   Massachusetts. Many beaches up and down the coast have been closed to swimmers during the weekend because there may be
30   strong rip currents. These strong seaward flows of water can carry even the strongest of swimmers out to sea.

By Sunday night, the
35   hurricane will have passed by Massachusetts.

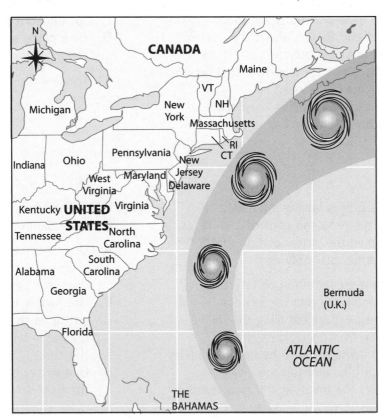

Reading

30 From information in the article and on the map, where are beaches likely to remain closed on Monday?

- A. Bermuda
- B. North Carolina
- C. Florida
- D. Canada

31. In the past week, three storms have been named. Before that, no storms were named. Why were the last three storms named?

- A. The National Hurricane Center decided that these storms would cause heavy rain along the East Coast of the United States.
- B. The winds were strong enough to classify the storms as tropical storms or hurricanes.
- C. The storms were near enough to land masses, such as Bermuda, to cause extensive damage.
- D. The National Weather Center was warning that the storms would cause heavy surf.

32. Assume that the storm will pick up strength and have winds greater than 110 miles per hour when it reaches Canada. What would you expect to happen?

- A. Workers at an offshore energy plant will be evacuated and brought to shore.
- B. Swimmers will go out in the ocean to ride the large waves created by the storm.
- C. The storm will be out over the ocean about 75 miles from the coast, so there will be no affects on shore.
- D. Small boats and ships will sail out to sea to experience the swells and high surf.

33. Why does the writer give this information from the National Hurricane Center: "hurricane-force winds can extend 85 miles outward from the eye of the storm. Tropical-storm winds can extend 275 miles outward" (lines 14–16)?

- A. to explain why the eye of this hurricane did not pass over Bermuda
- B. to explain what rip currents and high swells are and why they are dangerous
- C. to warn that a hurricane is dangerous even if it does not pass directly overhead
- D. to define a hurricane and explain what makes it different from other storms

34. Which readers stand to benefit the most from information in this article?

- A. vacationers on the eastern coast of Florida
- B. readers living inland in up-state New York
- C. people living in coastal Massachusetts
- D. forecasters at the National Hurricane Center

35. The writer mentions rip currents twice (lines 22 and 30). What is a rip current?

- A. a hurricane with 100–250 mile-per-hour winds
- B. a tropical storm that stays over water
- C. a wave that is 10–15 feet high
- D. a flow of water that goes out to sea

Reading

Directions: Questions 36–40 refer to the following informational text.

Grand Canyon National Park offers several options for sightseeing. Private vehicles are permitted along parts of the highway. Tourists can park at the Visitors Center and use the free shuttle-bus system for guided tours. Day hikers may stroll along the trails. The Greenway Trail is open for bicycles. The more adventurous can schedule multi-day backpacking trips or burro rides into the Canyon. Pets are permitted in certain areas, with some restrictions.

Visitors are encouraged to participate in the park's sustainability project by using the recycling bins and water stations.

The lodges, campgrounds, and trailer villages in the park fill up quickly, so it's best to make reservations several months, or even a year, in advance. Nearby towns also offer a variety of overnight accommodations.

Bryce Canyon and Zion National Parks are relatively close by. Consider adding a visit to the Kaibab Indian Reservation, Lake Meade, or the town of Sedona.

36. Which of the following is the best resource to use for planning a route from the Grand Canyon to the other nearby attractions?

   A. a glossary
   B. a manual
   C. a thesaurus
   D. an atlas

37. What information about the Grand Canyon would you expect to find in an encyclopedia article?

   A. the number of visitors in the last year
   B. the geological history
   C. current sales in the gift shop
   D. the names of the park rangers

38. Which of the following is the best resource to use find out the park's policies about dogs?

   A. an accommodations directory
   B. the employee handbook
   C. a trail map
   D. the park guidebook

39. You want to use a dictionary to look up the meaning of the word *sustainability* (line 13). Which guide words should you use to find the page?

   A. suspense – sway
   B. surprise – sushi
   C. sympathy – system
   D. stuck –support

40. What information would you get from a political map of the area?

   A. climate and weather
   B. shuttle bus schedules
   C. the park boundaries
   D. entrance fees and passes

Answer Key

1. **D.** Macomber is looking at an opening. Then he points to the animals he sees. The author describes three bulls in the prairie. The opening must be the prairie, which is a large grassy area.

2. **B.** In lines 13–14, the author compares the bulls to big black tank cars.

3. **C.** The author describes the wart-hog holes and the ants' mud castles that the driver avoids. The description helps the reader visualize the road.

4. **B.** Wilson was looking for the animals when he says, "There they are!" He is probably excited to see them.

5. **A.** The writer uses descriptive words to tell about the bulls and to explain what the bulls are doing. The writer wants the reader to be able to imagine the bulls.

6. **C.** All the details in the passage are about Babe Didrikson and the statistics that prove her athletic ability.

7. **B.** Lines 3–4 state that the results of sporting events are measurable. Then the authors contrast sports with art, music, and literature. Intangibles, therefore, are things that cannot be measured. They are abstract.

8. **C.** The last paragraph states that although Babe Didrikson tied for the highest jump, she was awarded second place because one of her dives was illegal.

9. **D.** You can conclude from the statistics in the excerpt that Babe Didrikson won a lot of competitions. Most people who compete and win are competitive. Babe might have been intelligent, lazy, or insecure, but the passage does not give facts to support those descriptions.

10. **A.** Paragraphs 2 and 3 describe events that Babe Didrikson won. The statistics support the opinion that Babe Didrikson was a great athlete.

11. **B.** Since the authors believe that statistics prove the greatness of an athlete, they would include other statistics. The number of golf tournaments that Babe Didrikson won is a statistic.

12. **D.** The first paragraph says that "greatness is a matter of intangibles" in the arts, literature, and music; however, statistics (scores and measurements) define greatness in sports.

13. **D.** The form serves as "a clear and permanent record of a worker's job performance" (paragraph 1).

14. **C.** *Exceeds* means "goes above and beyond what is expected." If the worker exceeds expectations, the person works harder than expected.

15. **C.** The definition of Average on the form is that the worker does not often exceed expectations. That implies that the worker does the work expected but little more.

16. **A.** A Below-Average worker does not meet the expectations of the company. If the company needs fewer workers, the first workers to be laid off will probably be those whose job performance has been rated Below Average.

17. **B.** The form evaluates job performance. Job quality, or how good your work is, is part of job performance. The other choices do not evaluate work.

18. **D.** The women have to drive to get to the store. Mariana thinks that "in gringo neighborhoods everything was a little better" (lines 10–11), so the store must be in a gringo neighborhood.

19. **C.** In line 1 Minnie says, "Where do they get vegetables like this?" when she sees the quality of the tomatoes and grapes. She realizes that when she shops in her neighborhood, she is paying the same price for fruits and vegetables that are not as fresh as the produce in this store.

20. **C.** Mrs. Jameson says "It's worth driving over here" (lines 6–7). Minnie says she will take Mrs. Jameson shopping next week after she gets a Cadillac (lines 27–29). Therefore, you can infer that this week Mrs. Jameson drove and took Minnie along with her.

21. **A.** Minnie wants Mrs. Jameson to think that she is accustomed to buying expensive items at nice stores.

22. **B.** Mrs. Jameson has "shown her that shopping near home was not good enough for someone with taste" (lines 24–26). Minnie probably thinks Mrs. Jameson believes she is superior to Minnie.

23. **C.** The narrator describes what Mariana thinks her mother is feeling about the gringo shop and about Mrs. Jameson's saying the shop was much better than shops in Minnie's neighborhood.

Answer Key

24. **B.** The writer is addressing residents of the city. The writer wants the residents to consider adding bike lanes to the city streets.

25. **A.** The writer mentions that studies support the argument for bike lanes (paragraph 2), so the writer might include statistics from those studies.

26. **D.** The writer of Editorial 2 does not think bike lanes will solve the traffic problem. The writer would rather see improvements to public transportation. Therefore, the writer would probably go to the meeting to express that opinion.

27. **B.** The writer thinks there will be more bikes in the city if there are bike lanes. Bikes are hard for motorists to see. Therefore, the writer is concerned that cyclists will not be safe.

28. **A.** Both writers want to persuade readers to support their opinions on how to reduce traffic problems in the city.

29. **C.** Both writers agree traffic is a problem in the city. The first writer thinks a good solution is to add bike lanes. The second wants to improve public transportation.

30. **D.** The article says that the hurricane will have passed by Massachusetts. Canada is north of Massachusetts, so the hurricane will be traveling along the Canadian coast.

31. **B.** When storms have strong enough winds to be classified as tropical storms or hurricanes, they are given names by the National Weather Center.

32. **A.** The article states that even if the storm is not over land, the offshore areas and beaches can be dangerous. People working just offshore would not be safe, so they would need to be evacuated. Swimmers and small boats would not be in the water during this storm.

33. **C.** People might think that a hurricane is not dangerous if it stays out to sea. That is not true. The facts from the National Hurricane Center would convince people of the possible dangers.

34. **C.** People living in coastal Massachusetts would benefit most from this information because they live where there will be effects from the storm. From the map, you know this storm is not hitting Florida, and it will not affect inland parts of New York as much as it will affect the coast.

35. **D.** In lines 30–33, the writer defines *rip currents* as "strong seaward flows of water that can carry even strong swimmers out to sea."

36. **D.** An atlas has maps showing the routes to the various attractions.

37. **B.** An encyclopedia provides general information. An encyclopedia article about the Grand Canyon would include a geological history of the park.

38. **D.** The park guidebook explains all policies, including rules for bringing dogs into the park.

39. **A.** The word *sustainability* comes after *suspense* and before *sway* in the dictionary.

40. **C.** A political map shows the boundaries of the park as well as the boundaries of nearby states. It also shows the location of cities and towns in the area.

Evaluation Chart

Check Your Understanding

On the following chart, circle the number of any question you answered incorrectly. Under each content area you will see the pages you can review to learn the content covered in the question. Pay particular attention to reviewing those lessons in which you missed half or more of the questions.

Chapter	Item Number	Review Pages
Functional Texts	13, 14, 15, 16, 17, 36, 37, 38, 39, 40	12–83
Expository Texts	30, 31, 32, 33, 34, 35	86–113
Persuasive Texts	24, 25, 26, 27, 28, 29	116–152
Literary Nonfiction	6, 7, 8, 9, 10, 11, 12	156–185
Fiction	1, 2, 3 4, 5, 18, 19, 20, 21, 22, 23	188–247

Answer Key

CHAPTER 1 Functional Texts

Lesson 1.1

Think about Reading, page 17

1. **C.** The purpose of this form is to request a review of an employee's behavior. The title of the form states this.

2. **B.** If a manager submits the form, only one signature is needed. This information is stated in the introductory paragraph.

3. **C.** Revealing confidential information is the only choice not listed in Section B.

4. date, time, context of incident, witnesses, prior attempts at correcting behavior

5. Completing Section D, Additional Comments, is optional, so this section does not need to be filled out.

Vocabulary Review, page 18

1. categories

2. encounter

3. functional

4. optional

5. violation

Skill Review, pages 18–19

1. **C.** The last sentence in the first paragraph states that an employee who has worked six months at the zoo can take a medical leave of absence.

2. **A.** An employee on medical leave will not required to attend physical therapy sessions.

3. An employee handbook is the place where employers can state their policies about various issues. Then employees know what is required of them.

4. The Medical Leave of Absence form should include the name of the employee, reason for medical leave, length of medical leave, dates of medical leave, date of employment, employee's signature, and manager's signature.

Skill Practice, pages 20–21

1. **B.** This document is a business memo that describes a company policy on shoplifters.

2. **D.** Store employees are advised to follow their manager's instructions. They are told not to follow the shoplifter.

3. **D.** Peyton is the owner of the store. This information is included in the "From" line of the memo.

4. **A.** Employees should discourage shoplifters by being visible to shoppers. They should not risk their own safety, however, by confronting shoplifters.

5. **C.** The main purpose of the memo is to inform employees about a policy. Memos are not written to entertain, confuse, or criticize.

Writing Practice, page 21
Use the memo on page 14 of this lesson as a guide for writing your memo.

Sample Response
To: All Employees
From: Beverly Griswold, President
Date: June 1, 2014
Subject: Excellent News

As a result of your efforts, our company has been without a lost-time accident for six months. We appreciate your concern for safety. The extra care you take around machinery benefits all of us. As a result of your outstanding efforts, each employee will receive an additional 8 hours of vacation time that can be used any time this year.

Lesson 1.2

Think about Reading, page 24

1. **B.** Option A is incorrect because you must remove the hub cap before loosening the lug nuts. Option C is incorrect because you should lower the car before tightening the lug nuts. Option D is incorrect because you should turn on your hazard lights after you safely pull the car off the road.

2. where to place the jack before jacking up the car

Think about Reading, page 25

1. Try to find the location of the paper jam.

2. If the paper jam isn't clear or if the copy machine gets another paper jam right away, you should repeat these steps.

Skill Review, pages 26–27

1. Write your name, address, phone number, and e-mail address at the top of the page. This is important because it tells the employer how to contact you.

2. Your objective tells the employer what kind of job you want.

3. List any special skills you have.

4. The diagram shows how a résumé should look.

5. Your work experience should come after the objective.

Answer Key

Vocabulary Review, page 27
1. diagram
2. résumé
3. sequence
4. instructions

Skill Practice, pages 28–29
1. **D.** The clue word *first* tells you that the first thing to do is to organize the people into a group. The other options all come after that step.
2. **C.** If you don't leave space for yourself, there might not be room for you in the picture. The first step does not relate to focusing the camera or using the self-timer button.
3. **A.** Paragraph 3 explains that pushing the shutter button down halfway allows you to focus the picture. If you push the button down all the way, you would not be able to check whether the picture is in focus. You would use a different button to set the timer. Using the shutter button will not affect getting into the picture or putting your camera on a flat surface.
4. **C.** After pushing the button down halfway, check to make sure the picture is the way you want it. You should not push the button all the way down until you know the picture is in focus. Getting into the picture is the last thing you will do. Setting the camera on a flat surface should be done before you push the shutter button.

Writing Practice, page 29
Keep the sequence of steps in mind as you write your instructions. When you finish, ask yourself if someone could follow your instructions.

Sample Response
How to Prepare Your Garden for Spring Planting
1. Make sure the ground has thawed completely.
2. Trim back any dead plant stalks.
3. Rake up leaves, twigs, or other debris.
4. Dig up at least 6 to 8 inches of the soil. Use a pitch fork or a machine tiller, whichever works best for your space.
5. Apply fertilizer to cover the area. Work it into the soil.
6. Add topsoil, if necessary.

Lesson 1.3

Think about Reading, page 31
1. A website address ending in *.com* belongs to a business. Its purpose is to sell something or give current information about the company.
2. Websites with addresses ending in *.edu* or *.gov* will be the most reliable sources of information.

Think about Reading, page 32
1. The paragraph at the bottom of the web page says you can click on the links to learn more about Anytown Science Center. You should click on the Observatory link.
2. *Sample answers:* tabs (at the top of the web page), headings, left-margin column

Think about Reading, page 33
1. *Sample answer:* You can learn about the history of the White House.
2. The Blue Room is where presidents formally receive guests. You would click on the link "White House Rooms" to learn more about various rooms in the White House.
3. The website is reliable. Its address ends in *.gov*, which means it's an official government website.

Vocabulary Review, page 34
1. **C.**
2. **A.**
3. **B.**
4. **D.**
5. **E.**

Skill Review, pages 34–35
1. There are seven dog groups. The author numbers the dog groups so you can easily find the various kinds of dogs.
2. *Possible responses:* Herding Dogs, Hounds, Non-Sporting Dogs, Sporting Dogs, Terriers, Toy Dogs, Working Dogs
3. The first site would be best. It provides facts and general information about many types of dogs.
4. **A.** Both websites say boxers, which are not sporting dogs, need to be trained.

Skill Practice, pages 36–37
1. **C.** Naismith is known for being the creator of basketball, so the date he invented the game would be the most important information to include.

(Lesson 1.3 cont.)

2. **A.** Website 1 gives general information about the history of basketball. This would make it most useful for a basketball report. Information about soccer would not be helpful. Website 2 would not be a good source for a report because its purpose is to sell basketballs.

3. **B.** Website 2 advertises a variety of basketballs, including colored basketballs, but it does not offer autographed basketballs. It does not sell other equipment.

4. **D.** The purpose of website 1 is to give information about basketball. If you want to learn the rules of the game, buy a basketball, or learn about other sports, you would have to visit a different website.

Writing Practice, page 37

Be sure your letter answers all the questions in the prompt. Include both positive and negative thoughts about the website.

Sample Response

Mr. Grant:

I have recently browsed your company website. I think the home page is neat and mostly easy to read. However, it would be helpful if you put the company's e-mail address and phone number in a more prominent place. Right now they are at the bottom of the page in small type, and they are hard to find. The links to other pages work well. The photos are really interesting. All your employees seem to be proud of their work.

Sincerely,
Rhonda Leven

Lesson 1.4

Think about Reading, page 40

The purpose of this document is to describe the job of an administrative assistant. The document tells what skills someone with this job must have. The audience might be someone who has this job or someone who wants the job.

Think about Reading, page 41

The purpose of this document is to request a conference room reservation. The form gives employees information so they can plan ahead for how the space will be used and gather the necessary equipment. It also gives contact information that employees can use if questions arise.

Think about Reading, page 43

1. **B.** This e-mail is from a supervisor to an employee. The purpose is to the check with the employee about an upcoming meeting.

2. **D.** The questions are intended to help Brian plan ahead for any equipment he needs for his presentation at an up-coming meeting.

3. **C.** An e-mail is a written message, not an oral message. Generally e-mails are casual, everyday forms of communication.

4. The lines below Carolyn's name tell that she is the director of resources at ABC Corporation in New York. From the questions she is asking, you can infer that she is most likely Brian's supervisor.

Vocabulary Review, page 43

1. **C.**
2. **G.**
3. **D.**
4. **E.**
5. **A.**
6. **B.**
7. **F.**

Skill Review, pages 44–45

1. The purpose of the first document is to communicate the safety policy of the company. The audience includes all the people who work at ABC Company.

2. Both documents are about safety in the workplace. The first document is a memo from the company's management to all employees. This letter explains that safety is important. The second document lists the company's safety rules. It communicates workplace rules to employees.

3. The first document says that ABC Company wants to develop a high standard of safety. The company values employees' health and safety and expects employees to be responsible for their own safety and health. The second document lists the safety rules described during orientation. Work must be done in a safe and responsible way. All accidents should be reported.

4. The first document is a letter. It delivers the information in a quick and personal way. The second document is organized as an outline. The bullet points make it easy to read the rules.

Answer Key

Skill Practice, pages 46–47

1. **B.** The level of schooling required for this job is described in the "Education" section. The applicant's work experience, the need for confidentiality, and the variety of tasks do not relate to the schooling required.

2. **C.** This document is a job announcement. Its purpose is to describe a position that someone searching for a new job might be interested in.

3. **D.** The "Special Qualifications" section mentions that the applicant must have the ability to keep records and follow department procedures. These duties require organizational skills. Public speaking, advanced computer expertise, and the ability to speak a second language are not mentioned in the announcement.

4. **C.** This is a job announcement, so it is written for someone looking for a new job. The intended audience is a future employee. This announcement is not written for a supervisor.

Writing Practice, page 47

Your summary should state the main points of the document. In a second paragraph, give the author's purpose for writing the document, and explain what action should be taken after reading the document.

Sample Response

   The workplace document on page 44 is a company memo. The author lists company safety rules regarding general safety, operating machinery, and workplace behavior.

   The author wrote the document so employees will pay careful attention to safety on the job in order to prevent accidents. Employees are supposed to read the rules and follow them at the workplace.

Lesson 1.5

Think about Reading, page 51

1. Both the first-aid sign and the fire-extinguisher sign include pictures and text. Both would be used to show the location of items needed for workplace safety.

2. **A.** Graphic 2 must be placed above a fire extinguisher, or the sign would have no meaning. Graphics 3, 5, and 6 do not depend on their location for meaning.

3. Graphics 3 and 6 are both safety warnings. Both include text and a symbol for a person.

4. These safety signs are effective because they can be quickly and easily understood by everyone. This is important when safety is at risk.

5. *Answers will vary.* Ask your fellow students to "read" your sign so you are sure the message can be figured out quickly and easily. If people have difficulty determining your message, revise your work.

Think about Reading, page 53

1. **D.** Graphic 4 shows how a workplace is organized. The manager is at the top, and the junior coworkers are at the bottom. Graphics 1, 2, and 3 do not represent the structure of a group.

2. **C.** The purpose of Graphic 2 is to show how a decision is made. By asking yourself a series of questions, you can make wise decisions. Graphics 1, 3, and 4 do not ask a series of questions.

3. Both graphics categorize a large group of data into smaller chunks. Graphic 1 categorizes the students in a class according to the month of their birthdays. Graphic 3 categorizes sales according to the territory where the sales occurred. Graphic 1 uses bars to represent the number of students. The taller the bar, the greater the number. Graphic 3 uses a circular pie image. The larger the "slice," the greater the percentage of sales in the area.

4. These documents show complicated information in a simple way. Written documents providing the same information would be longer and more difficult to understand. These graphic documents provide a lot of information very quickly.

Vocabulary Review, page 53

1. **B.**
2. **F.**
3. **E.**
4. **G.**
5. **A.**
6. **D.**
7. **C.**

Skill Review pages 54–55

1. Both graphic documents use art and text to provide information. "Soccer Field" has labels, but the labels are not explained. "Solids and Liquids" gives more information in words.

2. "Soccer Field" shows the layout of a soccer field. "Solids and Liquids" compares and contrasts solids and liquids.

Answer Key

(Lesson 1.5 cont.)

3. Both graphics present information in an easy, clear, and concise way. "Soccer Field" lets the reader visualize the field. "Solids and Liquids" makes it easy to see what characteristics are common to both solids and liquids.

4. *Sample answers for the Venn diagram:*
   Characteristics of cell phones—portable, lightweight, may have extra features, can send text messages.
   Characteristics of landlines—limited range, usually more reliable than a cell phone.
   Characteristic shared by both types of phones—used to send and receive calls.

Skill Practice, pages 56–57

1. **A.** This graphic document uses both art and text. Maps, such as this evacuation map, often have a legend that explains what each symbol represents.

2. **C.** The title of the map says that the purpose of this document is to help people evacuate the building in case of an emergency. While the document is a useful map and it might help workers find fire extinguishers and offices, these are not the primary purpose of the map.

3. The drawing can be "read" quickly. A written evacuation plan might be more detailed, but it would also be much less convenient. In an emergency, people need to quickly understand what to do.

4. Your map should clearly show all possible exits and the route a person should take to find each exit.

Writing Practice, page 57

After describing one of the graphic documents in the lesson, ask a friend to read your paragraph without looking at the sign. If your reader has difficulty understanding your written directions, revise your work.

Sample Response

The purpose of the "Fire/Use Stairs" sign on page 49 is to give instructions on what to do if there is a fire.

If there is a fire in your building, do not use the elevator or escalator. Instead, walk down the stairs.

Lesson 1.6

Think about Reading, page 61

Sample answer: An encyclopedia will give information about the history, major industries, educational institutions, and population of a city. An atlas will show features such as nearby cities, rivers, lakes, and parks.

Think about Reading, page 63

1. **C.** A directory contains names and addresses of people and organizations. Neither a manual nor a handbook will help you find a doctor. A map might show the location of hospitals, but it will not provide a list of doctors' names and phone numbers.

2. **D.** The purpose of a technical manual is to provide details and how-to information about assembling, using, and repairing a product.

3. Information about company policies and procedures, as well as product information, may change from time to time. Old handbooks and manuals may contain incorrect or outdated information.

Vocabulary Review, page 63

1. **G.**
2. **B.**
3. **C.**
4. **D.**
5. **A.**
6. **F.**
7. **E.**

Skill Review, pages 64–65

1. creaky, crease, creature, credence
2. meaning 2
3. crazy, credible
4. the *a* in *cape*
5. two
6. Like a dictionary, a glossary lists words in alphabetical order and gives their meanings. A dictionary provides more details, such as pronunciation and parts of speech. A glossary includes only words used in the text that the glossary appears in.
7. You use a dictionary to find the meaning, pronunciation, or other information about a word. You use a thesaurus to find a synonym when you already know the meaning of the word.

8. C. A key word Is needed to find information In an encyclopedia index. A dictionary does not have an index. Thesauruses and atlases may have indexes, but you do not need a list of topics to use these sources.

9. D. Headings are text features that help you find the information you are looking for. Reading the entire article or studying all the illustrations could take a long time, and very little of that information might relate to your topic. The first and last paragraphs are unlikely to give you the information you need.

10. A. Political maps show borders around states and between countries. The other references will probably not help you find which states border a particular state.

11. C. Directories list names and addresses of people in organizations. The other references provide other types of information.

12. B. People use directories to find businesses. Businesses are not required to be listed in directories. Directory publishers do not pay businesses to be listed; in fact, businesses may pay to be listed in the directory. Any business can be listed in a directory.

Skill Practice, pages 66–67

1. glossary
2. thesaurus, synonym
3. volumes, alphabetical
4. quickly see what words or information is on each page
5. atlas
6. *Sample answer:* Political maps show boundaries between countries, capitals, major cities, and roads, for example.
7. a technical manual
8. the address and phone number of the business
9. *Sample answer:* Company handbooks often include work hours, performance review forms, emergency procedures, employee benefits such as vacation time, contact numbers for the Human Resources Department, and holiday schedules.
10. Both print and digital dictionaries provide definitions, pronunciation guides, parts of speech, and information about the history of the word. Digital dictionaries may also offer audible pronunciation of entries. They may offer links to synonyms.

Writing Practice, page 67

Your paragraph should include data about the area's history, people, physical features, climate, tourist attractions, and culture.

Sample Response

I would like to visit the Historic Triangle area of Yorktown, Jamestown, and Williamsburg in the state of Virginia. Jamestown is the site of the first permanent English settlement in the United States. Williamsburg was the capital of the Virginia colony for several years. Yorktown is the site of the battle that ended the Revolutionary War.

Lesson 1.7

Think about Reading, page 70

Sample answer: I think the video version is more effective than the print version because the video shows workers doing a variety of tasks and many types of workplaces.

Think about Reading, page 73

Sample answers:

1. I can take my bike on the train and then bike from the station to school. Or I can store my bike at either Big Lake Station or Fridley Station and then walk from the station to school.
2. I cannot commute by train to the parade. Memorial Day is a holiday, and trains do not run that day.
3. There is a Park & Ride lot at Big Lake Station where parking is free.
4. The map shows the addresses of the stations and the major highways that are near the stations.

Vocabulary Review, page 73

1. B.
2. E.
3. D.
4. F.
5. C.
6. G.
7. A.

(Lesson 1.7 cont.)

Skill Review, pages 74–75

Sample answers:

1. The video version of the recipe shows the ingredients. The chef explains why the homemade sauce is healthier than store-bought sauce. She makes the recipe sound easy, and it looks like a meal I could serve my family. Watching the video makes me interested in trying the recipe.

2. The video version gives more information about how to do each step of the recipe. It shows what equipment to use, and it provides serving suggestions, such as adding a salad. The print version gives complete ingredient measurements so I can cook the recipe accurately.

3. I would use the idea of sprinkling Parmesan cheese over the top of the dish. I would like to add chopped black olives and ground beef to the sauce.

4. People reading a text use their imagination to "see" and "hear" what is described. However, people viewing a video version see a real cook, real food, and real cooking equipment. They hear real sounds. These sights and sounds show how the video director and the performers interpret the text.

5. The television director usually needs to shorten the demonstration, so the cook time or refrigeration time must be cut. The director cuts to the finished dish to show the results of the recipe. Sometimes the TV show will end with people enjoying the meal.

6. The print version may provide clear step-by-step instructions that can easily be read over and over. However, adding audio and animated video can make it easier to understand how to follow the steps and easier to imagine what the dish will look like.

Skill Practice, pages 76–77

Sample answers:

1. A video about the fair could show all the events that the flyer just mentions by name. People would see the carnival rides, hear fair-goers laughing and having fun, and get a look at the parade and the rodeo. This would inspire them to come to the fair.

2. I would feature the parade, the flat-track racing, the rodeo, the carnival midway, and the fireworks.

3. Both the print train schedule and the online train schedule show the times that trains stop at the stations. The online schedule has a link to a detailed route map that includes station addresses and information about parking, transporting bikes, and days that trains do not operate.

4. On a printed road map, there are roads, towns and cities, and geographical features such as lakes or rivers. On an online interactive map, the same roads, towns and cities, and geographical features appear. An interactive map might have additional information such as road closures and suggestions for alternative routes.

Writing Practice, page 77

Follow the prompt for describing one functional document. First, tell what document you are describing, state the purpose, and describe the audience. Then, summarize the document in your own words. Do not state your opinions. Finally, describe how the message might be more effective in another medium.

Sample response

I chose the online version of the travel advisory from page 69. The author's purpose is to give information about road conditions during the storm. The audience is anyone who is driving on the roads.

The document describes current road conditions in various areas. It also tells what the weather will be like the next day.

The text might be more effective as a multimedia document because viewers could see maps that would help them locate the problem areas and plan routes around those areas.

Chapter 1 Review

Chapter 1 Review, pages 78–80

1. **A.** It is easier to return an item with a receipt because you have proof you purchased the item. Different stores have different rules for returning an item without a receipt.

2. **C.** Going directly to the customer service counter when you are returning an item prevents employees from thinking you took something without paying for it. This is not a guarantee that you will get a refund or that you will be served quickly, but it can prevent a misunderstanding.

3. **C.** This article gives advice to people who do not have receipts. A customer who has a receipt or is happy with a purchase would not need the advice.

4. **D.** Step 1 advises you to make sure you have all the parts for the item you are returning. Without all the pieces, you may not be able to return the item for a refund or store credit.

5. **B.** The company pledge promises to sell "cost-effective, high-quality mattresses."

Answer Key

6. **D.** The company's goal states that it wants to be the top mattress company in the world. Options A and C refer only to the United States. The company is not trying to sell the cheapest mattresses in the world.

7. **C.** The company's goal states that it will use innovation and new design to make superior mattresses. It does not say mattresses will be produced cheaply outside the United States.

8. **A.** The last sentence under the heading "Our Professionalism" states the company's expectations of its employees.

9. **C.** This website is not the best place to get the facts about the game because it gives the opinions of a Sonics fan. The website says the referees made many unfair calls. Tornadoes fans might not agree.

10. **A.** All the choices are links to more information, but *www.citysonicsnews.com* is the only link to news updates.

11. **C.** The website uses boldfaced type to help you find important information quickly.

12. **B.** The web page has a series of tabs across the top. The best place to find a list of games would be the "Schedule" tab.

Essay Writing Practice

Essay Writing Practice, pages 82–83
Answers will vary. Here are some points to consider.

Memos and Forms

- Your memo should open by clearly stating the information it contains. For example: *Here are the details of our company Family Day Picnic on Saturday, June 10.*
- The body of the memo should provide all the details employees will need to attend the picnic. Include, for example, the start time and likely end time; suggest equipment or gear employees will need; describe the menu; give the location, with a description of available facilities; and provide directions. Include contact information for any questions.
- Edit your essay. As you proofread the essay, use your computer's spell-checker to check for spelling errors. Double-check the spelling and capitalization of names of people and places.

How-To and Instructions

- Your instructions should open by stating their purpose. For example: *Here is our process for taking customer orders. It has been developed over time, and we have found it to be highly effective.*
- The steps in the process should be numbered. They should include details that will help the person complete the task independently. For example: *To check whether stock is available, enter the item's order code in the search box on the customer order form. If the item is out of stock, ask the customer if you should like to back-order it.*
- Edit your instructions. As you proofread the instructions, use your computer's spell-checker to check for spelling errors. Double-check the spelling and capitalization of names of people and places.

Workplace Documents

- Your meeting summary should open by stating the date and purpose of the meeting. For example: *The sales managers met on March 4 to discuss strategies for new projects.*
- The summary should list each agenda item from the meeting and describe what decisions were made about each item. Include names of people who will be following up on the decisions.
- Edit your summary. As you proofread the summary, use your computer's spell-checker to check for spelling errors. Double-check the spelling and capitalization of names of people and places.

Reference Texts

- The reference texts you select will depend on your topic. For example, encyclopedias give basic information about a broad range of topics. Handbooks and manuals provide instructions.
- To explain the advantage of each type of reference text, look at sample reference texts online or in a library. Do some research on your topic so you see what kind of information you find in various types of reference texts.
- Edit your list of reference texts and your description of the texts. As you proofread the list, use your computer's spell-checker to check for spelling errors. Double-check the spelling and capitalization of the titles of your references.

CHAPTER 2 Expository Texts

Lesson 2.1

Think about Reading, page 87

2   Ask yourself questions.

5   Write answers to your questions.

1   Scan titles, headings, and boldface words.

3   Read for facts and ideas.

4   Look again at main ideas, details, and concepts.

Think about Reading, page 88

1. *filial piety* and *extended family*

2. How important is family in China?

3. The family was the basic unit of Chinese society and the most important.

Think about Reading, page 89

1. This topic is Egyptian society and daily life.

2. *Scribes* and *hieroglyphics* are in boldfaced type.

Vocabulary Review, page 90

1. C.

2. D.

3. A.

4. E.

5. B.

Skill Review, pages 90–91

1. Because the title is "Religion of the Byzantine Empire," you can assume the passage will be about the religions practiced in the Byzantine Empire.

2. Underline the second part of sentence 1. It states the most important idea in the paragraph— disagreements over religion occurred.

3. D.   "There was also a disagreement about the power of Rome over the Eastern churches."

4. Caste, Members, Work

5. Brahman, Kshatriya, Vaishya, Sudra, and Untouchable

6. Brahman

Skill Practice, pages 92–93

1. D.   This word *codify* appears in boldfaced type, which tells you that it is an important word or a vocabulary word.

2. B.   This section is mostly about what happened if a law was broken and how much control the law had over society. The other options are all mentioned in the excerpt, but they are details, not the main idea.

3. C.   The main idea of the first paragraph is that Hammurabi created an empire. The other choices are supporting details.

4. A.   The title explains that the table shows the achievements of Mesopotamia.

Writing Practice, page 93

Choose a topic that is interesting to you. Check to make sure you have used transitions to link your ideas.

Sample Essay

Ever since I saw a television documentary about the Everglades, I have wanted to learn more about this interesting place. I have a list of things I want to research, including the history, the types of animals and vegetation that live there, and how modern life is affecting the area. The first resource I will check is the Everglades National Park website. I will read Frequently Asked Questions and check out some of the links. I may also use an online search engine to find more websites. After that I will talk to the reference librarian at the county library. She is always helpful, and she should be able to help me find books to read. Also, I have a friend who used to live in Florida, so I will talk to him.

Lesson 2.2

Think about Reading, page 96

1. The article is mostly about the possibility that Napoleon may have been poisoned. The title shows that this is the topic of the article.

2. The most surprising evidence was how well Napoleon's body was preserved. This information can be found under the heading "Shocking Evidence."

3. The painting is of Napoleon. The caption tells the reader who is in the painting.

Think about Reading, page 97

1. "Experience Counts"

2. adults ages 18 and 19

Answer Key

Vocabulary Review, page 98

1. E.
2. A.
3. C.
4. D.
5. F.
6. B.

Skill Review, pages 98–99

1. In "Making Better Choices" the author explains how menus showing calorie counts affect the choices people make in restaurants.
2. The headings show three important ideas in the article: the importance of menu labeling, your right to know, and making better choices.
3. how people react to the idea of labeling menus
4. **A.** The graph shows that 76% of people (which is most people) would make better choices.

Skill Practice, pages 100–101

1. **D.** People who are from countries as different as these would have very different cultures. Coming from different countries does not necessarily mean that they have different levels of education or that they come from different economic classes. They would not have similar languages and experiences.
2. **A.** "Shattered Dreams" is the best choice because the paragraph tells that most miners did not fulfill their dream of striking it rich. The paragraph mentions traveling to California, but that is not the main idea. The paragraph is about California in the past, not the present.
3. **B.** People from diverse backgrounds came to California, so the population became more diverse. Many people stayed in California even if they didn't find gold. Although the passage mentions that foreign miners were taxed, it does not say that taxes caused them to leave California.
4. **C.** The purpose of the article is to give information about the gold rush. Dates, numbers, and facts are clues that the purpose is to inform.
5. **C.** The graph shows that Mexicans/South Americans were the second-largest group in California in 1852.

Writing Practice, page 101

Your review of a newspaper or magazine article should include a summary of the article, your opinion of the article, and examples to support your opinion.

Sample Response

A recent article in a cooking magazine explains the health benefits of some cooking oils. The article is useful and informative. A simple, easy-to-read chart shows which oils to use for cooking and baking and which oils to use for salad dressings. The article gives recipes that use various types of oils. The last part of the article describes the benefits of various oils. It also names a few recommended brands. After reading this article, I plan to purchase several of these oils.

LESSON 2.3

Think about Reading, page 105

1. **A.** *Monitor*, *inspect*, *require*, and *allow* are all words that have to do with making and enforcing rules. The other words might be found in instruction manuals, consumer information documents, and process flowcharts.
2. **C.** Numbered sections show the order and importance of information. Flowcharts use symbols to show a repetition of events, while regulations often use outline style. Poetic language is not used in technical documents.

Vocabulary Review, page 106

1. D.
2. A.
3. C.
4. B.

Skill Review, page 106

1. *Sample answer:* This information might be in a how-to book or an article about laying a hardwood floor. It could also be in an instruction manual for laying a floor or in the instructions that come with flooring materials.
2. The illustration shows how and where to place the first long board.
3. *Sample answers:* debris, chalk line, long board, pilot holes, base, random lengths, grooved

(Lesson 2.3 cont.)

Skill Practice, page 107

1. **D.** A technical document is written to provide information on a specialized subject. Texts that persuade, entertain, and tell about a person's life all have other purposes.

2. **B.** The format of a technical text varies depending on why the text was written. A technical text might have diagrams, numbered steps, or boldfaced headers, for example.

3. **A.** Looking for context clues in surrounding sentences is a good way to figure out the meaning of an unfamiliar word. Skipping the word or removing it would not be useful. Substituting another word can be done after you think you know the meaning of the unfamiliar word.

4. *Sample answer:* Consumers need clear information about how to use the products they purchase. Using products incorrectly can be unsafe. It can also damage the product.

Writing Practice, page 107

Choose a document describing a task that is unfamiliar to you so you can evaluate how effective the format, explanation of technical terms, and graphics are.

Sample Response

I chose a text that gave instructions for programming my DVR remote to control the volume and power functions on my TV. The instructions were laid out in numbered steps with illustrations showing the buttons on the remote. Bulleted points gave details that made it easy to follow the directions. Because most of the language was simple, I could understand the technical words and abbreviations such as "sat" and "sel."

Chapter 2 Review

Chapter 2 Review, pages 108–110

1. **C.** Black Hawk believed the chiefs had been drunk when they signed the contract to give up their land. His refusal was not because of hunting, a contract, or land won from another tribe.

2. **A.** He fought for his land to protect it. He gave up his land only after losing the battle. He did not sign a contract.

3. **B.** The Black Hawk War took place in 1832. None of the other events took place in 1832.

4. **D.** Black Hawk was fighting for his land. If he had won the war, he probably would have kept the land.

5. **C.** According to the article, 85% of newspaper advertising is done by local businesses and individuals. Therefore, it would make sense to advertise a refrigerator in the newspaper.

6. **A.** The company's goal is to advertise nationally. The article says that television and magazines are good ways to reach a national audience. Since magazines are not one of the options, television is the best answer.

7. **A.** According to the graph, about 4 billion dollars is spent every year on outdoor advertising in the United States. This is the lowest amount listed.

8. **B.** The main idea of this section is that advertising is important to the economy.

9. **C.** The article explains that rising temperatures are melting the ice blocks that polar bears live on, so polar bears are drowning.

10. **B.** The quotation is included to show that an expert supports the author's argument about what is happening to the polar bears.

11. **C.** The article states that using coal and oil releases carbon dioxide. The carbon dioxide helps raise temperatures. If people used less coal and oil, there would be less carbon dioxide in the air. The other options would not decrease the amount of carbon dioxide in the air.

12. **C.** The graph shows that the amount of carbon dioxide in the air has increased over time.

Answer Key

Essay Writing Practice

Essay Writing Practice, pages 112–113
Answers will vary. Here are some points to consider.

Textbooks and Other Educational Materials

- Before you begin writing your guide, follow the directions to access the site. Take notes about each step. For example: *American History link is organized by time periods from 1492 to present.*
- To select a topic, choose a time period and click on the link for a collection that interests you. Take advantage of "Explore More" links to see a wide variety of topics.
- Edit your guide. As you proofread the guide, make sure each sentence starts with a capital letter and ends with a punctuation mark.

Magazine and Newspaper Articles

- Your article should open with a clear description of one NASA mission, including NASA's goals for the mission. For example: *NASA is working with the European Space Agency (ESA) on the Euclid mission. Euclid is scheduled to launch in 2020. It will put a new telescope in space to explore the mysteries of dark energy and dark matter.*
- Your paragraphs should explain the mission's contribution to science and describe how the mission will be conducted. For example: *Scientists on the mission want to understand the nature of dark matter, an invisible substance that has a gravitational pull on other matter. They will analyze the shapes of galaxies to find dark matter.*
- Edit your article. As you proofread the article, make sure each sentence starts with a capital letter and ends with the appropriate punctuation mark.

CHAPTER 3 Persuasive Texts

Lesson 3.1

Think about Reading, page 118

1. Sentences 1, 3, and 4 are facts. They name the stores and give specific prices.

2. Sentences 2 and 5 are the opinions of the shopper.

3. The words *It seems to me*, *cheapest*, and *best* signal personal opinions.

Think about Reading, page 119

1. F   3. O
2. O   4. F

Think about Reading, page 120

1. **C.** It can be proven that StormStand homes are raised off the ground. The other choices are opinions.

2. **A.** This statement is meant to persuade you that you need a StormStand home because your home would not be safe if there were a violent storm.

3. "Ask anyone" does not provide evidence that StormStand homes are the best homes built. Most people would not know whether StormStand homes have the best record of storm survival.

Vocabulary Review, page 121

1. fact   4. argument
2. advertisement   5. opinion
3. slogan   6. logo

Skill Review, pages 121–122

1. **B.** By looking at the pen, you can see whether it has an applicator. The other choices are opinions that cannot be proven.

2. **C.** The ad assures you of a bright future if you use TruWhite. It does not show a celebrity using the product. No facts are provided. The ad never claims the product will save you money.

3. *best* and *most*

4. The ad tries to convince you that people are happy with this product and that it gives good results. However, you have no way to knowing how many people would agree with this opinion.

5. *Sample answer:* The ad does not tell how much whiter TruWhite makes your teeth or give data about other whiteners. The ad mostly states opinions. Therefore, it is impossible to tell if TruWhite is the best and most effective whitener available.

Skill Practice, page 123

1. **B.** Some people may not agree that bread, spaghetti, and cake represent all the good things in life. Therefore, this part of the sentence is an opinion.

2. **C.** The first sentence is a question addressed to someone who wants a new diet. People who are satisfied with other diets would not need Easy Diet. The ad mentions worrying, but it is a casual reference to people who are worried losing weight.

3. **D.** Data on how much weight people have lost using the product would be the most helpful information to have. A graph created by the FDA, an independent government agency, would be more reliable than a graph created by the company trying to sell the product.

4. **A.** Many people reading the ad are already on a diet. The ad wants readers to try Easy Diet. It is not trying to convince people that certain foods are bad. The ad says Easy Diet has the flavor of a milk shake, but it doesn't say Easy Diet is a milk shake.

Writing Practice, page 123

Be sure your advertisement uses facts and opinions effectively. Make your ad interesting and informative.

Sample Response

M & L Birthday Party Service

Do you need help thinking of an exciting theme for your child's next birthday party? Let us help you! We are two enthusiastic grandmothers who like kids and have lots of creative ideas. We have hosted more than 100 parties with themes that include dancing, costumes, science experiments, arts and crafts, and nature hikes. One young boy told us his party was "the best I've ever been to." A fourth-grade girl told us, "This party shows me that science really rocks!" A guest at one party asked her mom to have us give her next party. Parents give us high praise for our caring and creativity. Call 555-1111 and ask for Martina or Lisa.

Lesson 3.2

Think about Reading, page 125

When reading editorials, you should consider whose opinion is being expressed and what evidence supports the writer's opinion.

Answer Key

Think about Reading, page 126

A. In the last two paragraphs of the editorial, the author argues that citizens will be defenseless if handguns are banned.

C. The author says this in paragraph 6. The other statements are from the editorial, but they do not support the author's conclusion.

Think about Reading, page 127

1. They both discuss a ban on handguns.

2. The first editorial is against banning handguns, and the second editorial supports a ban.

Think about Reading, page 128

1. The letters are less formal than the editorials. They have a conversational tone.

2. *Sample answer:* I think the first letter is more persuasive because it includes facts and statistics from reliable sources.

Vocabulary Review, page 129

1. B.	4. C.
2. E.	5. A.
3. F.	6. D.

Skill Review, pages 129–130

1. **C** The writer of this article states that the driving age should be lowered to give teens time for more driving practice. The author would not agree with the other options.

2. **B** The author gives statistics from the Insurance Institute for Highway Safety showing how raising the driving age saves lives. The other options do not support the author's conclusion.

3. The writer of "Is 16 Too Young to Drive?" does not give supporting facts. The writer provides only opinions. "I think it is a lack of experience" is one of the writer's opinions.

4. The writer of "It's Time to Raise the Driving Age" provides statistics that compare the crash-related deaths of New Jersey (where the driving age is 17) to Connecticut (where the driving age is 16).

5. **C** Options A, B, and D are each mentioned by one of the writers, but not by both.

6. **B** Only one writer thinks the driving age should be raised. The other writer thinks the driving age should be lowered.

Skill Practice, page 131

1. **A.** The editorial includes details about Palmer's fashionable clothes and expensive car while explaining that farmers are borrowing money to keep their land. The editorial does not imply that farmers aren't hardworking or don't keep their promises. Farmers borrow money and work hard, so they certainly care about their future.

2. **B.** The editorial is biased against Representative Palmer. Details imply that she is more concerned with re-election than with farming. The author is not against farming, picnicking, or homegrown food.

3. **B.** By not meeting the farmers at the Powell farm, Palmer shows she doesn't care much about farmers. People usually take time to meet those they care about.

4. **C.** Farmer are likely to agree with this editorial, but Representative Palmer and her supporters probably won't. Voters must make their own decision about the ideas in the editorial.

Writing Practice, page 131

Be sure your opinion is supported by facts and statistics.

Sample Response

Members of the Board of Supervisors:

Three months ago, you ended weekly recycling pickups in our community and went to monthly pickups. I believe this was a mistake. Many people in the community agree with me. Too many people now put their recyclables in the regular trash rather than save them for four weeks. Your effort to save money means that we are doing less recycling. Please consider weekly or biweekly pickups—so we all do a better job of protecting the environment.

Sincerely,
Cheol Kim

Lesson 3.3

Think about Reading, page 133
1. T
2. T
3. F
4. F

Think about Reading, page 134
1. She was dynamic and determined and worked tirelessly.
2. to thank Lavinia and Walter for their vision for the center

Think about Reading, page 135
1. *super cool* and *You won't be disappointed!*
2. **C.** The store sells Stella Marie Soaps and Scrubs. The author of this passage is the creator of those soaps. She will benefit if people buy them at Elisia's on Broadway.
3. **A.** The author is trying to persuade people to buy her soaps at Elisia's on Broadway. She is not trying to inform, entertain, or describe.

Vocabulary Review, page 136
1. endorse
2. blog
3. qualifications
4. persuade
5. judgment

Skill Review, pages 136–137
1. **B.** The author calls the message boards a "gimmick." He does not think it is necessary to tell fans to cheer. He does not like message boards, and he does not think Fenway Park should use them. He never says he likes the sound of cheers.
2. **C.** "Way to tell it like it is!" indicates that the author feels that Rose is telling the truth. The other options are statements of fact. They do not reveal the author's opinion.
3. The author agrees with the announcer's opinion that telling New York fans to cheer is a gimmick. He says that Fenway Park, home of the Red Sox, has never done this. You can infer from this that the author is a Red Sox fan.
4. The word *rowdy* means "wild, loud, or out of control."

Skill Practice, pages 138–139
1. **A.** The author wants the superintendent to let him have a Monday off, even though it is against the official policy. He does not expect the superintendent to plan his travel or let him use two personal days. The superintendent has no control over the date of the game.
2. **C.** The author wants to get a fair hearing. He knows the superintendent can make exceptions to the policy. He presents his arguments about why he needs an extra day off. He also offers some bargaining ideas.
3. **D.** The author would be biased toward a rule that lets teachers use personal days at any time.
4. **B.** The author says he would be willing to write about his trip for the school paper. This option would have the most direct benefit for the school.
5. **D.** The audience would be anyone who reads the blog. The author does not know whether of Manchester United team members, the superintendent, or fellow teachers read his blog.

Writing Practice, page 139
Review the contents of a blog and make comments about the blogger's writing style.

Sample Response

I have been reading the *Green It Up* blog by Emily. She is involved in the city's efforts to improve our green living efforts. Emily's writing style is simple and easy to read. She is sometimes funny; she's never nasty or critical of others. She gives helpful suggestions about recycling and reusing things. In one entry, she posted a map of all the city's bike routes. In other entries, she reviews local restaurants that are doing their part to help the environment. I have eaten at a few of these places. The food is tasty and the workers support our efforts to promote green living. I will continue to read this excellent blog.

Answer Key

Lesson 3.4

Think about Reading, page 142

1. Poetry can be a valuable tool to explore personality. Paragraph 1 states that students are using poetry to explore who they are.

2. Readers will be hooked by Grimes's creative premise. The reviewer makes no negative comments about poetry.

3. *Sample answer:* "As always, Grimes gives young people exactly what they are looking for—real characters who show them they are not alone."

Think about Reading, page 143

Sample answers:

What I Know: People work hard at things they love or things they think are important.

Inference: Aldo Castillo thinks it's important to showcase Latino art.

Vocabulary Review, page 144

1. criticized
2. implied
3. commentary
4. review
5. analysis

Skill Review, pages 144–145

1. **A.** At the start of the review, the reviewer states that the author got his ideas from more than 40 years of working with leaders in many fields, so you can infer that the author is very experienced.

2. This sentence means that you should prevent problems before they happen. Then you will not have problems to solve.

3. **C.** The reviewer clearly thinks the play is good and the acting is excellent.

4. *Sample answer:* The reviewer is giving the play a good recommendation and is implying that people should support their local community theater by going to see it.

Skill Practice, pages 145–146

1. **B.** The review provides an opinion about the show, so you could use the review to determine whether to see the show. It does not describe steps for becoming a sculptor or Davis's skill as a barber. It would not be useful for a report because it has more opinions than facts.

2. **D.** The author thinks that Davis is so talented that he cannot be categorized in one simple way. The other options tell facts about Davis rather opinions about Davis's work.

3. **A.** Ads are written to persuade people. Option A is the best choice because it presents a good reason to see the exhibit.

4. **C.** It is the reviewer's opinion that the show is *excellent. Love* describes what Davis thinks about barbering, *Treasure* is part of the title of the show, and *quoted* does not express an opinion.

Writing Practice, page 147

Respond to a review of a book or a movie that you are familiar with. Include explanations of why you agree and disagree with the reviewer.

Sample Response

The review I read of the movie *Lincoln* says that the scenery is authentic and well done. I certainly agree with this statement. I also agree that the director was right to include only real people in the movie; there are no added fictional characters. However, I disagree with the reviewer's opinion that some scenes are overly dramatic. I think the scenes about the passage of the 13th Amendment add suspense to the movie.

Answer Key

Chapter 3 Review

Chapter 3 Review, pages 101–103

1. **B.** The writer uses description to remind readers of clutter in their homes. Finding out what readers need or reminding them to organize are not the goals of advertising. The paragraph would be too long to be used as a tagline, or slogan, for a business.

2. **C.** The writer is selling organizing services and wants readers to purchase them. There is no evidence that the writer wants readers to clean and organize their homes on their own.

3. **D.** "25% more effective" looks like a statistic, but effectiveness not something that can be measured; it is an opinion. This number is misleading and meaningless.

4. **D.** The article describes both benefits and criticisms. It carefully looks at both sides of the issue of nuclear power.

5. **B.** Bill Kerby is part of a group that wants to be sure the plant is safe. A person concerned about radiation hazards would be most likely to agree with him.

6. **D.** Stanley Novak is president of the company that owns the plant. Therefore, he would support it.

7. **B.** The author presents two opinions about the opening of the nuclear power plant, so the purpose is to compare opinions. The author does not say that the plant should not be opened, nor does the author focus on why nuclear power is beneficial.

8. **C.** The author talks about why she likes to blog and she tells about her grandmother, but her real purpose is to encourage bloggers to be safe.

9. **C.** The food and cake are safe details that the author would share. The author advises against giving addresses and the names of children. She also cautions against writing anything that might be "hurtful."

10. **C.** The author warns against giving your address because that would make it easy for readers to find you. The other options do not relate to your home address.

11. **B.** The author enjoys feeling connected. She would not agree with any of the other options.

Essay Writing Practice

Essay Writing Practice, page 152

Answers will vary. Here are some points to consider.

Editorial

- Your editorial should open with a clear statement of your claim. For example: *Violent video games should be outlawed.* Your introduction may include an anecdote, or story, about your topic as a way to interest readers.

- The paragraphs in the body of your editorial should provide facts and reasons to support your opinion. This may include quotations from experts or well-known people. You can also use statistics, or data, as support. Use persuasive language.

- Acknowledge opposing opinions. Use facts to show why your opinion is better. Conclude your editorial with a brief summary that restates your opinion. Encourage readers to take positive action that supports your opinion.

- Edit your editorial. As you proofread your editorial, check that you have correctly spelled the names and job titles for any individuals you have quoted. Make sure the titles of publications you have mentioned are spelled accurately.

Answer Key

CHAPTER 4 Literary Nonfiction

Lesson 4.1

Think about Reading, page 157

1. The author is watching what is happening on the streets of the ghetto where he lives. He may be looking out a window or sitting on a park bench.

2. He is disgusted with the police, who dress up in new clothes and act important.

Think about Reading, page 158

1. *Sample answers:* "nearly half-dead," "I have just slept sixteen hours at a stretch," "I am all right again," "My eyes are still tired"

2. *Sample answer:* Despite being ill, Van Gogh worked with great energy and purpose.

Think about Reading, page 159

This excerpt is written to sound like normal speech, so it is prose. It is about real people and real events, so it is nonfiction.

Think about Reading, page 160

1. **C.** Author Stephen King seems surprised by the amount of money he will receive for his book. This implies that this is the first time he has sold a book to a major publisher.

2. **D.** He says, "The strength ran out of my legs" and "I kind of whooshed down to a sitting position there in the doorway." This all implies that he was shocked by the news.

Vocabulary Review, page 161

1. Nonfiction
2. Prose
3. genre
4. essay
5. diary
6. memoir

Skill Review, pages 161–162

1. **B.** Elizabeth's problem was that her skirts kept blowing up when she walked outdoors. With her skirts weighted down, she could walk about the post (military fort) even when it was windy. *Constitutionals* must mean "walks."

2. In the passage, the author mentions the Civil War, so the event must have taken place after the Civil War. Also, the women's skirts are described as being very large, which is what women wore after the Civil War.

3. **C.** Adams is referring to mail when he says the delivery of the post was later than usual.

4. **B.** Adams states he was very happy because of the "favorable Account . . . of all the Family."

5. **C.** This is a letter. There is a date at the top, and the writer says he is responding to a letter he just received from his wife.

Skill Practice, page 163

1. **B.** The purpose of this excerpt is to inform. Mortenson wants to tell people about a time in his life when he was trying to find a way to raise money from rich Americans. He is not criticizing, persuading, or entertaining.

2. **B.** Greg Mortenson is very determined. He saved money by sleeping in his car rather than paying rent. He looked up names of famous people he could ask for money. There is nothing in the passage to suggest that he is reckless, flighty, or fearful.

Writing Practice, page 163

Start by choosing an experience you have had that others might enjoy hearing about. Explain why you chose a particular genre.

Sample Response

I chose a journal entry because I like to jot down details about my experiences.

I was stopped at the traffic light near the airport when police motorcycles blocked all traffic. I heard a loud rumbling and looked up to see Air Force One coming in for a landing. Amazing! A few minutes later, the President's motorcade roared down the street and turned in front of me. What a day!

Answer Key

Lesson 4.2

Think about Reading, page 164

1. F
2. T
3. F
4. T

Think about Reading, page 166

Sample answer: I think the author believes Mandela was a good, kind, and just leader. The quotations and other information show that Mandela respected people and their opinions and that he was compassionate.

Think about Reading, page 167

1. **B.** The information included in this excerpt shows that Derek was dedicated to baseball at an early age. He loved playing baseball and watching professional games.

2. **B.** This excerpt shows that Derek Jeter was special from an early age. It does not describe his baseball technique or his warmup routine.

Vocabulary Review, page 168

1. biography
2. unauthorized
3. authorized
4. emphasize
5. chronological

Skill Review, pages 168–169

1. **A.** False
   B. True
   C. True

2. **A.** The excerpt begins with the word *politics* in all capital letters. The author does this to emphasize the importance of politics in Clinton's life.

3. **B.** An atlas includes maps, which would show where Park Ridge, Illinois, is located. An almanac, an encyclopedia, or a magazine would not help you locate Park Ridge.

4. **D.** Magazines feature current events and interviews with famous people. You would probably not find this type of text in an almanac, atlas, or encyclopedia.

5. **C.** An encyclopedia has articles on a variety of subjects, including famous people and historical events. An almanac, an atlas, and a magazine would not be the best resources for this type of information.

Skill Practice, pages 170–171

1. **C.** Harriet saw her mother resist efforts to sell her brother. This would have helped her understand that resistance was an option. She did leave Maryland, she was around slaves for most of her life, and she returned to Dorchester County many times, so the other options are not correct.

2. **D.** Harriet was determined that her people should have the freedom she found in St. Catharines. She was willing to do whatever she could for the people she loved.

3. **A.** We can infer that when Harriet made trips between Canada and the Eastern Shore of Maryland, she was helping fugitive slaves reach freedom.

4. **C.** The author thinks Harriet Tubman was brave and hardworking. She includes details about the difficult conditions Tubman faced and the many jobs she had to support herself. Tubman was not foolish, and she was not a county official. She did understand the value of freedom.

Writing Practice, page 171

Describe an event that will make your readers interested in knowing more about the subject of the biography.

Sample Response

Erma Rombauer (1877–1962) was the author of *Joy of Cooking*. In 1995 the New York Library put the book on its list of the 150 most influential books of the 20th century. As a young bride, Rombauer was not a good cook. After her husband died suddenly, she decided to write a cookbook to support herself. She collected recipes that she and her daughter tested. Her daughter illustrated the recipes, and they self-published the first version of the cookbook. In 1936, Bobbs-Merril took over publication. *Joy of Cooking* is still one of the most popular American cookbooks.

Answer Key

Lesson 4.3

Think about Reading, page 174

1. The words *I* and *my* show that this passage was written from the first-person point of view.

2. *Sample answer:* The narrator tells what he was thinking and uses chronological order to tell about events in his life. These are characteristics of an autobiography.

Think about Reading, page 175
Sample answer:

What the Character Does	What This Shows about the Character
He worried about how he looked.	He wanted to impress girls.
He cracked jokes in school.	He wanted people to like him.
He listened to his teacher.	He valued what his teacher said.

Think about Reading, page 176
Sample answer: Orman might have tried to hide the fact that she had difficulty learning foreign languages.

Vocabulary Review, page 177
1. pattern
2. perspective
3. subjective
4. characteristics
5. autobiography

Skill Review, pages 177–178

1. *Sample answer:* As two children escaped Vietnam in 1982, they saw their father for the last time.

2. SEQUENCE CHAIN

    1. Two children were awakened at 4 a.m.
    2. They were told to act natural so no one would know they were escaping.
    3. They arrived at the bus station.
    4. Their father bought them tickets for the trip.
    5. The children took their seats; the narrator was sad.
    6. The narrator watched her father as the bus drove off.

3. *Sample answer:* Two children were escaping from Vietnam in 1982. Their parents woke them up early, and their father took them to the bus station. They tried to act natural so no one would know they were escaping. Their father bought them bus tickets, and they said goodbye. Both the children and the father were upset and feared they might never see one another again.

4. If this story were written as a biography, it might not have included details such as what Kim-Hue Phan was thinking and feeling as she watched her father stare at the bus.

Skill Practice, page 179

1. **D.** The author and his mother had a close and affectionate relationship. They spent time together and talked about their feelings and wishes. The author describes his mother lovingly.

2. **B.** The car was "rust-spackled," so it was probably old. If it "sounded like a Civil War cannon," it was loud. It could not have been built during the Civil War, and it was not shiny or new.

Writing Practice, page 179
Include details about what you were thinking and what you learned from your experience. These are details that no one else could know.

Sample Response

I was born in New Jersey in 1974. My parents were in the military, so we moved frequently. By the time I graduated from eighth grade, I had lived in South Korea, Japan, Germany, and Italy. I learned languages easily, and I liked speaking in a foreign language, even if it was only a few words. My parents made friends with many local people, and I was happy to learn about different foods and cultures. We spent my high school years in California, and I also went to college there.

Chapter 4 Review

Chapter 4 Review, pages 180–182

1. **B.** To Maya Lin, landscape is an important element in design. She wanted her design to fit the beautiful park where the monument would be.

2. **C.** Winning the contest was Lin's major achievement. The other options tell how she prepared her entry and what she did after winning.

3. **A.** The purpose of the memorial is to honor the dead. Lin's design was chosen because it would help people remember the men and women who lost their lives fighting in Vietnam.

4. **C.** The words *howl, moo, creaking,* and *bang* are all sound words. The author includes them to show how the ranch sounds.

5. **A.** The author includes vivid, descriptive details to help readers picture the sights and sounds of the ranch. She does not tell what life is like on a ranch or help readers find the ranch. She does not include persuasive language.

6. **A.** The author clearly values the culture and traditions of the Ojibway. She talked to her children when they were small and continues to tell them stories about their culture.

7. **D.** The details shared by the author all show she thinks knowledge of the past is important.

8. **A.** The author says that her children want her to tell stories about the past and that she plans to do that, so it is likely she will tell stories to her grandchildren.

9. **B.** The author uses the image of the chain to show that she is linked to the past because she thinks the past is important. She is not a prisoner of the past, and she does not want to be free from the past. It is not possible to travel back to the past.

Essay Writing Practice

Essay Writing Practice, pages 184–185
Answers will vary. Here are some points to consider.

Biography

- Your biography should open with an interesting story that shows others why this person is important to you.

- Your paragraphs should be organized in time order. Each event should support a central idea. For example, if your central idea is that this person is your role model, you can tell stories about how the person showed qualities you value, such as courage and persistence.

- Edit your biography. As you proofread the biography, check sentences to be sure that subjects and verbs agree in number. For example: *She has helped many people*, or *Many family members have helped him.*

Autobiography

- Your autobiography should open with an interesting story that will make others want to read about your life.

- Your paragraphs should be organized in time order. Use details of sights and sounds to keep your readers engaged. For example: *When I dove into the sparkling blue water of the pool, all my troubles floated away. I didn't realize I'd won the race until I heard my mother screaming my name.*

- Edit your autobiography. As you proofread the autobiography, check sentences to be sure that subjects and verbs agree in number. For example: *The kids were cheering*, or *I was cheering too.*

Answer Key

CHAPTER 5 Fiction

Lesson 5.1

Think about Reading, page 190

1. Bill and Mary, who dated years earlier, meet in Washington Square in New York City.

2. Mary and Bill do not know quite what to say to each other.

3. Mary and Bill say good-bye to each other as Mary gets on her bus.

4. Mary realizes that she and Bill do not know how to contact each other, so it is unlikely they will meet later.

Think about Reading, page 193

1. The story takes place on an isolated island. "He must explore this island quickly."

2. The time is in the past. Pentaquod is using a canoe to explore the island.

3. The mood is quiet and cautious. "With extreme caution he started inland, noticing everything."

Vocabulary Review, page 193

1. C.
2. E.
3. B.
4. A.
5. D.

Skill Review, pages 194–195

1. A. The exposition includes information about the characters (an old lady and Tom), the setting (the lady's house), and the conflict (the lady is looking for Tom). Aunt Polly's finding Tom and her looking away are part of the rising action. Aunt Polly's laughter is part of the resolution.

2. B. The high point of the action occurs when Tom gets away from Aunt Polly. The other three events are part of the exposition and rising action.

3. B. Most of the passage takes place inside Aunt Polly's house. The bedroom, the jam closet, and the tomato garden are all parts of her property.

4. C. Aunt Polly's words, actions, and reactions create a humorous mood in the story. There is nothing scary, angry, or mysterious going on.

5. D. Tom scrambles over a high board-fence. Most likely Aunt Polly, who is an old lady, would not be able to chase Tom over a high fence. The other details do not relate to Tom's escape.

Skill Practice, page 196–197

Exposition: Gwen (a passenger), Anson Harris (a pilot), and several other passengers are on a damaged plane.

Plot: Passengers are losing consciousness as their plane loses oxygen. The pilot makes a dive for a lower altitude.

Climax: The plane reaches 10,000 feet in two and a half minutes.

Resolution: The dive restores oxygen to the plane. All passengers except Gwen regain consciousness.

1. The story takes place in a damaged airplane. The action occurs in modern time.

2. The damaged plane requires the pilot to take action.

3. The mood is tense and suspenseful.

Writing Practice, page 197

Be sure your story contains all the elements of a plot.

Sample answer

One evening a few years ago, I borrowed my dad's car so Larry, Sergio, and I could go to the movies. The problem was that the theater was sold out of tickets for the film we wanted to see. So we were left with the question of what to do for the next few hours.

"Let's drive over to Elmdale," suggested Larry. "Something's always going on there."

Elmdale was farther than my dad would have wanted me to drive. But both Larry and Sergio nagged me, so I reluctantly agreed. With radio blaring, we set out on the interstate for Elmdale.

"Hey, Ken, quit poking along," whined Sergio after a little while. "Let's put on some speed!"

"Yeah, Ken, we'll never get to Elmdale at this rate," Larry chimed in.

"Will you guys quit ragging on me?" I complained. However, I did put my foot on the gas, and the car leaped forward.

It didn't take long. The flashing lights of the highway patrol car looked like a sudden display of fireworks.

When the highway patrol officer came over to the car, Larry made some smart remark that did not help our situation. Soon we found ourselves sitting in the sheriff's station, waiting for our parents to arrive and for the fireworks to begin all over again.

Lesson 5.2

Think about Reading, page 201

1. **D.** You can tell that the speaker is a person who is part of the story because the speaker uses the pronouns *I* and *we*.

2. **A.** In paragraph 1, when telling Estella about the day they met, the speaker asks, "Not remember that you made me cry?"

3. **B.** Estella acts cold and distant toward the narrator. She says, "I have no heart" and "I have no softness there, no—sympathy—sentiment—nonsense." There is no evidence to suggest she is warm and tenderhearted, easygoing and friendly, or bitter and angry.

4. Estella seems to have no regret about being heartlessness. She accepts herself as cold and unfeeling.

Think about Reading, page 202

1. Phoenix Jackson is an old, wrinkled African American. She is small, and she walks slowly, using a cane. Her hair is black, and her eyes look blue. Her head is tied in a red rag, and her clothes are simple. She is not wearing a coat, even though it is a cold day.

2. She is strong and proud. She looks straight ahead as she walks. The noise of her cane makes a steady tapping sound as she moves with determination.

3. Phoenix Jackson is wearing an apron made of old sugar sacks. This suggests that she is a poor woman who knows how to make do with what she has. Although her clothes are poor, she looks "neat and tidy." This shows that she cares about her appearance.

Vocabulary Review, page 203

1. adjust
2. prediction
3. reasonable
4. familiar
5. characters

Skill Review, pages 203–204

1. *Sample answer:* Mama will send Pepé again. If the father gets sick, there is no one else who can go to town to get medicine.

2. *Sample answer:* He may meet someone he knows on his way to get the medicine. This could delay him so he would have to stay overnight and return the following day.

3. Mama feels worried and proud of Pepé. Pepé feels confident and anxious to get going.

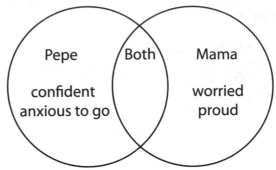

Skill Practice, page 205

1. **D.** Having the character speak to himself about his feelings is the most effective technique. He tries to encourage himself by saying, "I have no cramps. He'll be up soon and I can last. You have to last. Don't even speak of it."

2. **A.** The story says that the old man is tired. Pouring water on his head would revive him. There is no indication that he was trying to do anything else.

3. **B.** He is determined to catch the fish. He may be tired, but he is not faint. He is not angry or sad.

4. **B.** The old man is trying to reel in the fish. This is his sole purpose. He is not trying to reposition the boat, and he is not letting go of the fish.

Writing Practice, page 205

Describe a favorite character, and explain why you like the character.

Sample Response

Mr. Spock from the Star Trek series is one of my favorite characters. Spock is the science officer on the Starship Enterprise. He is part human and part Vulcan. I like watching the way he struggles with blending the two parts of his being.

Answer Key

Lesson 5.3

Think about Reading, page 208
1. P
2. O
3. P
4. O
5. P

Think about Reading, page 209
The story is told from the first-person point of view. The narrator uses the pronoun *I*. He is describing the event as he saw it.

Think about Reading, page 210
1. **A.** The clue that tells you this is written from the first-person point of view is the use of the pronouns *I* and *me*.
2. **C.** The narrator is clearly anxious about what Pap is going to do. He is afraid that Pap will let him be given back to the widow.
3. He is very independent. He does not want to go back to the widow because he would be forced to follow some rules (become civilized). He wants his freedom.

Vocabulary Review, page 211
1. first-person
2. logical
3. third-person
4. perspective

Skill Review, pages 211–212
1. **C.** In the first paragraph, Aunt Rosie says that "Anger is just hurt covered over." This is the main idea of the passage.
2. **B.** Aunt Rosie's advice was good, which shows she is a wise woman. No details in the story support the other options.
3. **D.** Aunt Rosie says that you should "stay in touch with the hurt." When you are upset, you feel hurt. She would advise you to tell your neighbor that you feel hurt.
4. The narrator has learned a good lesson from Aunt Rosie's advice. She will probably not change her mind about the advice.
5. *Sample answer:* Aunt Rosie's advice is important because it teaches the narrator to deal with her anger rather than bury it. By speaking about her anger, she is able to avoid a big fight with Les, and Les is able to understand how she feels.

Skill Practice, page 213
1. **B.** This story is told from the first-person point of view. The narrator is describing how miserable he felt while on the coach ride.
2. **D.** When a story is told from the first-person point of view, the narrator uses the pronouns *I* and *me* to tell about an event as he remembers it.
3. **C.** The coach ride was uncomfortable and upsetting. The narrator was cramped between two men and had to hold his legs above the lady's basket.
4. **D.** If the story were told by the elderly lady, the readers would know her thoughts about the fidgety boy who was taking up space in the coach.

Writing Practice, page 213
Be sure at least one of your stories is told from the first-person point of view.

Sample answer
Scene 1

I ran down the hall as quickly and quietly as I could. I knew I was late, and I knew the meeting wouldn't start without me. I have to remember that it takes time to take the elevator from the 4th floor down to the 1st floor and then another elevator up to the 44th floor.

Mikayla was glaring at the door when I entered. Everyone else seemed to be holding their breath, probably hoping no harsh words would come from a boss known from her impatience. As I took my seat, Mikayla tossed a folder toward me. Questions started flying at me. I felt more like hiding under the table than looking at the numbers in the report.

Scene 2

It was a regular Tuesday morning meeting, scheduled to begin at 9 a.m. sharp. Eight deparment chairs would discuss sales from the previous week. The new company was trying hard, but sales were slow.

Everyone's input was important, so the meeting didn't start on time because Jonah was missing. Promptness was a highly rated quality in this company. Seven people waiting for one latecomer was not acceptable. Finally Jonah arrived, hair flying and shirttail untucked. The boss started the meeting without waiting for him to get settled in his chair.

The first scene is told from Jonah's point of view. He is late and nervous. He is aware that all eyes are on him, and he wishes he could hide. The second scene is told from the third-person point of view. The narrator recognizes that Jonah is creating a problem but does not tell how Jonah feels about the problem.

Lesson 5.4

Think about Reading, page 214

1. D.
2. G.
3. A.
4. B.
5. F.
6. C.
7. E.
8. H.

Think about Reading, page 216

1. **B.** The first paragraph describes tractors that are plowing the land.

2. **C.** Insects crawl on the ground, so the machines were crawling along.

3. **A.** The narrator uses figurative language to describe the driver as though he were a machine. He feels that the driver does not care about the people whose jobs he is destroying.

4. This is an example of figurative language. Tractors do not really create thunder when they move. They do, however, make a loud noise.

Vocabulary Review, page 217

1. emotion
2. figurative
3. Connotation
4. Denotation
5. literal

Skill Review, pages 217–218

1. This is an example of figurative language. The darkness of the night and the sounds of the woods seem to be tightening up the space around him.

2. As the character continues walking, he becomes frightened. He starts seeing faces with hard eyes. As he walks faster, he begins to hear whistling and pattering.

3. *Answers will vary.*

4. *Answers will vary.*

5. **B.** The phrase "hard eyes" has a negative connotation. The character is clearly afraid of the eyes, and he calls the faces "evil."

Skill Practice, page 219

1. **D.** Trees do not actually have arms, so this is an example of figurative language. The other options all mean exactly what they say.

2. **C.** This means that the dog was as large as a man. A dog that looked like a man would not be small, funny, or playful.

3. **C.** The sheepdog really does have two names, so this is an example of literal language. The other options all use figurative language—limbs are not shoes, steps are not teeth, and floors do not go up and down hills.

4. **A.** Using figurative language is the best way to develop Meme's character. For example, it provides a picture of the dog's "limbs flopping all over the place like untied shoes."

Writing Practice, page 219

Be sure to use figurative language in your description.

Sample Response

    I waited outside, hoping a cab would drive by to pick me up. The trains were shut down, and people wandered around, confused like cattle that had been let out of their pen. The crowds were thick with locals and tourists looking for a beacon to guide them home. If I waited much longer, I would be swallowed whole.

    Finally a sliver of hope drove down the street in yellow metal. A taxi with its light on came nearer. I waved my arms around and pushed my way through the mass. This was my taxi, and I would battle for it.

Lesson 5.5

Think about Reading, page 222

C. War brings pain and misery. The text describes the corpses as well as the sights and sounds of the wounded men.

Think about Reading, page 223

The theme of the passage: facing the unknown takes courage.

Think about Reading, page 225

1. **B.** Paragraph 1 says Pete "could just see himself in a new home." The passage describes Pete's effort to buy a new home.

2. **C.** Paragraph 2 says Pete believed he could live wherever he chose because he was earning a good salary (had "financial success").

Answer Key

3. **A.** The real estate salesmen avoid telling Pete the truth—that he is not welcome in the development because of his race. Their responses to Pete do not answer his questions.

4. **C.** Although Pete can afford to live where he wants, racial discrimination keeps him out of this neighborhood.

5. *Sample answer:* Pete's thoughts tells us that he is financially able to buy a home outside the ghetto. His conversation with the salesman makes clear that no one is going to sell Pete a house. If Pete currently lives in a ghetto, he probably belongs to a racial minority. That is the reason no one will sell him a home.

Think about Reading, page 227

1. Passage 1 is poetry, and passage 2 is drama.

2. Freedom is the American Dream.

3. "I Hear America Singing" is a list of people singing as they go about their various tasks. They all have the freedom to do what they want to do. Walter in *A Raisin in the Sun* has the freedom to dream of becoming a business executive and sending his son to the best college.

Vocabulary Review, page 228

1. **B.**
2. **D.**
3. **A.**
4. **C.**

Skill Review, pages 228–229

1. The narrator says that rich people have a hard time understanding that there are people who have to share their rooms with brothers or sisters and may not have their own places to swim. Poor people have a hard time understanding that someone could be rich enough to own a pond.

2. The narrator lives in the gatehouse of an estate, which means that his parents probably work for Ernest's wealthy parents—so the narrator is poor and Ernest is rich. The two boys grow up riding bikes and playing ball together. Ernest does not understand the important differences between the rich and the poor, but the narrator understands there are lines that society draws between the rich and the poor.

3. *Sample answer:*

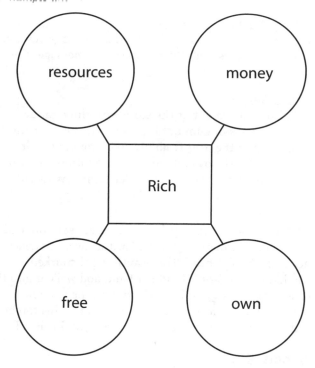

4. Benny Briggs is someone that the narrator knows. Benny and his family are not rich. He does not understand there are things that poor people are not suppose so do—like swim in a pond where rich people swim.

Skill Practice, pages 230

1. **C.** The passage states that the man does not realize how cold it is, that he has no supplies or shelter, and that his cheek bones and nose are unprotected. The dog instinctively knows that it is too cold to travel. Using this information, you can logically conclude that the man and dog are in danger.

2. **D.** The man is not cruel or overly cautious. Though the man may think he's bold, the narrator makes it clear that he is foolish, or misguided, about being out in the extreme cold.

3. **A.** The dog knows that this type of weather is dangerous, but the man pushes on ahead. Humans react to nature differently than other animals do.

4. **D.** The man's nose is "eager" and "aggressive." This shows that the man is fearless and adventurous.

5. **C.** The author's message is that an animal's instinct can be more accurate than a man's judgment.

(Lesson 5.5 cont.)

Writing Practice, page 219

Before writing your story, decide what message you want readers to understand. Do not state this message (the theme) in your story.

Sample Response

Carlton walked out of the store with three candy bars and a pack of gum in his pocket. He pulled them out quickly so the heat from his body wouldn't melt the chocolate. He loved it when Mrs. Whitmore was at the register at the corner store. Her sight was so bad he probably could have taken the whole magazine rack without her noticing.

Suddenly a beautiful girl he had never seen rounded the corner. Trying to look cool, Carlton swept his hair back from his forehead. The beautiful girl smirked at him, hiding her face behind her hand and walked into the store. When he caught his reflection in the window, he noticed a huge smear of melted chocolate on his forehead. He'd forgotten all about the stolen candy in his hand.

Lesson 5.6

Think about Reading, Page 235

1. This text is a poem. It is organized into four stanzas. Each stanza focuses on a different idea about the tree.

2. This is a play. Each set of lines in the play has a different speaker.

3. *Sample answer:* If "Woodman, Spare That Tree!" was a novel, the author might include a chapter telling about the narrator's great-grandfather planting the tree. Other chapters might describe family gatherings near the tree. The final chapter might discuss protecting forests from developers who want to chop them down. The ideas and events in the poem and the novel might be similar. However, the novel would have room for more details.

Think about Reading, Pages 237

1. **B.** Short stories are organized in paragraphs. Novels have chapters, poems have stanzas, and plays have scenes.

2. *Sample answer:* The tone is sad. The author uses the words *dreary, weak, weary, bleak December, dying ember,* and *sorrow* to give the poem this tone.

Vocabulary Review, Page 238

1. **B.**
2. **A.**
3. **D.**
4. **C.**
5. **E.**

Skill Review, Page 238–239

1. This is a play. The writer uses the text structure of a play: the name of speaker is followed by the speaker's words. Stage directions are written in italics.

2. **D.** Plays are organized into scenes. Often a new scene means the action is taking place in a new place or at a different time.

3. This is probably the beginning of the play. Peter and Wendy ask each other their names, so they are meeting for the first time.

4. The information would be organized in paragraphs. The words that the characters speak would be similar, but the words would appear in quotation marks. Descriptions would be more detailed. The author might also include more of the characters' thoughts.

Skill Practice, Page 240–241

1. This passage is from a long story or novel. The text is organized in paragraphs.

2. *Sample answer:*

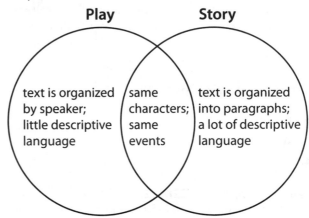

Play   **Story**

text is organized by speaker; little descriptive language

same characters; same events

text is organized into paragraphs; a lot of descriptive language

3. *Sample answer:* The play focuses on the characters' words. Its tone is light and playful. The story includes more descriptive language and narration. Its tone is more serious.

4. *Sample answer:* I enjoyed reading the novel because the writer tells what the characters are thinking and the descriptions make it easier to visualize the action.

Answer Key

Writing Practice, Page 241
Follow the text structure of plays in this lesson.

Sample Response
Cast of characters
BOY, 11 years old
SISTER 1, 9 years old
SISTER 2, 8 years old
MOTHER, a loving person
FATHER, a generous and kind person
(SCENE—a sunny day in the backyard of the family home. A tall oak tree shades the house and yard. A picnic table sits in the shade of the oak. On the table are a pitcher of lemonade and five glasses. MOTHER and FATHER sit at the table, sipping lemonade. BOY leans against the trunk of the tree. SISTERS 1 and 2 are playing tag.)
SISTER 1: (*catching up with SISTER 2*) Hah! You're "it"!
SISTER 2: (*panting and laughing*) Oh, Sissy, it's too hot to play. I'm not going to chase you again!
MOTHER: Girls! Don't run yourselves silly. Have a rest and come drink some lemonade.
SISTER 2: (*fanning herself with both hands as she approaches the table*) Whew! I *am* thirsty. (*MOTHER hands her a full glass.*) Thank you, Mom. Mmmm, this is delicious!
FATHER: (*handing a glass to SISTER 1*) Here you go, Sissy. Now, you girls cool yourselves off.
SISTER 1: (*takes a big sip*) Thanks, Dad!
BOY: Bring your glasses over here. Sit by the tree, where it's shady.
(*SISTERS 1 and 2 walk over to the oak tree and sit down beside BOY.*)
BOY: (*to the girls*) See? Isn't it cooler here? Our old oak tree sure is a great place to hang out.
FATHER: Well, you can thank your great-grandfather for that. You know he planted that tree there before I was born.
MOTHER, BOY, SISTER 1, and SISTER 2: (*laughing*) Yes, we know. You have told us before!
FATHER: (*grinning*) And? What do you say?
BOY, SISTER 1, and SISTER 2: (*laughing in unison*) Thank you, Great-Grandfather!!

Chapter 5 Review

Chapter 5 Review, pages 242–244

1. **C.** The passage is about Simple's long life of suffering. There is nothing in the pasage to indicate that Simple is lying or that most people in Harlem have sore feet.

2. **D.** The author seems affectionate toward Simple and understanding of his problems. Simple is a likable character.

3. **C.** Simple had to work hard and long, so he wore out many socks. Simple is exaggerating when he says he could have built a knitting mill because of all the socks he had to buy.

4. **A.** Paragraphs 1 and 5 make it clear that this scene takes place in the kitchen at breakfast time.

5. **C.** The young man's words always have a sarcastic tone, even when he tells his grandmother, "I'm nuts about you."

6. **B.** The grandmother cares about her grandson and is concerned about him. She stays up to be sure he gets home, she keeps his toast warm, and she worries about his getting a good night's sleep and avoiding a chill.

7. **B.** The author says the frozen trees are a cathedral. This is an example of figurative language. The author is using words to create a mental image.

8. **D.** Aunt Francine loves Alex and cares for her. In this paragraph, she pulls Alex close and kisses her hair.

9. **B.** The passage is organized into paragraphs. It is part of a longer story.

Essay Writing Practice

Essay Writing Practice, page 246–247
Answers will vary. Here are some points to consider.

Fiction
Whether you write a poem, a dramatic scene, or a short story, include these elements in your work:

- Your opening stanza or paragraph should introduce the setting and the characters. If you are writing a dramatic scene, a description of the setting and characters should be provided as stage notes.

- The plot should move forward in increasingly dramatic steps. Your passage should reach its climax when the main character finds the solution to the problem.

- Your passage should include both literal and figurative language. Example of literal language: *The boy ran quickly down the street.* Example of figurative language: *The boy flew like a greyhound.*

- Edit your passage. As you proofread your work, check that quotations are correctly punctuated. In a poem or short story, use quotation marks around the exact words of the speaker. In a play, all the speaker's words follow the name of that speaker. Descriptions of how the speaker looks or acts should be in brackets.

Glossary

A

act (akt) a part of a play

adapt (uh DAPT) to change

adjust (uh JUST) to change one's thinking

advertisement (AD ver TIZE munt) a persuasive message that tries to convince you to buy or use something, think something, or do something; also called *ad*

agenda (uh JEN duh) a list of things to do

alternative (awl TUR nuh tiv) a substitute or replacement

analysis (uh NAL uh siss) a careful study of something

analyze (AN uh lize) to study carefully

animation (an uh MAY shuhn) movement

apply (uh PLYE) to use

argument (AR gyuh munt) a reason given for or against something

assumption (uh SUMP shuhn) an unproven conclusion

audio (AW dee OH) a sound version of a text or performance

authorized (AW thuh rized) given permission

autobiography (AW toh bye OG ruh fee) the story of a person's life written by that person

B

bar graph (BAR GRAF) a type of graph that uses bars to compare two or more values

bias (BYE uss) a writer's personal opinions that give writing a positive or negative slant

biography (bye OG ruh fee) the true story of a person's life written by another person

blog (blawg) a personal web page that is used to express the writer's opinions on a subject

boldfaced (BOHLD FAYST) in dark type

border (BOR dur) a line dividing two areas

byline (BYE line) a line telling who wrote an article in a newspaper or magazine

C

categories (KAT uh GOR eez) groups of things that have something in common

chapter (CHAP tur) a section of a book

character (KAIR ik tur) a person, animal, or other being who performs the action in a story

characteristics (KAIR ik tuh RISS tiks) qualities that belong to a person or thing

chronological (KRON uh LOJ ik uhl) in time order

circle graph (SUR kuhl GRAF) a type of graph that is divided into fractions, like a pie

classify (KLASS uh fye) to arrange information into categories

climax (KLYE maks) the turning point in a story; the point of highest interest or suspense

commentary (KOM un TAIR ee) a review or essay that presents opinions

compare (kom PAIR) to examine two or more things to see how they are alike

conclusion (kon KLOO shuhn) a decision made by putting together several pieces of information

concrete (kon KREET) real

conflict (KON flikt) the struggle between opposing forces in a story

connection (kuh NEK shuhn) a link between a text and world events, one's personal experience, or another text

connotation (KON uh TAY shuhn) the positive or negative feeling associated with a word

connote (kon NOHT) to suggest a meaning

consumer (kon SOO mur) someone who buys things

context (KON tekst) the surrounding words or sentences that help explain the meaning of a particular word or expression

contrast (kuhn TRAST) to examine two or more things to see how they are different

criticize (KRIT uh SIZE) to tell what you like and don't like about something

D

defend (di FEND) to speak, write, or act in support of a position

denotation (dee noh TAY shuhn) a word's meaning, as found in a dictionary

design (dih ZINE) the way something looks

details (dee TAYLZ) words and phrases that give information

develop (dih VEL up) to change and grow

diagram (DYE uh GRAM) a drawing used to represent an idea or concept

dialogue (DYE uh LAWG) the words that characters in a story say, which are usually enclosed in quotation marks

diary (DYE ur ee) a record of a person's thoughts, activities, and feelings

dictionary (DIK shuhn AIR ee) a book of word meanings

digital (DIJ uh tuhl) electronic

document (DOK yuh munt) a formal piece of writing

E

editorial (ED uh TOR ee uhl) a column in a newspaper or magazine expressing an opinion

emoticon (i MOH tuh KON) a symbol made by combining keystrokes or picture characters

emotion (e MOH shuhn) a strong feeling

emphasize (EM fuh size) to stress or give importance to

employee (em PLOY ee) **handbook** a book that explains company rules

encounter (en KOWNT ur) to come across

endorse (en DORSS) to give support to a position or a product

enhance (en HANSS) to improve or add to

entry (EN tree) a word listed in a dictionary

essay (ESS ay) nonfiction writing that deals with a single subject

evaluate (i VAL yoo ayt) to make a judgment about the accuracy, truthfulness, or worth of something

evidence (EV uh duns) information that helps someone make an inference or come to a conclusion

examine (eg ZAM un) to look closely at

exposition (eks puh ZISH un) the beginning of a story, where the characters and the setting are introduced

extended family (ik STEN did FAM uh lee) all related members of a family

F

fact (fakt) a true statement that can be proven

falling action (FAWL ing AK shuhn) events occurring after the climax of a story that tie up loose ends

familiar (fuh MIL yur) easily recognized because of being similar to something known

figurative (FIG yur uh tiv) **language** words chosen for effect, not literal truth, to express a speaker's message

filial piety (FIL ee uhl PYE uh tee) the responsibility of family members to one another

first person point of view the perspective in a story told by a character in the story who uses the pronouns *I*, *me*, and *we*

forms (formz) documents employers use to gather information

functional (FUNGK shuh nuhl) having a specific purpose or use

G

genre (ZHAHN ruh) an artistic or literary category

Global Positioning System (GPS) a device that uses satellites to track location

glossary (GLAWSS uh ree) a feature in a nonfiction book that identifies important vocabulary words and phrases

grammar (GRAM ur) **handbook** a book that lists rules of language usage

graph (graf) a visual that shows or compares information

graphic (GRAF ik) a document in visual format

guide word (GIDE WURD) either of two words at the head of a page of a dictonary

H

heading (HED ing) a text feature that states an important idea or main topic of a section of text

hieroglyphics (HYE ruh GLIF iks) a picture writing system

I

identify (eye DEN tuh fye) to recognize or name

illustrate (IL uh strayt) to show or demonstrate

implied (im PLIDE) suggested without saying directly

index (IN deks) an alphabetical list of subject matter at the end of a book

infer (in FUR) to figure out

inference (IN fur uns) a conclusion that is made by putting together text clues with information that is already known

instruction (in STRUK shuhn) an explanation of how to do something

interact (in tur AKT) to communicate or work together

Internet (IN tur net) a worldwide system of computer networks

interpret (in TUR prut) to understand the meaning of

italics (ih TAL iks) slanted type

J

judgment (JUHJ munt) an opinion or a decision about something

K

key words words that are central to a document's main idea, such as definitions, dates, headings, and specific examples

L

layout map (LAY owt MAP) a floor plan

legend (LEJ und) the key in a graph, chart, or map that helps readers understand what is shown

line graph (LINE GRAF) a type of graph with points connected by a line to show how a value changes over time

literal (LIT ur uhl) meaning as found in a dictionary

logical (LOJ ik uhl) using sound reasoning

logo (LOH goh) the symbol for a company or organization

M

main idea what a book, chapter, or paragraph is mostly about

margin (MAR jun) the narrow column on the side of a page

media (MEE dee uh) systems of communication

memo (MEM oh) a document used to share information

memoir (MEM wahr) a story of a writer's personal experiences

metaphor (MET uh for) a comparison made without the use of the word *like*, *as*, or *than*

mood (mood) the emotional response or tone of a story

motivate (MOH tuh vayt) to make someone behave in a certain way

motivation (MOH tuh VAY shuhn) the reasons for doing something

multimedia (MUHL ti MEE dee uh) a presentation that uses two or more types of media

N

narrative (NAR uh tiv) writing that gives an account of real or imagined events

nonfiction (non FIK shuhn) a type of writing that focuses on real people and real events

O

online (AWN line) on the Internet

opinion (uh PIN yun) a personal judgment or belief

optional (OP shuh nuhl) not required

organization chart (OR guh nuh ZAY shun CHART) a chart showing the roles or functions of company employees

P

paraphrase (PAIR uh FRAYZ) to restate ideas in your own words

part of speech (PART uv SPEECH) a category of words; for example, noun, verb, or adjective

pattern (PAT urn) a repeated arrangement or order

perspective (pur SPEK tiv) the viewpoint from which events in a story are told

persuade (pur SWAYD) to convince

physical map (FIZ i kuhl MAP) a map that shows landforms, oceans, and other natural features

pie chart (PYE CHART) a circular graph divided into sections

plot (plot) all the events that take place in a story from beginning to end

plot diagram (PLOT DYE uh gram) a graphic organizer that shows the key parts of a story's plot

point of view the way a particular event or a series of events looks to a specific individual; also, the perspective from which a story is told

political map (puh LIT i kuhl MAP) a map that shows the boundaries between countries

prediction (prih DIK shuhn) a statement that tells what might happen next

presentation (PREZ un TAY shuhn) a demonstration

preview (pree VYOO) to look at something in advance

process (PRAH sess) a series of actions for doing something

pronounce (pruh NOWNS) to say

pronunciation key (pruh NUN see AY shuhn KEE) text that explains the sounds used for saying a word

propel (pruh PEL) to drive or move forward

prose (prohz) the ordinary language people use in writing and speaking

Q

qualification (KWAHL uh tuh KAY shuhn) professional experience and education

question (KWESS chun) to ask about something in order to get information

R

read (reed) to interpret written material

reasonable (REE zun uh buhl) showing good sense

recite (ri SITE) to say aloud

reference source (REF uh renss SORS) a document containing factual information

reference text (REF uh rens TEKST) a source of factual information

regulation (reg yoo LAY shuhn) rule

relationship (ri LAY shuhn ship) connection

reliability (ri LYE uh BIL uh tee) the accuracy or dependability of a reference source

reliable (ri LYE uh buhl) trustworthy

resolution (rez uh LOO shuhn) the point in a story when the conflict, or problem, is solved

résumé (REZ uh MAY) a document that describes a person's educational and work experience

reunion (ree YOON yuhn) a gathering of family members or friends who have been apart for some time

review (ri VYOO) a personal critique of a movie, book, play, or television or radio program

rising action (RIZE ing AK shuhn) the events in a story that lead to the climax

S

safety sign (SAYF tee SINE) a visual representation of a potentially dangerous environment

scan (skan) to read quickly to find a specific fact or detail

scene (seen) a part of a play

scribe (skribe) someone who writes or copies text

search engine (surch EN jun) a software code that looks for information on the World Wide Web

sensory detail (SEN suh ree DEE tayl) language in a story that appeals to one of the five senses

sequence (SEE kwuns) logical time order

setting (SET ing) the place, time, and atmosphere in which a story takes place

slogans (SLOH gunz) phrases or mottos used by companies or groups

specialized (SPESH uh lized) focusing on just one subject area

stanzas (STAN zuhz) verses or several lines that stand together in a poem or song

stated (STAY ted) explained in words

strategy (STRAT uh jee) a skill or plan

strong fortress (STRONG FOR tris) a building that can withstand storms

structure (STRUK chur) the way something is arranged or organized

subjective (sub JEK tiv) affected by personal views

summarize (SUM ur ize) to tell only the most important information about a story, article, or experience

survey (SUR vay) to scan

synonym (SIN uh nim) a word with the same (or similar) meaning as another word

synthesize (SIN thuh size) to combine ideas to create a new idea

T

technical (TEK nih kuhl) belonging to a specialized area

technical manual (TEK nih kuhl MAN yoo uhl) a reference text containing details and instructions on how to repair something

technique (tek NEEK) a process or method for doing something

testimonial (TES tuh MOH nee uhl) a statement about the high quality of a product

text feature (TEKST FEE chur) a part of a text

text structure (TEKST STRUK chur) the way a text is arranged or organized

text-to-self-connection (TEKST too SELF kuh NEK shuhn) a link between what a person reads and something in the person's life

text-to-text connection (TEKST too TEKST kuh NEK shuhn) a link between what a person reads in two or more texts

text-to-world-connection (TEKST too WURLD kuh NEK shuhn) a link between what a person reads and something that is happening in the world

theme (theem) the general message in a work of fiction or a poem that gives meaning to the text

third person point of view the perspective in a story told by someone outside the story who uses the pronouns *he*, *she*, and *they*

tone (tohn) the emotion in a piece of writing or in a character's voice

topic sentence (TOP ik SEN tens) the sentence in which the main idea of a paragraph is stated

U

unauthorized (un AW thuh rized) without permission

universal (yoo nuh VUR suhl) general, widespread

URL a website addres

V

vary (VAIR ee) to change

version (VER zhuhn) an account of something

violation (VYE oh LAY shuhn) a failure to follow policies

visual (VIZH uh wuhl) information in the form of a photograph, illustration, chart, or graph

visualize (VIZH uh wuh LIZE) to form pictures in one's mind

volume (VOL yoom) one book in a set of books

Index